The
Chronic Pain Control Workbook

A Step-by-Step Guide for Coping With and Overcoming Your Pain

by Ellen Mohr Catalano, M.A.

With an Introduction by Harold Carron, M.D.

and Contributions from Gregg A. Korbon, M.D., Douglas DeGood, Ph.D., Richard Gevirtz, Ph.D., Stephen Wegener, Ph.D., William Stewart, Ph.D., Patricia Wolskee, Ph.D., Glenn H. Catalano, M.S.

Illustrations by Shelby Putnam-Tupper
Edited by Kirk Johnson

Publisher's Note

This publication is designed to provide accurate and authoritative information in regard to the subject matter covered. It is sold with the understanding that the publisher is not engaged in rendering psychological, financial, legal, or other professional services. If expert assistance or counseling is needed, the services of a competent professional should be sought.

Copyright © 1987 by Ellen Mohr Catalano
New Harbinger Publications, Inc.
5674 Shattuck Avenue
Oakland, CA 94609

ISBN 0-934986-45-2 paperback
ISBN 0-934986-46-0 cloth

Printed in the United States of America

First Printing May 1987, 5,000 copies
Second Printing January 1988, 7,500 copies
Third Printing May 1990, 3,000 copies
Fourth Printing April 1991, 5,000 copies
Fifth Printing July 1992, 10,000 copies

To Glenn—My constant source of love and encouragement

Acknowledgments

I wish to thank these professional people and friends for their supportive time and attention: Doctors Harold Carron, John Rowlingson, and Douglas DeGood; Dr. Leeland Cross, Department of Orthopedics and Rehabilitation, University of Virginia, for his generous editing contribution; Doctors Joe Gieck, Athletic Trainer, University of Virginia, and Doug Cox, Chiropractor, Charlottesville, Virginia, for their clear, concise, and patient explanations of complex subjects; Anna Corbin and Mary Totin, Massage Therapists, Marci Silvermetz, Exercise Physiologist, and the rest of the staff and patients at the Pain Management Center, University of Virginia Medical Center, Charlottesville, Virginia. Also thank you to Elizabeth Robinson for her boundless enthusiasm throughout this project and careful reading of the initial stages of the manuscript. And finally, Matt McKay, Pat Fanning, and Kirk Johnson, New Harbinger Publications, for their endless patience, editorial support, and belief in this project.

Table of Contents

Introduction

Pain is a personal experience. Usually initiated by injury or disease, the discomfort it produces on movement or at rest is amplified by the patient's emotional response to the meaning, persistence, intensity, and debilitating aspects of the experience. Most acute pain is limited in duration, amenable to treatment, and usually can be cured. But for reasons unknown to medical science, pain may persist following healing and despite the absence of any demonstrable pathology. This kind of chronic pain is poorly understood by both the patient and the treating professional.

With its demands and commands for rest, chronic pain leads to the additional hardships of muscle weakness and atrophy, tendon and ligament shortening, and joint immobility. Normal physical activities then become painful, further limiting the sufferer's ability to function. With no relief in view, many patients fall into the traps of doctor shopping in search of a cure, overdependence on medication, depression, and social withdrawal. Family and sexual relationships are also commonly damaged by the sufferer's unrelenting pain.

This text is designed for the chronic pain sufferer, but offers health professionals at all levels a rational approach to understanding chronic pain and its management. Throughout, it emphasizes the key point that the patient must take responsibility for carrying out his or her own treatment, a responsibility that can be accomplished by setting realistic goals and learning specific skills.

While there are few controlled studies on the management of any chronic pain syndrome—nor even a confluence of opinions as to the value of any specific therapeutic intervention—this workbook is based on many years of experience by specialists in the management of patients with chronic pain. The programs outlined reinforce the fact that chronic pain is seldom cured, and that one must "learn to control the pain rather than let it control him" as an alternative to disability. The text covers the development of coping skills through stress management and relaxation training and examines approaches to physical rehabilitation through appropriate exercise programs and use of body mechanics to avoid further injury.

Several chapters are devoted to the more common pain problems, of which back and neck pain lead the list. Also covered in depth are headache, temperomandibular pain, arthritis, abdominal pain, and the neuralgias. A final section is devoted to a description of pain clinics and their role and that of governmental agencies in rehabilitation.

This text is pragmatic in its approach. The reasons for particular self-help treatments are explained, the steps to take are detailed, and additional supportive measures that will enhance the patient's response to treatment are explored. The book should serve as a useful tool for health professionals working with chronic pain patients. And in this volume, many pain patients will find answers to their questions and a better understanding of chronic pain and its control.

Harold Carron, M.D.
Clinical Professor of Anesthesiology
Pain Consultant
Georgetown University Medical Center and N.I.H.
Washington, DC

1

Learning To Cope

This workbook may have caught your attention because you have chronic pain or know someone who does. You know, then, that chronic pain can be terribly difficult to manage, both physically and emotionally.

Chronic Pain Control is designed to help you assess your particular situation, learn methods of managing chronic pain, and try out some new options that you may not have considered before. Most importantly, each chapter encourages you to look at how your pain affects you as a whole person. Most pain sufferers go into treatment viewing their pain as a separate problem, unrelated to the rest of their lives. But a real ability to cope with your pain begins when you learn to see it as a complex interweaving of your own unique physical and emotional reactions.

Physically, as the pain drags on, you often begin to avoid even the smallest movement for fear of reinjury. You hold your breath and tighten your muscles in anticipation of the pain, as if that stiffness and constriction would keep it from returning. The pain wakes you up in the middle of the night, and so it's a chore to get out of bed in the morning, and you frequently feel groggy and half-alert during the day. The pain interferes with your work and your home life, and it is on your mind almost constantly. Often your friends and family can't understand it, since there are no visible broken bones or torn muscles and you still look like you used to look. But you look in the mirror and see the bags under the eyes and the pale, gaunt look of a face that is fighting pain.

The physical hardships of chronic pain may force you to withdraw from friends and family. And this further contributes to your feelings of frustration, isolation, and loneliness. People say, "Exercise . . . " "Try hot tubs . . . " "Use tiger balm . . . " And you do try, but at the first sign of pain you're not sure how much is too much and you stop for fear of doing any more damage. And so you hold yourself very still and wait, hoping that someone will come along who has a cure, or at least a definite answer, so that you can get off this vicious pain cycle.

Emotionally, those of you who suffer from chronic pain may feel depressed about your prospects for recovery. You think to yourself, "This will never get better," and sometimes you despair that you will ever again be your old self, able to enjoy, able to be spontaneous. Sometimes you feel plain scared. You imagine the pain continuing until you are overwhelmed or crazy, until everything you love or count on is lost. You may feel resentful that this is happening to you, that your pain is making you weak, unacceptable, useless. Or you may lash out at others, blaming them for not helping you or for putting you in a difficult situation.

As a result, your family and work relationships suffer. Your family wants you to get well but feels helpless. Maybe they try to be supportive, but turn on you or sulk when you get angry or complain. Children in the family may get confused about the change of pace at home—why is Dad staying home and Mom going to work? Or perhaps the children and spouse begin to feel neglected and strained because your pain has taken up so much time, attention, and money. Those of you who live with or counsel chronic pain sufferers are probably well aware of the frustrations in helping someone adapt to the major life disruptions that pain causes. You may feel manipulated, stuck, or discouraged in your efforts to help the person cope.

When you're wrapped up in your pain, it's hard to make decisions like you used to. If you've stayed out of work for a while, you may find it increasingly difficult to imagine returning. If you do go back, you know that you will have to face the boss and request certain changes so you can continue to do your job. And you're not sure what his or her reaction will be. On top of it all, you consult with several different doctors or health care professionals about your condition, only to find that you get widely varying opinions. No one agrees on how to treat your pain, or how and when you can resume work.

Traditionally, medicine has excelled at treating symptoms, curing acute problems, researching and prescribing drugs, and perfecting diagnostic techniques. But chronic pain frequently falls through the cracks of modern medical science. A pain symptom that may be diagnosed as one thing in clinic A is diagnosed as another in hospital B. Doctors sometimes fail to clearly communicate with one another or with their patients. It's not uncommon to find a chronic pain sufferer who takes one drug prescribed by one physician and another drug prescribed by another, and the doctors have no idea that their patient is getting conflicting drug treatments. Or one doctor cannot diagnose your problem and so refers you to another doctor, who refers you to another department which in turn refers you somewhere else, until you begin to feel like a hot potato being passed from hand to hand. And if you were hoping that the doctors would know what to do, you feel mounting frustration as you realize that you're not going to be fixed or cured and the doctor whom you trusted really has no answers at all. And the doctors who see or at least sense your frustration react in various ways—some try harder and harder to help you, others get defensive, and others prescribe still more drugs because it makes them feel bad to see you in pain.

The traditional medical model is that the doctor has the burden of control—he or she must DO SOMETHING to remedy your situation. But this traditional approach to chronic pain management is rapidly being replaced by a newer and more effective strategy. This strategy involves working with the WHOLE person, not just the symptoms. Methods are being developed that attempt to return control of pain to you, the patient. Pills are replaced with skills—stress management, self-hypnosis, biofeedback, and exercise, among many others. You can internalize these skills—that is, learn them so well that they become natural to you. With them, you can learn to effectively manage your pain.

These approaches are *not* designed to replace your doctor. They are presented here as alternatives you should include as part of a full treatment plan—a plan that you and your doctor can work out together. In the process, you will come to depend less on doctors and more on yourself. And you will find that most medical professionals prefer to work with patients who are informed about their condition and willing to take a variety of treatment approaches, and who have chosen to take responsibility for their own pain management.

Although the enormous scope of this subject necessitates simplified and brief explanations of the various techniques, this book will provide a comprehensive overview that will help you pick and choose among the available pain control options. You will be in a better position to ask educated questions of your doctor or health care professional, as well as design a treatment program that meets your needs. Suggested readings at the end of each chapter will help you pursue the topics that interest you most.

This book is divided into four sections:

1. Physical management of pain, including medical interventions, exercise, and stress management
2. Psychological management of pain, including examination of attitudes and beliefs about chronic pain
3. Techniques for managing specific pain conditions, with basic information about current medical treatments and medications
4. Strategies for using outside resources available to help you cope with pain and pain-related changes in your life

Most people find it helpful to begin with physical management. When pain is constantly reminding you of its presence, it can be extremely difficult to concentrate on anything else. This section is designed to teach you valuable exercise and relaxation skills to get you through your difficult times so that you can move on to other aspects of coping. First read chapter two, which acquaints you with medical terms and current practices in treating chronic pain. Chapters three and four on exercise and basic stress management skills are indispensable and need to be read carefully. The passive stretches and strengtheners in chapter three and the basic relaxation techniques of breathing and progressive relaxation in chapter four complement each other and lay a firm foundation for the rest of the skills you will learn in the book. When you feel yourself becoming more comfortable with relaxation, you will be ready to try out the advanced relaxation techniques in chapter five and move on to the psychological management section of the book.

Chapters six and seven examine some common attitudes and beliefs about chronic pain and teach you effective skills for dealing with pain-related situations. In chapter six, you will first learn to identify your internal messages and responses to pain by examining your negative thoughts and how they may be obstacles to progress. In chapter seven you will learn to productively handle many of the interpersonal situations that pain sufferers face through assertiveness training and conflict management.

Following these chapters is a section devoted to medication and specific chronic pain conditions. You can pick the chapters here that address your specific questions.

The last three chapters will help motivate you to use other resources available to chronic pain sufferers, such as your state's vocational rehabilitation system and other existing programs designed to aid you in career decisions. Chapter sixteen provides general guidelines in using pain clinics and support groups as additional resources for getting better. The last chapter is a pep talk for you to remember as you learn these new skills.

A pep talk is appropriate here also. I want you to regard chronic pain management as you would learning a new skill. Do you remember learning to ride a bicycle? You wanted to ride off down the street with the big kids. You knew the time had come to graduate from your tricycle, but the two-wheeler looked ominous. As you clumsily tried to balance yourself on the seat while searching for the pedal with your foot, you wondered if you would ever learn. You may even have considered forgetting the whole thing. But you remembered your basic goal . . . to ride with the big kids. So you tried, and from clumsy motions and awkward falls came balance. Your body finally learned to harmonize with the wheels and frame underneath. You worked hard to get there, but you knew it was worth it.

There is a close analogy between managing chronic pain and the learning process you went through with your bicycle. At first your pain looks like an insurmountable obstacle, and the time it will take to "fix it" seems astronomical. You may feel like giving up before you start. The exercises may feel awkward to you, or the slightest bit of exercise may aggravate your pain to the point that you have to stop. You may feel too distracted to try stress reduction exercises, or feel just plain silly doing them. Or maybe you don't know how to fit it all into your lifestyle. But you have your basic goal in mind. You want to get better. And so you persevere.

One crucial key to pain management is to formulate clear, realistic goals and keep them in your mind at all times. By realistic, I mean that you should set reachable, appropriate goals, ones you know you can strive for and keep. Don't tell yourself that you'll be a marathon runner one year after your injury, when you never ran before your injury. And if you promise yourself that you'll become TOTALLY pain free, that pain will never bother you again, you are setting yourself up for disappointment. But if you promise yourself that you will stick to the program, not give up at the first flickering of pain, and realize that you will have occasional relapses that you *can* manage . . . those are realistic goals.

Here are three good overall goals for anyone who is suffering from chronic pain and is seeking help:

1. Get basic information about the best methods of controlling *your* pain.
2. Decrease the level of pain you are experiencing while also decreasing the inappropriate use of medical interventions.
3. Work toward a return to full or partial functioning.

The first goal starts with reading this book and creating a pain control plan with your doctor or a nearby pain clinic. Your second goal is to help yourself feel less pain by using specific medical and psychological interventions. For example, by working with your doctor, you can implement a treatment plan where you use a combination of nerve blocks, appropriate medications, exercise, and stress reduction strategies to help you cope with the pain and get on to your other goals. In order to pursue this goal efficiently, it is important for you to decrease the amount of time you spend going from doctor to doctor in search of the perfect cure. The inappropriate use of medical interventions, or doctor shopping, wastes a lot of time and energy on your part—time better spent accomplishing goals two and three. Finally, you can accomplish your third goal by making use of available resources, such as physical therapy and vocational rehabilitation, to help you return to partial, if not full activity.

As with all major goals, you will find it helpful to formulate some mini-goals to help you accomplish your overall agenda. Mini-goals are tasks or activities that are laid out chronologically and have a specific time frame. For example, in order to satisfy your second overall goal, to decrease the level of pain you are experiencing, a mini-goal could be to take several deep, diaphragmatic breaths each time you begin to experience the pain. Another mini-goal might be to allow yourself to take this process step by step, go at the pace your body allows, and not force yourself to go faster than you are ready to go.

Remember though that requiring yourself to perform perfectly is one point where chronic pain management and learning to ride a bike are *not* similar. Stubborn perseverance paid off when you were a kid. But with chronic pain, trying too hard to control your pain is like saying to yourself, "Hurry up and relax." Pushing yourself too hard is counterproductive. Instead, adopt a "passive perseverence" attitude, one that allows you to experience the control *in time.* Gradually, all the pieces will fall into place, and parts of the puzzle will fit together. But the change will take some time, patience, and open-mindedness on your part. You will also need a plan to accomplish your goals.

Following a written plan of action can be a useful tool in getting started. Unless you have already had experience managing pain, you may not be ready to actually sit down and formulate a plan. But as you go through this workbook, jot down ideas that appeal to you that you might want to pursue in your plan. I suggest that you read through the workbook once, pick out the sections that you would like to work on, and then write out a contract for yourself using the following format.

Sample Chronic Pain Action Plan

Goal 1. Get basic information about best methods for controlling my pain

Activity 1.   *What:* Look for a pain clinic or institution that specializes in pain management.

When: Call this week for the next available appointment. Do not put it off.

Where: Research the available clinics in my area. Ask friends. Locate one within a reasonable distance. Arrange for at least one or two follow-up visits.

Activity 2. *What:* Set up an appointment with my regular doctor to discuss my concerns and learn about available pain management resources in my area.

Activity 3. *What:* Find out where I can learn stress management, self-hypnosis, biofeedback, or related techniques to help manage pain. Make an appointment and give it at least two or three tries.

Goal 2: Decrease level of pain—physical management

Activity 1. *What:* Start the special back exercise program
When: Right after morning bath
Where: On the soft bedroom carpet

Activity 2. *What:* Take the anti-inflammatory medication prescribed by my doctor
When: Four times a day

Activity 3. *What:* Use the TENS unit
When: Two hours after lunch when pain is the worst
Where: Home or office

Goal 3: Decrease level of pain—relaxation training

Activity 1. *What:* Progressive muscle relaxation
When: Once in the morning, once in the afternoon or evening
Where: In easy chair in den

Activity 2. *What:* Self-hypnosis
When: Practice right after PMR
Where: In easy chair

Goal 4: Decrease level of pain—psychological management

Activity 1. *What:* Learn to handle my anger and frustration by confronting any negative thoughts and remembering my coping thoughts
When: Every time I'm aware of growing anger

Activity 2. *What:* Learn to handle my anxiety by confronting any catastrophic thinking
When: Every time I'm starting to feel anxious about my back

Activity 3. *What:* Learn to say no and set limits
When: People ask me to go beyond my limits
Where: At the physical therapist's office, at home when my wife asks me to do certain tasks, and when negotiating with the plant concerning my return to work

Goal 5. Get back to partial functioning

Activity 1. *What:* Arrange to return half-time within four weeks
When: Now

Activity 2.   *What:* Arrange modified duties: no travel, no carrying during first two months
When: Now

Activity 3.   *What:* Explore permanent reassignment to a "desk job" at the plant
When: Now

Your Plan

Goal 1. Get information about best methods for controlling pain

Activity 1.   *What:* _____

When: _____

Where: _____

Activity 2.   *What:* _____

When: _____

Where: _____

Activity 3.   *What:* _____

When: _____

Where: _____

Goal 2. Decrease level of pain—physical management

Activity 1.   *What:* _____

When: _____

Where: _____

Activity 2.   *What:* _____

When: _____

Where: _____

Activity 3.   *What:* _____

When: _____

Where: _____

Goal 3. Decrease level of pain—relaxation training

Activity 1.   *What:* _____

When: _____

Where: _____

Activity 2.   *What:* _____

When: _____

Where: _____

Activity 3.   *What:* _____

When: _____

Where: _____

Goal 4. Decrease level of pain—psychological management

Activity 1.   *What:* _____

When: _____

Where: _____

Activity 2.   *What:* _____

When: _____

Where: _____

Activity 3.   *What:* _____

When: _____

Where: _____

Goal 5. Back to full or partial functioning

Activity 1. *What:* _____

               When: _____

               Where: _____

Activity 2. *What:* _____

               When: _____

               Where: _____

Activity 3: *What:* _____

               When: _____

               Where: _____

Once you have drawn up a plan, show your desired contract to a doctor or health care professional who you feel can give you helpful feedback and assist you in setting realistic goals. It can also be very helpful to share your contract with a spouse or friend who can give you support and encouragement.

A Final Note

Don't give up! The information presented here has been gleaned from hundreds of chronic pain sufferers who have learned to stick with it, bolster themselves when things get tough, and design for themselves a workable plan for coping. After applying some or all of the principles laid out in this workbook, they tell us that they have learned these things:

- To put the pain in perspective
- To relax away some or all of the pain
- To make new decisions based on changes the pain has caused in their lives
- To set realistic goals
- To minimize the disruption the pain has caused

Before you say to yourself, "You don't know what kind of pain I have," give yourself another chance and read this book.

Further Reading

Kushner, Harold. *When Bad Things Happen to Good People.* New York: Avon Books, 1983.

Bresler, David. *Free Yourself From Pain.* New York: Simon and Schuster, 1986.

2

Theories of Pain

A biofeedback patient with a very painful neck problem once came to me to learn about pain management. At the beginning of our program I told her that I would keep my discussion of the theories of pain very short and simple. "Good," she replied. "This pain wears me down. I'm too exhausted to hear any long explanations."

This chapter is about theories of pain, kept short and simple. But no simplification can avoid the fact that pain is an extremely complex interaction of the mind and the body. Among the many theories and suggested treatments for chronic pain, one basic rule stands out:

WHEN YOU HAVE CHRONIC PAIN, YOUR MIND AS WELL AS YOUR BODY IS INVOLVED.

First, you'll need to understand five basic concepts.

1. *Acute pain is a signal to the body that it has been or is being damaged in some way.* It is an alarm that requests immediate attention. The sensation of acute pain protects you from getting too close to a flame or from walking on a fractured foot. Burns and broken bones are examples of acute pain.

2. *Acute pain is different from chronic pain.* The word "acute" comes from the Latin word meaning "needle" and basically means "sharp." When acute pain occurs as a result of a wound, a broken bone, or a bite, it requires immediate attention because of the tissue damage. When treated with the appropriate medical care, the wound heals, the bone mends, and usually the pain goes away.

The word "chronic" is derived from a Greek word for time. Chronic pain means persistent pain that tends to be constant rather than intermittent and can become a pattern of painful sensations that persist long after the initial injury.

In your reading, you may have seen the word "subacute." The Harvard Medical School *Health Letter* defines this as "not quite acute—not sudden, but also not something of long standing." A subacute illness has its onset over a period of weeks to months, as opposed to hours or days. In contrast, a chronic illness hangs around for months to years.

You can usually get decisive medical care for your acute pain, but treating chronic pain can become a maze of misunderstanding and misdiagnosis.

3. *Chronic pain is real.* All pain is real, whether it is acute or chronic. Your pain may not be obvious to someone else, but you know when you hurt.

4. *Pain is a subjective experience.* Everyone is a unique individual, and everyone handles pain in different ways. You have probably seen some people cry out loudly at what seems to be a minor injury, while others are stoic and keep a "stiff upper lip." These variations in pain reaction will be examined in the following chapters from a physical as well as an emotional perspective.

5. *Chronic pain is influenced by your environment.* Because it involves far more than tissue damage and a physical diability, chronic pain is not a simple problem. Chronic pain can be affected adversely or positively by your family, your job, and your world in general. The fact that your pain can be influenced by the environmental and emotional factors listed in diagram 2.1 does not make it any less real. But these factors can frustrate treatment efforts and confuse and depress not only you, the sufferer, but also your family and your health care professional.

DIAGRAM 2.1

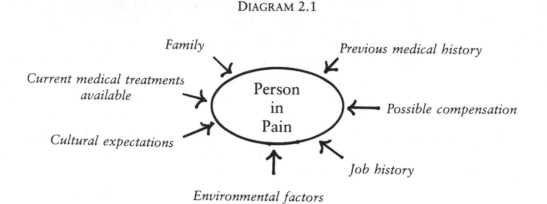

Beyond the Physiology of Pain

Pain has been the subject of study and controversy for centuries, but only in the last several decades has careful research revealed illuminating new concepts about our perception of and reaction to pain. In 1956, a researcher named Beecher compared the reactions to pain of soldiers in battle to the reactions of a comparable number of civilians about to undergo an operation. Amazingly, he found that soldiers who had severe wounds complained less of pain and required less medication than the civilians did. To the soldiers, their severe wounds meant an end to battle and a sure trip to the safety of the hospital and home. To the civilians, their wounds meant removal from the safety of home to the anxiety of being in the hospital and facing surgery. According to Dr. Beecher, the soldiers perceived less pain because they had reduced anxiety. This classic study showed that there is more to pain than mere sensation. A painful war wound means an end to battle and a quick ticket home. The pain of surgery means disease and an uncertain future. The meaning of pain affects the experience of pain.

Specificity theory. Until fairly recently, pain has been regarded as a straightforward mechanism—an individual gets hurt somewhere and that message is relayed directly to the brain. This simple stimulus-response concept, known as the specificity theory, is still taught in many medical schools. The theory assumes that the intensity of the pain is directly proportional to the amount of damage. In other words, if you have an obvious injury, you are expected to hurt; an unseen injury cannot hurt as much. This theory supposes that if surgery or medication can eliminate the cause of pain, then the pain should disappear.

But when the pain drags on and there seems to be no obvious medical solution for it, this stimulus-response concept of pain is clearly an inadequate explanation.

A broader approach. More recent theories have shown that the experience of pain is not a simple cause-and-effect relationship between the body and the brain. Rather, the experience is a complex interweaving of pain signals, emotions, and thoughts involving several different pathways of pain. These pathways can transmit the pain signal at lightning-fast speed, or slowly and continuously. The pathways can continue to transmit a pain signal after the injury has supposedly healed, or even when an injured site has been entirely removed (as in the case of phantom limb pain). Sometimes the pain sensation is transformed along its pathway so that when the signal reaches the brain it is perceived as something other than pain. Or the brain can send messages back to the injured area to stop the pain sensation. In other words, there is a continuous feedback motion from pain to brain and back again.

This fluid and constantly changing motion can be prevented or relieved by surgery and medication. You can have a surgeon sever a nerve in hope of cutting off the transmission of pain, or you can take drugs to try to block the pain. But more often than not, the pain is somehow regenerated even after surgery. Furthermore, you can develop a tolerance for drugs and find that you have to take higher and higher drug dosages. And drugs and surgery are very costly. So in most cases you are left with what is usually offered as the last alternative, but is actually the best alternative— learning to control that fluid motion of pain to brain by changing *your attitude toward the pain*. You *can* change the way your pain feels by changing how your body and your brain react. But in order to make this change happen, it will help you to know some basic facts about the physiology of pain. The following simplified descriptions of pathways for pain transmission will show you *why* pain sensations can be changed internally and *how* your attitudes can make a difference. They will also explain how such therapies as nerve blocks, acupuncture, and nerve stimulators can work.

Pain Pathways—Going Up and Down

Going up: fast and slow pain. Pain starts with a physical event—a cut, burn, tear, or bump. Nerve endings in the periphery of your body (limbs and organs) pick up the pain. These nerve endings are called *pain receptors*. These receptors cable the pain information from one bunch of nerve fibers to another to cells in the spinal cord where the message is relayed to the brain. This pathway is called the *ascending tract*.

This process can happen at different rates of speed because the nerve fibers that transmit the pain messages come in different sizes. Large diameter A-beta nerve fibers transmit pain quickly along the cable network. This is commonly known as "fast pain." You know it as the kind of pain that feels like pressure and touch. Two smaller diameter A-delta and C nerve fibers transmit pain information at a slower rate of speed. You know the A-delta pain as the sharp and stabbing pain you feel from a cut or burn. The C fiber pain is typically called "slow pain" or secondary pain. As a sufferer of chronic pain, you are all too familiar with C fiber slow pain. This is the dull aching sensation usually associated with chronic problems.

The spinal cord is the central concourse along which all pain messages travel to and from the brain. When you stub you toe and your peripheral nerves register alarm, this pain is immediately relayed along the nerve fibers of your foot and leg to a special area within the dorsal horn of the spinal cord called the *substantia gelatinosa*. The cells within the substantia gelatinosa relay this "fast pain" message along a pain tract called the *neospinothalamic* pathway. The trip ends at specific locations in the brain, namely the *thalamus* and the *cortex*. The cortex is the portion of the brain where most of your thought processes take place. A pain message arrives, and the cortex prompts you to say "Ouch!" and to begin rubbing the affl icted area.

By contrast, chronic pain tends to move along a different, slower tract called the *paleospinothalamic* pathway. This "slow pain" tends to be dull, aching, burning, and cramping. Initially it travels the same route as the fast pain through the dorsal horn on the spinal cord. But once there, the slow pain message separates in the brain stem area to turn toward a final destination in a different portion of the brain, the *hypothalamus* and *limbic structures*. The hypothalamus is the gland responsible for instructing the pituitary gland to release certain stress hormones. It is sometimes referred to as the central clearing house of the brain. The limbic structures are the place where your emotions are processed. Their involvement at this stage of the process helps to explain how your feelings can influence your pain.

Going down. Just as there is a pain-to-brain motion, there is also a brain-to-pain motion whereby your brain attempts to counteract the pain message trying to make its way up. You have probably heard stories about athletes who sprain or strain something during a game but continue to play seemingly unaffected until the game is over. Or recall the study mentioned earlier in this chapter about soldiers wounded in battle who did not complain of pain because they were so relieved to be off the battlefield. In both of these cases, the brain instructs the body not to register the pain until later, if at all.

This downward pathway from the brain is called a "descending tract"; the brain uses it to send chemical substances and nerve impulses back down to the cells in the spinal cord to act against the pain message sent up by the pain receptors. Dr. John Rowlingson, Director of the University of Virginia Pain Management Center, notes that although not much is known about these descending systems, they have been found to be largely chemical in nature and can be described as acting centrally to close the gates in the spinal cord to ascending messages. These characteristics of the descending tract help explain why therapies that act primarily in the brain, such as hypnosis and biofeedback, work so well to control pain.

Neurotransmitters. Another essential link is needed to forge the chain of pain events. This link is the presence of chemical substances within each cell of the nerve tract. These substances are called neurotransmitters; they can either pass the pain message along its way or make sure that it is stopped. Neurotransmitters can act as painkillers or pain producers. A commonly known neurotransmitter is *serotonin,* one of the most important chemicals involved in pain relief.

A group of neurotransmitters believed to be the body's own natural painkillers are called *endorphins* and *enkephalins.* These substances are produced in the brain and can have the same powerful effect as morphine or heroin. New research indicates that different people produce different amounts of these natural painkillers, which may explain why some people experience more pain than others do. For example, when an athlete is performing with an injury, he or she may be producing enough endorphins to override the pain message.

The Gate Control Theory

Have you ever bumped your shin and then instinctively rubbed it to make it feel better? You probably noticed that when you did, the shin seemed to ache a little less. Why is this so?

In 1965, Drs. Melzack and Wall proposed that there were "gates" on the bundles of nerve fibers on the spinal cord that can either open to allow pain impulses through to your brain or close to cut them off. This gate control theory proposes that a sufficient amount of stimuli can close the gate to the pain sensation. Specifically, the large diameter nerve fibers close the gate to the small diameter fibers, so that A-beta pain supersedes the pain of the A-delta and C fibers. This gating mechanism can also be influenced by other factors, such as messages sent from the brain instructing certain gates to close to the pain sensation.

The rubbing that you do after you bump your shin is a fast pain sensation, transmitted more quickly over the large fibers; it cancels out the sharp pain of hitting your shin, transmitted more slowly by the small fibers. The result is that you feel the rubbing, rather than the sharp pain. This mechanism explains why stimulators and acupuncture can be so effective in managing pain—they operate on the gating mechanism to close out slower pain sensations.

Many studies have attempted to prove the gate control theory, but none have shown conclusively that all facets of the theory are valid. Still, the importance of this theory should not be underrated, since it has served to stimulate much thinking on the subject of pain and helped us come to the conclusions we have today about effective treatment of chronic pain.

Pain Treatment Strategies

Every day you can read in newspapers and magazines about some new technique for managing chronic pain. Some of these techniques have just appeared on the scene, while others have been around for centuries. Some are very conservative or traditional in nature, while others strain your imagination as to their connection to pain control. You can be massaged by a masseuse, whirlpooled in a jacuzzi, operated on by a surgeon, medicated by a medical doctor, exercised by a physical therapist or exercise physiologist, analyzed by a psychiatrist, behaviorally modified by a psychologist, or rehabbed by a social worker! The possibilities are mind-numbing, and explanations so confusing and conflicting, that you may feel like giving up before you start.

To guide you through this maze, this section discusses techniques usually associated with a medical setting, such as nerve blocks and electrical stimulators. The next chapter deals with physical techniques such as exercise, and the four chapters after that deal with psychological techniques such as relaxation and assertiveness training.

Take time to discuss with your doctor any of the techniques described in this book that you would like to use. Try to educate yourself as much as possible about each technique, so that you know what you are getting into. Don't be afraid to ask questions! If your doctor is too rushed to explain, or doesn't know something, get another opinion. It's crucial for you to become informed in order to take charge of your own healing process.

Also, be aware that all the techniques will not work for everyone. What works for your best friend may not be the key to your recovery. You may know instinctively that a certain technique is not for you, while others may seem quite natural to work with and adapt. Or you may need to try each technique once, to get a feel for it, before deciding which ones work best for you. In any case, this process of pain management takes time. Explore all your options and choose the strategies that fit your life and your situation. Most importantly, keep an open mind, be patient, and be persistent.

Electrical Stimulators

If you have gone to a pain clinic, you may have been prescribed an electrical stimulator for pain relief. These small box-shaped devices are also known as transcutaneous (across the skin) electrical nerve stimulators (TENS). The small box is a transmitter that can be carried in the pocket or worn around the waist. It transmits electrical impulses through wires to surface electrodes taped to the skin surrounding the painful area. When the unit is turned on, most people feel an electrical buzzing or tingling sensation, the intensity of which they can control by a dial on the transmitting box.

The device is designed to work on the principle of the gate control theory, discussed above. The electrical impulse is picked up and transmitted over the large nerve fiber tracts, which in turn inhibit the small nerve fiber tracts from transmitting pain. In other words, you feel a tingling sensation rather than a pain sensation. You can increase or decrease the intensity of the tingling sensation as your pain increases or decreases.

TENS also works in two other ways. First, in addition to inhibiting the pain sensation, the tingling sensation also helps to distract you from it. Second, some researchers feel that TENS stimulates the release of endorphins in the brain and spinal cord. As noted above, endorphins are your body's own natural painkillers.

Some people find that brief periods of stimulation can provide hours, days, or weeks of pain relief. Others find that they need to wear the device continuously in order to feel some relief. Daily stimulation sometimes provides gradually increasing pain relief over periods of weeks or months. A great advantage of a TENS unit is that once you locate the point on your body that provides you the greatest amount of pain relief, you can use this method at home or work as needed, giving you a significant measure of control over you own pain therapy.

TENS units are simple and easy to use and can be purchased through your doctor. These devices are safe and are found to have virtually no harmful side effects even with continuous use. Some people may find that they develop a skin irritation from the unit's electrode paste or tape. Check with your doctor for types of nonallergic paste and nonabrasive tape. TENS units are not to be used around water or microwave ovens or while sleeping or driving.

TENS units have been found to be most useful as an adjunct to other forms of therapy commonly found in multimodal pain clinics, such as exercise, physical therapy, appropriate medication, and relaxation techniques.

Acupuncture

Acupuncture is an ancient and time-tested method of pain and disease control discovered in China as early as 3000 B.C. Chinese folklore has it that a warrior discovered the principle of acupuncture during a battle. He was pierced by an arrow in his leg and found that the wound from the arrow made another wound in his shoulder feel better.

Acupuncture works on the principle of "meridians" or imaginary lines drawn on the body that represent internal organs and the trunk. Points on these lines are thought to connect different parts of the body. For example, a point on the skin between the thumb and index finger connects to various parts of the head for control of headaches; a point on the leg is specified for control of gastric disorders. When one of these points is stimulated by an acupuncture needle or deeply massaged (acupressure), a headache or stomachache can be relieved. In practice, a thin steel or gold needle is inserted at the acupuncture point and gently twirled. The round-tipped needle simply spreads the skin rather than puncturing it, thereby reducing the chance of infection. Some needles are twirled for brief periods of from ten to twenty minutes and then removed; others are left in over a longer period of time.

Remember the gate control theory? Here is another direct application of it. The stimulation of the needles is thought to set off a series of electrical impulses that travel the large nerve fiber tracts, cutting off the more painful sensations sent along the small fiber tracts. With acupuncture you feel a pleasant, tingling, warm sensation, much like the sensations you get from a TENS unit.

There are three other explanations for the effectiveness of acupuncture. First, acupuncture has been shown to stimulate better circulation to tissues; often the effects of poor circulation to an injured area can increase pain and retard the healing process. Second, acupuncture can release tension in the muscle surrounding the acupuncture point. Third, recent research suggests that acupuncture stimulates the production of endorphins, the natural painkiller, in the brain and spinal cord.

A related acupuncture method has served to further renew Western interest in the field. Electroacupuncture involves stimulation of body tissues through needles hooked up to battery-driven stimulators. In modern China, this method is used to produce intense analgesia during surgery. "Films of such operations are extremely dramatic, and the feeling arose that if acupuncture could produce sufficient analgesia for surgery, it must surely be effective for chronic pain of all kinds." (Melzack and Wall, 1982)

Consult your doctor for help in contacting trained and licensed acupuncture specialists.

Trigger Points

When a trigger point is pressed, it causes a great deal of pain, sometimes reproducing an exact chronic pain sensation. Trigger points in muscles or ligaments can also be identified by muscle spasms or contractions. They are known to lie above or near the point in the muscle where the motor nerves are firing most intensely (that is, producing pain).

Although the exact mechanism of trigger points is unknown, they are probably caused by a direct stress to your muscle such as trauma (tear during an injury), chronic tension, abnormal posture, or muscle fatigue. Sometimes trigger points lay dormant for many years after recovery from an injury. You may not experience chronic pain complaints, but instead be accumulating unsuspected latent trigger points. These can be activated by chronic strain from sedentary living habits, minor stresses from daily living, anxiety, or overstretching or fatigue of your muscles.

Trigger points are thought to be very similar to acupuncture points. A study done by Melzack, Stillwell and Fox (1977) showed that every trigger point has a corresponding acupuncture point and that there is a close correlation between the pain syndromes associated with each point. In other words, the Western medical world labels these points differently from the Eastern medical world, but they represent the same underlying nerve mechanisms.

Trigger points are often injected for pain relief. These trigger point injections are a form of nerve block.

Nerve Blocks

When you have chronic pain, you are tempted to tense your muscles in an attempt to brace yourself against the pain. This very common and automatic response can lead to the *pain-spasm-pain cycle*. As a result of this response, your muscles remain in a tense or contracted state, blood flow is decreased to the muscles, and your posture can become abnormal. In other words, your muscles become immobile and inflexible, which further contributes to your pain.

Local anesthetic nerve blocks and trigger point injections can interrupt this cycle. An anesthesiologist specially trained in the area of pain management injects a local anesthetic solution into the painful area, causing the nerve fibers to become numb or anesthetized and to stop sending pain signals. You should feel an alleviation of your pain immediately following each injection. This is a good time to do gentle stretching exercises to improve your mobility and relax your muscles and to return to normal posture. Sometimes the mere insertion of the doctor's needle can aid in pain relief, much as an acupuncture needle would do.

If you have acute pain, the effect of the nerve block will often outlast the duration of the painful stimulus from your injury or surgical incision. However, local anesthetic blocks for chronic pain often do not produce long-term benefits. An exception to this is the use of repeated blocks for causalgia (burning pain) or causalgia-like symptoms such as reflex sympathetic dystrophy. In these cases, permanent pain relief can often be achieved.

Heat and Cold Therapy

Getting you back to full or at least freer movement is a very important goal of chronic pain management. The pain-spasm-pain cycle reinforces immobility—you brace yourself against the pain and hold your muscles stiffly for long periods of time, which further contributes to your pain and makes even menial activity a chore. A physical therapist or an exercise physiologist can help you reverse this process by gradually increasing your mobility through strength and flexibility exercises. Exercise is such an important part of pain management that all of chapter three is devoted to it.

Both heat and cold therapy can also reduce muscle tension or spasm. If you try heat, the physical therapist will usually apply hot packs for twenty minutes under six to eight layers of towels. Cold packs are also applied for twenty minutes, but under two layers of towels. An ice block massage involves lightly rubbing the painful area with a cake of ice for at least ten minutes or until numbness occurs. In one study, the ice block massage was considered more effective than the cold pack because it provided more intense stimulation to the painful area; the cold pack cooled tissues more slowly.

Both heat and cold therapy reduce muscle spasming and swelling from an injury or inflammation. Both also decrease the number of nerve impulses from the painful area to the spinal cord, which means that less small fiber input (carrying the pain message) is available to open the pain gate.

You can decide for yourself which temperature provides more relief. Both are considered equally effective methods of pain reduction.

Massage

Massage can be a relaxing and revitalizing experience and an excellent addition to a pain management program. It not only soothes aching muscles, but also has therapeutic benefits as well, such as stimulating blood flow and releasing toxins from muscles and tissues. Massage can help to break the pain-spasm-pain cycle by relaxing muscles that are tight or in spasm, increasing circulation, improving oxygen and nutrition flow to the painful area, increasing your range of motion, and finding and relaxing your trigger points. For people who have to be inactive due to injury, illness, or age, massage can compensate for lack of exercise and muscular contraction.

Massage systematically works with each muscle in your body to look for and relieve areas of tension and trigger points. Trigger points, which often reoccur in the same places, are relieved through sustained pressure. As you find out which ones contribute to your pain, you can learn to massage them yourself to help decrease your pain.

Your massage therapist may use a light stroke or deep kneading action, depending on what he or she thinks is right for you. A well-trained therapist will take a medical history from you to determine the acute or chronic nature of your problem, extent of medication use, and other pertinent information. A massage is usually not suggested in cases of inflammation, edema (swelling), herniated discs, fever, and other conditions that require you to wait until their acute symptoms have subsided.

You can do massage for yourself, especially for neck and headache pain. This will help when you're feeling tense, but for a more relaxing and effective experience try letting your spouse, trusted friend, or massage therapist give you a massage. Make sure that they listen to your feedback and do not massage spasms or painful areas too heavily when it hurts. You want your massage to be a pleasant experience.

To locate a trained massage therapist in your area, write to Robert King, National President, American Massage Therapy Association, 1329 West Pratt Bouldevard, Chicago, IL 60626. Several of the many excellent references on the subject of massage and chronic pain are included in the further reading section at the end of this chapter.

Your Internal Resources

This chapter has covered medical approaches to the problem of pain, from the basic foundation of pain anatomy to the current medical technology of nerve blocks and TENS units. These methods can be considered "external" approaches—you have something done to you, such as an ice massage or a nerve block. These medical approaches are, of course, extremely important elements in any pain control effort.

But there is an even more important element in pain control—that of managing your "internal" resources. In the following chapters you will read about identifying and making use of your own internal resources to reduce pain through relaxation and exercise.

To show how these approaches can be applied, let's return to the woman with the neck problem described in the opening of this chapter. She can apply her new knowledge of pain theory by making sure she is not unconsciously bracing against her neck pain and contributing to the pain-spasm-pain cycle by holding her neck, shoulder, and arm stiffly. She can use the external approach of a TENS unit or a nerve block to gain some pain relief so that she can begin to gently stretch her muscles and increase her circulation and flexibility. She can take medications prescribed by her doctor specifically for pain relief. Or she can draw on her internal resources to send soothing, pain-free messages to her painful area by distracting her attention from the pain and focusing on something pleasant with the aid of relaxation training or self-hypnosis.

All of these are valid and effective means of reducing pain. They can be used alone or in combination with each other. If you maintain an open mind to them, you can find an overall approach that will work best for you.

Further Reading

Aronoff, Gerald, ed. *Evaluation and Treatment of Chronic Pain.* Baltimore: Urban & Schwarzenberg, 1985.

Goleman, Daniel, and Tara Bennett-Goleman. *The Relaxed Body Book.* Garden City, NY: Doubleday, 1986.

Hendler, Nelson, and Judith Fenton. *Coping With Chronic Pain.* New York: Clarkson N. Potter, Inc., 1979.

Krieger, Dolores. *The Therapeutic Touch.* Englewood Cliffs, NJ: Prentice-Hall, 1979.

Lidell, Lucinda, with others. *The Book of Massage.* New York: Simon and Schuster, 1984.

Melzack, Ronald, and Patrick Wall. *The Challenge of Pain.* New York: Basic Books, 1983.

Raj, P. Prithvi, ed. *Practical Management of Pain.* Chicago: Yearbook Medical Publishers, 1986.

Sternbach, Richard, ed. *The Psychology of Pain.* New York: Raven Press, 1978.

3

Exercise

Exercise has become quite a fad in America, with booming marketing campaigns promoting the right clothes to wear, the right kind of place to work out in, and the right companion to meet while you're there. With so many facts and opinions flying around, it is no wonder that people are confused about the appropriate way to exercise. In fact, the seemingly arduous task of wading through the facts and figures (no pun intended) may tempt you not to start exercising in the first place. Throw in the burden of a chronic pain condition, and your uncertainty about what to do for your condition is perfectly understandable.

But amid all the many research theories, Hollywood promotions, and magazine suggestions, one thing is crystal clear. Exercise is extremely important. And if you have chronic pain, exercise should be a fact of life.

Research has shown that people who gradually introduce exercise into their daily routine after an injury or sprain or strain (a) return to a more normal lifestyle faster and (b) maintain a pain-free existence more consistently. Gradual stretching and strengthening exercises help recondition your muscles, a benefit which in turn aids in healing and rehabilitation, prevents reinjury, and relieves the stress of chronic pain.

Take stock of your exercise habits. Do you lead a sedentary life? If you have chronic pain, have you made a commitment to yourself to move your muscles at least a little every day?

Some people find that honestly evaluating their exercise habits helps motivate them to begin a regular program. Record your exercise activities for the past week below. Be sure to include your attitudes toward each activity. Negative, automatic thoughts can often become obstacles to starting something new. It will be helpful for you to uncover such thoughts early in your exercise program and to learn to dispel them so that you can avoid discouraging yourself. Examples of negative thinking about exercise are:

- "My parents were fat, so I'll be fat."
- "I'll never learn to cope with this much pain—exercise will make it worse."
- "I don't have time."

For more about the effects of negative thinking on chronic pain, refer to chapter five. For now, jot down your activities and your thoughts on the chart below. Share your list with a friend or relative who exercises regularly. Chances are that person has had the same or similar thoughts before and can lend a sympathetic ear.

Pre-Exercise Chart for the Past Week

Day	Physical Activity	Attitudes
_____	_____	_____
	_____	_____
_____	_____	_____
	_____	_____
_____	_____	_____
	_____	_____
_____	_____	_____
	_____	_____
_____	_____	_____
	_____	_____
_____	_____	_____
	_____	_____
_____	_____	_____
	_____	_____

When To Start Exercising

Because movement can make the pain feel worse, the initial temptation for most people in pain is to brace their muscles against the pain and hold them in a rigid position. In fact, during the initial stages of an acute pain condition, inactivity is usually recommended. Movement during an early stage can further aggravate a torn muscle, ligament, or bulging disc through swelling and inflammation, possibly retarding the healing process.

To allow maximum healing to take place, the common rule for acute pain is one or more weeks of bed rest, with aspirin or analgesic (pain killer). There are several recommended positions to make your bed rest more comfortable, especially for back injuries. You can support your legs behind your knees with enough pillows to ensure that your pelvis is flat against the bed. Or you can lay in the fetal position, bringing your knees towards your chest and placing a pillow between your knees. Both of these positions ease pressure on your spine. Make sure that you are sleeping on a firm mattress, not a sagging one.

When the pain becomes chronic (after approximately three months), the time has come for you to begin gradually exercising the painful area to increase your mobility, flexibility, and circulation and get you back on the road to healthy functioning. Before you start, follow these suggestions:

1. Check with your doctor prior to beginning any exercise program.

2. If you were a regular exerciser before your injury, do not expect yourself to be able to immediately resume the same strenuous exercise. Gradually build up your strength and tolerance. The healing and coping process takes time, and you may reinjure yourself if you push yourself too hard.

3. Educate yourself. Learn about your muscles. If you are new to exercise, take some time to learn about your body and how it responds to exercise. It has taken you this long to learn how your body responds to pain and stress; now give yourself some time to learn about and incorporate exercise into your daily life.

Some Basic Muscle Anatomy

A muscle is a strong type of body tissue that is capable of contracting and relaxing when instructed by nerves to make your body move. A *muscle spasm* is a muscle that is continually contracted due to tension or injury. You can create a muscle spasm by making a fist and holding your hand and arm tightly for as long as you can. Eventually your hand and arm begin to tremble, and you feel a cramping, burning sensation. Because you are squeezing the muscles, oxygen and blood cannot move through the muscle to remove a buildup of waste (in the form of lactic acid). The acid produces pain when it accumulates in the tissue, causing burning and cramping. Muscles that are chronically contracted, or in spasm, are caused by excessive demand from overuse, trauma, or tension.

When a muscle is *strained,* it is usually overstretched due to fatigue or overexertion. A muscle *sprain* actually refers to a partial tearing of ligaments, the tough fibers that hold the bones together at the joints. Both sprains and strains tend to go away spontaneously in a few days or weeks, with bed rest, proper medication, heat, and massage.

A healthy muscle can stretch or contract and then return to a normal resting state. A muscle is *shortened* or *weak* when it is contracted due to spasm or injury.

A shortened muscle is not able to withstand very much movement or bear very much weight. Its energy is gone because its blood supply is essentially squeezed out. An *overly stretched* muscle is also weak and unable to provide necessary support to the spine and other bones. For example, people with large bellies have overstretched abdominal muscles. Their other back muscles are forced to compensate and may in turn spasm or become fatigued. Stretching a shortened muscle helps to lengthen it and increase its blood supply; strengthening an overly lengthened muscle helps to build up fiber strength. This is why a balanced exercise program includes both a stretching and strengthening program to help contracted muscles become more flexible and overly stretched muscles become stronger.

Proper Posture

Poor posture is a major culprit contributing to lower and upper back and neck pain. Poor posture is often learned in childhood, when it's popular to order children to "Stand up straight—stick out your chest and hold your stomach in!" Both commands can force your spine into unnatural positions that fatigue and strain the back's muscles and joints.

Your spine is out of balance whenever it loses its natural curves—the cervical curve and the lumbar curve. Poor posture can distort these natural curves, because pressure is unevenly distributed along the spine, causing stress to the vertebrae, joints, and muscles.

You can test your posture by standing with your back against a wall. Put your hand in the small of your back. You should feel only minimal space between your back and the wall. People with poor posture either slouch forward, slumping their shoulders and rounding their backs, or they overly arch their backs, sticking out their chests and buttocks. Both postures unbalance the spine and stress the muscles and joints. As you are standing at the wall, tuck your pelvis into a pelvic tilt position (see diagram 3.1) and feel how the lumbar curve in your back is partially reduced. This is proper, balanced posture.

Here are five simple, common sense rules to follow to correct poor posture. You'll be surprised at how much they help relieve a backache and help you prevent further problems.

1. Slightly tuck in your chin.
2. Relax your shoulders and arms.
3. Tuck in your stomach (into the pelvic tilt position).
4. Tighten your buttocks.
5. Slightly bend your knees.

If you commit these rules to memory, it will become a habit for you to tuck your tummy instead of slump! You can practice good posture anywhere, but pay special attention to it while you're at your job, especially when sitting or standing in one position for a long time. If you have to stand awhile, prop up one foot on a low box or stool.

DIAGRAM 3.1

Feeling the Pelvic Tilt

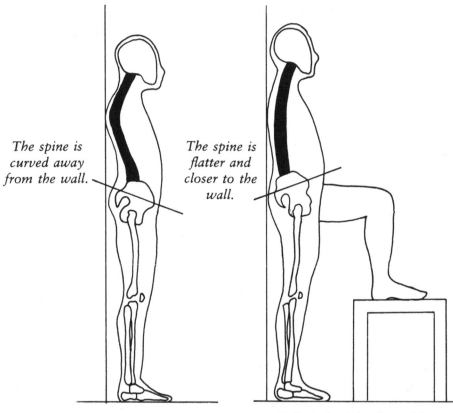

The spine is curved away from the wall.

The spine is flatter and closer to the wall.

Unbalanced pelvic position   *Balanced pelvic tilt position*

1. Stand with your back and buttocks against a wall.
2. Place your hands between the hollow of your back and the wall.
3. Place one foot on a chair seat in front of you.
4. Note that your pelvis is tilted up and your back is straighter and closer to the wall than it was when both feet were on the ground.
   YOU ARE NOW IN THE PELVIC TILT POSITION.
5. Tighten your stomach and buttock muscles to keep your back in this position.
6. Hold this balanced pelvic position as you lower your leg to the floor.
7. Walk around the room holding this position.

From Dr. David Imrie's *Goodbye Back Ache* (Toronto: Prentice-Hall/Newcastle Publishing, 1983).

Exercises

Stretching properly and sufficiently is a critical part of any exercise program. Many injuries or reinjuries occur during exercise because the muscle is "cold," or not properly warmed up before movement. A car runs efficiently when the engine is warm; so does the body.

If your muscles have not been physically active, they become atrophied—small and weak. Stretching and strengthening help the muscles to return to a more normal size, increasing their endurance and enabling them to withstand more twisting, turning, and sudden movement.

Proper stretching involves a "static stretch." This means a stretch which is a slow, gentle, continuous extension, rather than several quick bounces. Bouncing actually tightens the muscle, which can lead to tendon, ligament, and muscle tears if the muscle is cold. Have you ever suddenly sprinted for the bus and felt a sharp cramp in your calf or foot? Your leg was not ready for action, and the result was a spasm. Even muscles that are in good shape can cramp or spasm if subjected to a sudden shock such as twisting or sprinting. But conditioned muscles will withstand the shock better and return to a normal state faster than muscles that are out of shape.

Stretch for at least five minutes before you begin your conditioning exercises. If you are a new stretcher, hold each stretch for twenty seconds. Stretch to the point of gentle resistance, NOT PAIN. As you become familiar with the stretches and your body's responses, increase the stretch time gradually to between thirty and sixty seconds. Sometimes it is helpful to stretch lightly and easily first, ease up, and then repeat the stretch, holding for a longer period and pushing slightly beyond the first stretch. In his popular *Stretching* workbook, Bob Anderson reminds us that the object of stretching is to reduce muscular tension and promote freer movement—not to force yourself to attempt such extreme flexibility that you risk overstretching and injury. The key is regularity and relaxation.

Ten Rules for Proper Stretching

1. Do static stretches—no bouncing.
2. Start very slowly and gently. Move twice as slow as you think you should. Do ten minutes of slow stretching before starting any strengthening exercises.
3. Hold stretches at least twenty seconds.
4. Stretch to the point of gentle resistance, not pain. At the slightest pain, back off.
5. The object of stretching is to warm up your body and relax it, not to achieve brute strength or super flexibility.
6. Don't throw your head or body around. Move slowly and carefully even when getting into position for the next exercise.
7. Keep breathing during stretches. Begin and end exercise sessions with five to ten deep breaths.

8. Avoid exercise entirely right after acute injury.
9. Many short sessions are better than a few long sessions. It's better for your body to do 6 stretches 6 times a day than to do 36 stretches all at once.
10. Consult your doctor if soreness persists more than two days, of if your symptoms are worse immediately after exercise and don't get better the next day.

The following stretches and strengtheners have been chosen from the recommendations of experts in the field for overall body strength and flexibility. However, it is always wise to consult with your doctor, physical therapist, or athletic trainer before you attempt any of these exercises. Professional expertise will tell you whether you have a specific problem that needs special attention, or have the garden variety of musculoskeletal pain that responds well to these types of exercises.

A safe way to begin is on the floor with gentle stretching only until you and your doctor feel that you are ready to move on to strengthening exercises. Then you should do strengthening exercises only after you are warmed up from the stretching. As you become familiar with the exercises and feel your strength and flexibility increasing, add repetitions to your daily workout.

Consult chapter nine for more information about how to exercise.

Remember, if you are unused to exercise, you will probably feel some tightness and soreness at first. This is the normal microscopic tearing and rebuilding of muscle fiber associated with any exercise. However, if the soreness persists for more than two days, or if your symptoms are much worse immediately after exercising and remain worse the next day, consult with your doctor. Back off a bit from your exercise routine and decrease the number of repetitions of each exercise. But do not quit altogether. Keep moving, if only gently and gingerly. The movement will help you decrease the pain and stress and keep healing oxygen and blood nutrients circulating throughout your body. With relaxed persistence, in time you will be able to move about again more freely.

The following exercises are designed to be done in the sequence presented, but you are encouraged to add, delete, or modify the exercises based on your needs and body reactions. The sequence will take approximately twenty minutes to begin with, but will lengthen somewhat as your stretches increase above twenty seconds each. Make sure you perform your exercises at least once a day.

I. Leg Stretches

1. *Ankle and calf stretch* (seated or lying). Rotate ankles slowly, with feet relaxed, first clockwise, then counterclockwise, eight times in each direction.

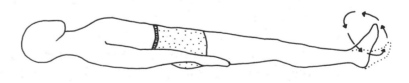

2. *Hamstring stretch*. Place your left foot against your right inner thigh. Slightly bend your outstretched leg, keeping your knee pointing toward the ceiling. Bend forward at the hips until you feel the stretch in the back of your legs (hamstrings). Hold for twenty seconds. Repeat three times on each side.

3. *Hip flexor stretch*. Lace your hands under your knee. Pull your leg toward your chest, keeping your lower back on the floor and your other leg slightly bent. Hold for twenty seconds. Repeat three times on each side. *Advanced hip flexor stretch:* To increase your workout, raise your head and shoulders slightly when doing the hip flexor stretch, tucking your chin to meet your bent knee and tightening your stomach muscles. Hold for five seconds to begin and gradually increase.

4. *Quadricep stretch*. (Note: If you have back or knee problems, take care as you get into this position.) Sit with your right leg bent backwards and your left leg bent with your foot touching your right knee. *Slowly* lean straight back until you feel the stretch in the muscle on top of the leg bent backwards (quadricep). Hold for twenty seconds. Repeat three times on each side. Keep your neck muscles relaxed as you perform this exercise.

II. Lower Back Stretches

1. *Cross leg rotation stretch.* (Note: IF YOU HAVE DISC PROBLEMS, CHECK WITH YOUR DOCTOR BEFORE DOING THIS EXERCISE.) Place your left leg on top of your right leg and gently pull left towards the floor. Feel the stretch in your lower back, sides, and the top of your hips. Hold for twenty seconds. Repeat twice on each side, pulling in the direction of the knee on top.

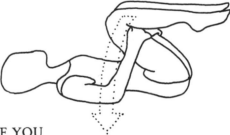

2. *Lower back stretch and roll.* (Note: IF YOU HAVE DISC PROBLEMS, CHECK WITH YOUR DOCTOR BEFORE DOING THIS EXERCISE.) With your hands laced under your knees, pull both knees to your chest, keeping your lower back flat on the bed or floor. Hold for twenty seconds. Keep breathing. Now rotate your knees slowly to the right, gently twisting as far as you feel comfortable. Keep your shoulders on the bed or floor. Hold for twenty seconds. Breathe. Slowly roll to the left and hold for twenty seconds. Repeat the sequence three times.

3. *Press-ups.* (Note: DO NOT DO THIS EXERCISE IF YOU HAVE DISC PROBLEMS. CHECK WITH YOUR DOCTOR FIRST.) Lie on your stomach with your arms bent at the elbow. Press up slowly, keeping your elbows bent. Keep your pelvis and legs relaxed. Repeat ten times.

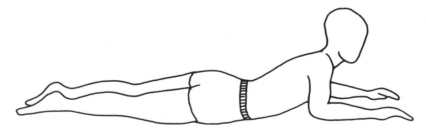

Advanced press-ups: As you are pressing up, slowly straighten your arms and lift your torso as far as feels comfortable.

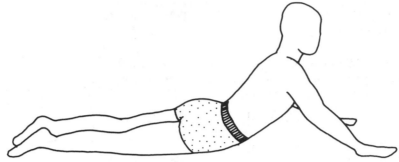

III. Upper Back, Chest, and Neck Stretches

1. *Middle-upper back stretch.* Raise your right arm and hold it below the elbow with your left hand. Pull your right elbow gently toward your left shoulder until you feel the stretch. Hold for five seconds. Repeat for the other side.

2. *Pectoral stretch.* Lace your hands behind your neck and press your elbows back as far as you can. Hold for five seconds. Return to your starting position, then drop your arms and relax. Repeat

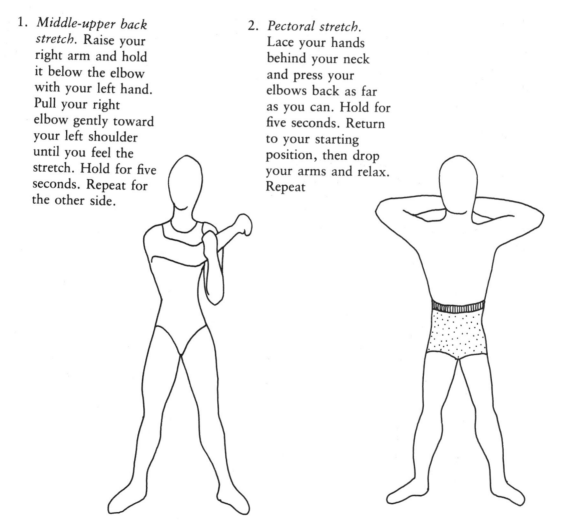

3. *Arm circles.* Stand with your feet shoulder-width apart. Inhale and cross both arms in front of your body, feeling the stretch in your upper back. Uncross your arms and raise them over your head. Exhale slowly while lowering both arms in an arc behind your body, feeling the stretch in your chest. Do the entire exercise as if in slow motion. Breathing is a very important part of this exercise. For this reason, it is an excellent warm-up and cool-down exercise. Repeat five to ten times.

4. *"Yes-no-maybe."* First stretch your head forward with your chin tucked, then stretch it from side to side, and at last at an angle on each side (the "maybe" position). Hold each stretch for ten seconds and repeat three times.

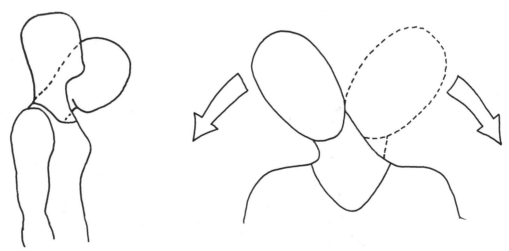

5. *Advanced neck stretches.* While seated, pull your neck forward (as shown, from the top of your head), and then to each side 30 to 35 degrees. Pull your head until you feel a slight stretch in the back of your neck and your upper back. Hold the stretch for twenty to thirty seconds.

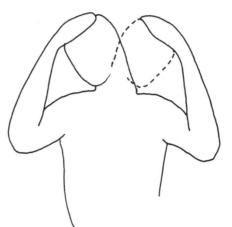

6. *Shoulder shrugs.* Pull both shoulders upward (but do not hunch your neck downward) simultaneously for ten seconds. Do this three times in a row. Gradually increase the time for each shrug.

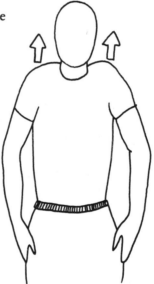

7. *Neck strengthener.* Lie down. Raise your head off the bed or floor and hold for five seconds. Lower your head slowly and press it into the bed or floor for five seconds. Repeat three times.

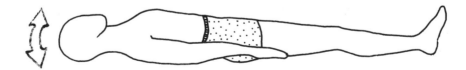

IV. Overall Body Stretches

1. *Chair stretch.* Place your feet wide apart on the floor. Drop both hands between your knees and slowly bend over to the point where you feel a stretch. Hold for twenty seconds. Relax and breathe.

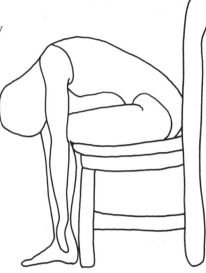

2. *Spinal twist.* (Note: DO NOT DO THIS EXERCISE IF YOU HAVE DISC PROBLEMS. CHECK WITH YOUR DOCTOR FIRST.) Bend your left leg over your outstretched right leg. Your left foot should rest on the outside of your right knee. Rest your right elbow on the outside of your upper left thigh. With your left hand behind you, slowly turn your head to look over your left shoulder, rotating your upper body toward your left arm and hand. Hold for twenty seconds. This is a good stretch for your upper and lower back, hips, and ribcage.

V. Back Strengtheners

1. *Lower back flattener (pelvic tilt).* Flatten the curve in your lower back by flattening against the floor with your lower abdominal muscles. Hold for at least five seconds. Start with only a few repetitions, but repeat many times during the day. Stop if you feel pain. This is one of the best exercises for lower back injuries and good exercise for practicing a correct pelvic tilt and strengthening the gluteus and abdominal muscles.

2. *Abdominal curls (curl-ups).* Lie down and bend your knees with your feet flat on the floor. While maintaining a pelvic tilt, slowly curl your head, shoulders, and upper back off the floor toward your knees. With your chin tucked, hold this raised position for a count of five. Slowly lower yourself back to the starting position. Repeat five times.

3. *Curl-backs.* (Note: This exercise should be tried after you feel comfortable and stronger during curl-ups.) Start by sitting tilted slightly back, with a C curve in your spine. Keep your arms folded, your knees bent, and your feet flat on the floor. Lean back one third to one half of the way to the floor, leaning back very carefully and only as far as you feel safe. Pull forward to your original position. Repeat five times. (Caution: When doing curl-backs, do not anchor your feet under a chair or bed. This causes you to use muscles other than your abdominals to lower yourself. Also, be sure to keep your chin tucked and your neck relaxed. Do not throw your head back.)

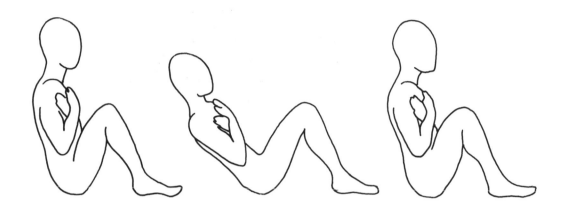

A Case for Exercise

"The worst thing about chronic pain for me was the loneliness, the isolation. There was nothing to look forward to."

These are the words of Mary Jo, a normally active mother of four who was totally unprepared for the disruption in her life that a riding injury would cause. But when I interviewed her a year and a half after her accident, she was up and moving around her kitchen, busy fixing me iced tea, wrestling with stuck kitchen windows, and tending to a sick child. Looking back at her progress, she was sure that doing consistent exercise was a major factor.

Horseback riding had always been one of Mary Jo's favorite activities. Although she was an expert horsewoman, a tree branch struck her in the shoulder one day on a cross-country ride. Nothing was broken, but she felt a severe burning pain ("It felt just like a branding iron") spreading down her arm.

Several weeks later, she couldn't use her arm and hand, and her fingers were numb. A doctor put her on complete bed rest with traction and a ten-day series of steroid medications. The medications relieved the burning sensation, but Mary Jo found herself nearly immobilized.

"I couldn't drive, cook, brush my teeth, or wash my hair. I would struggle to get up in the mornings to have coffee with my family, but the pain would drive me back to bed after fifteen or twenty minutes."

After three months in this situation, Mary Jo felt desperate. A doctor had prescribed more bed rest, with possible surgery, but Mary Jo realized that she would have to start moving to get better. She had a friend drive her to the physical therapy department of a local hospital. There she was given massages, whirlpool baths, and a series of exercises to do daily to begin loosening up her tense shoulder and neck muscles. After their many months of inactivity her muscles were weak, inflexible, and unable to withstand much movement before they were thrown into painful spasms.

She tried the easy exercises first—gentle shoulder shrugs, "yes-no-maybe" exercises, and neck stretches (all described earlier in this chapter). She did her exercises first thing in the morning, again after she had a hot shower and her muscles were more relaxed, and once more in the evening. At first she did only a few repetitions of each exercise, because her muscles would tire easily. As she got stronger, she increased the repetitions.

Mary Jo had also gone to a pain clinic, where the exercise therapist showed her how to strengthen her muscles by using gentle resistance exercises (see chapter nine) and arm circles with jelly jar weights. She was also given a TENS unit, which provided so much pain relief that she was able to greatly increase the time spent exercising.

"I began to exercise in earnest, doing more vigorous neck, shoulder, and arm exercises three times a day and after a hot shower. Instead of searing pain, all I felt during and after exercise was heat in my muscles.

"These days I still do a lot of shoulder shrugs, deep breathing, and neck exercises to loosen my neck and shoulders. I remember to drop my shoulders and let my arms and hands hang loose and heavy. I check the points in my body where I know I tense up. I still have some pain, but I know that exercise has really helped me get moving again and back into my life."

4

Pain and Basic Stress Management

Paulette suffered from a combination of tension and migraine headaches for years. At first her headaches seemed manageable, but then they grew worse and began to seriously disrupt her work and home life. She decided that she had to do something about them.

After visiting several different doctors, she reluctantly agreed to go to a pain clinic for biofeedback and stress management. She politely listened to the therapist's explanations of the program, with her face frozen into a smile, all the while thinking to herself that the therapist—and the other doctors—must all think her crazy. She finally blurted out, "What does stress management have to do with my pain? I'm not making this up. And anyway, I don't have time to learn anything new because my headaches take so much of my energy."

Many people have these same concerns. And if you've been sent from one doctor to the next and given different explanations for your pain each time, then it's reasonable to begin to wonder if they really think that you're fabricating your pain—or that you're truly crazy.

Odds are that you're not crazy or faking. But you do have an understandable amount of stress in response to a difficult situation—coping with chronic pain. And health professionals are often tempted to pin a label on you when they don't know what else to do. In your frustration, you may even begin to doubt yourself, thinking that your pain is all in your head and there's nothing you can do about it.

Self-defeating behavior and negative thinking are what this and the next three chapters are all about. In this chapter, we will examine ways to counteract self-defeating pain behavior by practicing relaxation strategies. You will learn to deal with the pain in your life much as you deal with other stressors. After all, your chronic pain drains your energy much like the stress of a demanding job or a nagging family problem.

When you have chronic pain, life stressors seem like insurmountable obstacles in your path. Your family harmony is affected, sexual relations with your spouse can be reduced or stop altogether, and your ability to do your job or chores around the house can be severely curtailed, perhaps leading to financial worries.

When pain flares up, it feels like it will never go away, which can make you feel depressed and angry. You find yourself facing not only your physical pain, but mental anguish as well. You feel helpless and alone. Sometimes you feel that your hopes for recovery are being chiseled away with every ache and throb. As Paulette said, "I feel like I use all my energy doing battle with the pain—I have no stamina or joy left over for important things in my life, like my family and job."

Ease Your Pain by Managing Your Stress

When you're in pain, you need to learn and practice stress management for two simple reasons. First, chronic pain is itself a stressor. It reduces your ability to function, to cope, and to feel good. If you can't function, you feel useless. If you can't cope, then other stressors begin piling up. Second, you tense your muscles in response to pain and its byproducts. You grit your teeth in anticipation of the pain. You hold your shoulders rigidly to brace against the pain. This increases your body's overall tension level, which only makes your pain worse.

Begin by realizing that there is a stress component to your pain. Physical tension and mental anxiety can make coping more difficult. You can minimize the domino effect of stress and pain by learning to manage the tension component in your life. Learn to identify stress in your body and its interplay with your pain.

Understanding the Stress Response

When your body is physically tense because of pain or other stressors, it usually reacts with what is termed the *stress response*. You may also know this response as the "fight or flight" response. In his popular book *The Relaxation Response*, Dr. Herbert Benson suggests that the fight or flight response had important evolutionary significance for human survival. We inherited this response from our ancestors, who put it to good use in the face of extreme physical danger. Among other things, their hearts pumped blood faster to their muscles and lungs, enabling them to strike harder or run faster than they normally would. But now, although you have the same physical response, your world seldom requires or even permits you to fight or run. For example, you cannot run away from or hit your boss when he or she yells at you. The same ancient physical response is turned on, but it doesn't benefit you in the same way. You don't have an appropriate outlet or release valve for the stress.

This doesn't mean that all stress is bad. The natural stress response can help you react quickly to protect yourself or give you a charge so that you think more quickly and clearly. The adrenalin that's suddenly pumped into your blood stream helps you swerve out of the path of an oncoming car. Similarly, a challenging project at work can motivate you to work harder. But when the adrenalin that gave you a quick reaction continues to course through your bloodstream for months or years, its effects are not so positive.

The danger of a prolonged stress response is its wear and tear on your body. And when stress is coupled with chronic pain, the wear and tear you experience is multiplied. Twenty years of a demanding job or six months of pain will both take a toll on your body. You may end up with circulation problems from decreased blood flow, or the chronic secretions in your stomach may eventually contribute to an ulcer. Or the shoulder, neck, and head muscles that you tense to brace against the pain may lead to tension headaches or temporal mandibular joint syndrome, a problem of the jaw resulting in part from chronically clenched teeth.

Here is what usually happens to the human body under stress and what you feel:

• Your heart rate increases.	You feel your heart pounding in your chest.
• Your blood pressure increases.	(Not detectable unless measured.)
• Your sweat level increases.	Your skin feels cold and clammy.
• Your respiration rate changes.	Your breathing becomes shallow or you breathe in gulps.
• Adrenalin and other hormones are released into the blood stream, causing vasoconstriction in the periphery and increase in muscle tone. Blood flows away from the periphery (hands and feet) to the heart, lungs, and muscles.	Your muscles contract; your hands and feet become cold.
• Certain acids are secreted in the gastro-intestinal tract.	You feel "butterflies" in your stomach.

Other organs such as the liver and spleen are also affected by stress, and some organs shut down altogether, such as the digestive tract and sexual functioning.

You can help yourself by learning to identify your typical unhelpful stress patterns and by beginning to eliminate them from your daily routine. This can be done with regular and consistent daily practice of one or more of the techniques discussed in the rest of this chapter and in chapter five. These techniques have different names and use different processes, but they are all designed to do virtually the same thing . . . to relax your body so that you can cope with your pain and stress better.

You can also manage your pain and stress levels by attending to your thoughts and feelings—that is, by identifying the negative self-talk which is part of your belief system. This highly important part of your coping repertoire will be discussed in chapter six. For now, you'll find it easier to branch out into other coping methods once you begin to take care of your immediate problem—your aching body. After that, you will have more energy to devote to other aspects of chronic pain management.

Deep Breathing

Deep breathing is one of the easiest, most effective ways to release tension in your body. Yet it's easy to take this important function for granted, and when you are in stress or pain, you are likely to forget to take this essential relaxation step.

Think for a moment about the last time you sat in a theater engrossed in a movie—you probably did not move or breathe deeply for a good part of two hours. That's why you stretched when you rose from the seat—your muscles had been deprived of oxygen and your circulation slowed, and stretching is a natural reflex to rejuvenate the muscles. Now think about the last time you had a bout with your pain. You probably sucked in your breath, clenched your teeth, and hunched your shoulders, as if doing these things would ward off the pain. In fact, these responses only make your situation worse, because you now have your pain *plus* tense muscles, a headache, and insufficient oxygen. As a muscle relaxer, deep breathing can help to release tension in the abdomen, neck, and shoulders, which are common places where people brace against the pain.

Deep breathing helps to make sure there is a sufficient amount of oxygen in your body. Oxygen is a nutrient carried in the blood, and it is necessary for metabolism in healthy tissues. Internal organs and muscles as well as injured areas need a sufficient daily amount of oxygen to survive, and a great deal more to heal.

Some people use deep breathing as their only relaxation exercise. Some use it as a cue to signal the start of their tension-relieving regimen. However you choose to use it, it is quick, pleasant, and readily available.

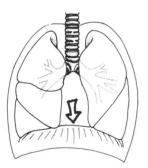
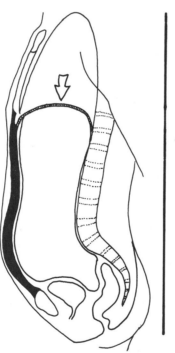
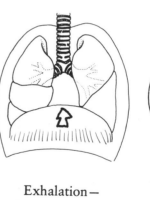
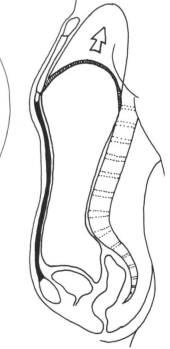

Inhalation—
diaphragm drops

Exhalation—
diaphragm rises

1. Breathing awareness
a. Lie down on a rug or blanket on the floor with your legs uncrossed and slightly apart. Allow your arms to relax comfortably at your sides. Close your eyes.
b. Bring your attention to your breathing and place your hand on the spot that seems to rise and fall the most as you inhale and exhale. Note that if this spot is in your chest, you are not making good use of the lower part of your

lungs. People who are nervous tend to breathe many short, shallow breaths in their upper chest.

c. Place both of your hands gently on your abdomen and follow your breathing. Notice how your adbomen rises with each inhalation and falls with each exhalation.

d. Allow yourself to breathe through your nose. Clear your nasal passages before doing breathing exercises.

e. Is your chest moving in harmony with your abdomen, or is it rigid? Spend a minute or two letting your chest follow the movement of your abdomen.

f. Scan your body for tension, especially in your throat, chest, and abdomen.

(Adapted from *The Relaxation and Stress Reduction Workbook*.)

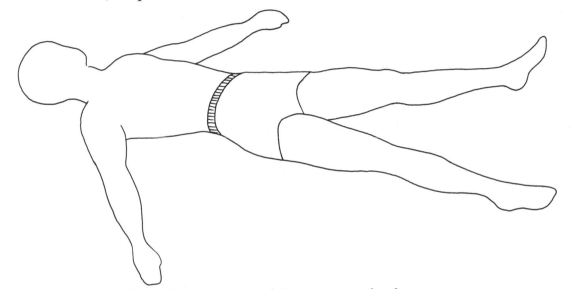

2. Abdominal breathing sitting or lying on your back

Abdominal breathing can be practiced anywhere—in the office, riding, the bus, driving, at home, before bedtime—while sitting, standing, or lying. But to become comfortable with the technique, it is recommended that you first focus your attention on abdominal breathing while lying on your back. After abdominal breathing has become automatic for you, it will take only seconds to use it anywhere, anytime, to help relieve tension and pain.

a. Lie on your back, place one hand on your chest, and the other on your abdomen. Uncross your legs, allowing them to spread comfortably apart or bend at the knees with your feet flat on floor.

b. Inhale slowly through your nostrils.

c. Feel the breath move through your chest, raising the hand on your chest slightly. As the breath reaches your stomach, push your abdomen upwards toward the ceiling, while completing your inhalation. Allow the hand on your abdomen to raise slightly higher than the hand on your chest.

d. Hold for a second and then reverse the process, allowing the breath to pass back out through your chest and nostrils. As you exhale, feel your muscles let go of tension. Allow your jaw to unclench as you exhale.

e. Focus on this breathing process twice each day, for a period of ten to twenty minutes each time. Your body will tell you when you are comfortable with this breathing, and you will soon be able to apply it automatically when your body tenses up from pain and stress.

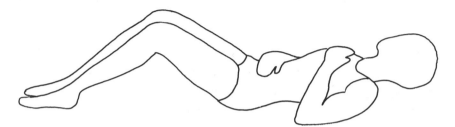

3. Abdominal breathing on your stomach

This is an excellent exercise for practicing abdominal breathing, especially if you have difficulty feeling the movement of the diaphragm while breathing in a sitting or lying position.

a. Lie on your stomach, placing your legs a comfortable distance apart with your toes pointed outward. Fold your arms in front of your body, resting your hands on your biceps. Position your arms so that your chest does not touch the floor.

b. As you inhale, feel the abdomen pressing against the floor. As you slowly exhale, feel the abdominal muscles relaxing. It is easy to feel the diaphragmatic motion while in this position.

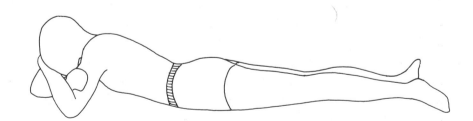

4. Deep breathing and imagery

As you become comfortable with deep breathing exercises, you can begin experimenting with imagery to combat pain in combination with your breathing.

a. When you notice the first twinges of pain, begin to calm your body by spending a minute or two doing three to four deep, natural breaths.

b. With the fourth or fifth breath, as you exhale, feel the muscles that are beginning to tighten and sink down into the rug or chair. Use imagery to represent the muscles relaxing. Imagine them as knotted ropes slowly loosening and becoming limp, or picture warming blood flowing into the muscles, making them heavy. Refer to the section on imagery in chapter five for other ideas.

c. Focus specifically on the area that is hurting. With each inhalation, assign an image to represent the hurting area. You might see it as a bright red pulsating light. With each exhalation, see the image change to a more pleasant and relaxing image. For example, see the bright light change to a dim, cool blue or green light.

d. Keep one hand on your abdomen and move the other hand to a point on your body that hurts. As you inhale, imagine energy coming in and being stored in your abdominal area. As you exhale, imagine the energy flowing to the spot that hurts. Inhale more energy, and when you exhale, imagine the energy driving out the pain. Imagine this process clearly, as you alternately send energy to the spot that hurts, and then drive out the pain.

(Adapted from *The Relaxation and Stress Reduction Workbook.*)

Points to remember about deep breathing:

1. Deep breathing can be extremely useful in combating daily stress, including the daily stress of pain. Deep breathing can serve as a preventative tool to help you guard against a buildup of tension levels. Monitor yourself throughout the day. At the first signs of stress or twinges of pain, take a few moments to do five or six breaths. You can do this anywhere, anytime, sitting or standing. Simply close your eyes and focus on your breathing, slowing it and deepening it. Do this as many times during the day as necessary to help calm yourself. With persistence, you'll begin to notice an accumulation of calm by the end of the day, rather than a buildup of pain and stress.

2. Develop the ability to "passively concentrate" on your deep breathing. The concept of passive concentration or passive volition is well known to Eastern philosophy, but less understood in Western culture, where striving for perfection is

emphasized. Passive concentration means focusing on what you are doing, but in such a way that you are observing yourself comfortably. In other words, *allow* yourself to breathe deeply, rather than *force* yourself to breath "just right" like the book says. A common problem with ambitious achievers who are attempting to relax is that they expect themselves to relax perfectly on schedule and on command. When stray thoughts of business or pleasure interrupt their task, they get frustrated and try to force the thoughts away. They work too hard! If you feel that you have to do the deep breathing and the other exercises in this chapter "just right" in order to be successful, then consider that "forcing" yourself to relax can only be counterproductive. Repeat to yourself over and over, "I am ALLOWING myself to relax." Watch your extraneous thoughts pass through your mind; observe them and let them go. Give yourself permission not to do it "just right" all the time.

Progressive Muscle Relaxation

Progressive muscle relaxation (PMR) was developed by Edmund Jacobson in the 1930s when he discovered that his hypnosis patients kept a good deal of tension in their muscles while attempting to relax. He taught his patients to release this residual tension by tightly contracting their muscles group by group and then releasing the tension slowly. He felt that deep muscle relaxation would help his patients to replace the habit of tensing their muscles in response to stress with the habit of releasing muscle tension.

PMR can be a very effective way to learn about the amount of muscle tension in your body and to feel the sharp contrast between tensed muscles and relaxed muscles. It's possible to walk around with clenched teeth or fists all day and not even realize it until the evening, when a tension headache or sore shoulder lets you know what you've been doing. Or you may think that you have relaxed your muscles even though they are still tightly contracted. Your unawareness of what state your muscles are in can lead to muscle fatigue, poor circulation, cramping, and stiffness. And chronic muscle tightness can lead to exacerbation of your pain condition. Inflexible muscles are more prone to spasming, which sets off the pain-spasm-pain cycle discussed in the first chapter.

One word of caution about progressive muscle relaxation: If you feel pain when you first try this exercise, take care! Avoid over-tensing your injured area and the muscles surrounding it. Ease into this exercise slowly and do not strain yourself.

Progressive muscle relaxation is also a more "active" exercise than the others described in this chapter. You physically tense and relax your muscles, pushing up the tension in order to feel the upward limit of your muscle contraction. If you are hooked up to a biofeedback machine, you will notice that the needle registers more muscle activity as you continue tensing the muscle group being monitored. These factors make PMR a valuable way to learn about the tension in your body and a good exercise for beginning relaxers, but also mean that it may not be as conducive to deep relaxation as other relaxation exercises. Experiment with PMR and the other exercises in this chapter; after you get to know your own responses, pick the ones that work best for you. The following exercise has been adapted from *The Relaxation and Stress Reduction Workbook* and from *The Relaxation Training Program* by Thomas Budzynski.

We will be focusing on four major groups of muscles in the body:

1. Hands, forearms, and biceps
2. Feet, calves, thighs, and buttocks
3. Chest, stomach, and lower back
4. Shoulders, neck, throat, face, and head

Spend at least twenty minutes per day for two to three days on each muscle group. Most beginners find it helpful to follow along with a tape at first. You can order a prerecorded tape, or make one yourself by recording the instructions given here.

Begin by lying down or sitting in a comfortable chair with your head supported. Take several deep breaths, releasing each breath slowly. Let the deep and natural breathing be your cue to begin your relaxation session.

a. Focus on the first group of muscles—your right hand, arm, and bicep. Make a fist, clenching as hard as you can. Hold that tension, feeling it creep up your arm towards your shoulder. Hold it till you begin to feel a slight cramping, burning sensation.

b. Now relax, feeling the muscles go limp. Feel the warming blood flow through your arm into your hand and fingers. Notice the contrast between what your muscles felt like when they were tense, and what they feel like now that they are relaxed.

c. Repeat this procedure twice more. Remember to pay attention to your breathing as you tense and relax. Does your breathing begin to get shallow? Make sure you are not unconsciously holding your breath.

d. Now notice how your right arm and hand feel in comparison to your left arm and hand. Now focus on your left hand, arm, and bicep and repeat the exercise three times.

After two to three days on the first muscle group, move on to the second group: feet, calves, thighs, and buttocks. Repeat the same procedure as above, alternating sides of your body.

a. Focus on your right foot and calf. Tighten them as hard as you can. You can either pull your foot upward, or stretch your foot outward by pointing your toe. Hold the tension, feeling it creep up your leg toward your torso. Hold the tension till you begin to feel a slight cramping, burning sensation.

b. Now relax, feeling the muscles go limp. Feel the warming blood flow through your calf and foot. Notice the contrast between what your muscles felt like when you were tense, and what they feel like now that you are relaxed.

c. Repeat this procedure twice more. Remember to pay attention to your breathing as you tense and relax. Does your breathing begin to get shallow? Make sure you are not unconsciously holding your breath.

d. Now notice how the right calf and foot feel in comparison to the left calf and foot. Focus on your left calf and foot and repeat the exercise three times.

e. Now focus on your right leg again. Tense your thigh and buttocks as you tense your foot and calf. Tense as hard as you can, until you begin to feel a slight cramping and burning sensation.

f. Now relax, feeling all the muscles in your right leg go limp. Feel the warming blood flow through your buttocks, thigh, calf, and foot. Notice the contrast between what your leg felt like when it was tense, and what it feels like now that it is relaxed.

g. Repeat this procedure twice more. Remember to do relaxed and natural breathing. Notice how your right leg feels in comparison to your left leg.

h. Now focus on your left leg, tensing your buttocks and thigh as you tense your left foot and calf. Repeat the exercise three times.

Spend the next two to three days of your practice on the third group: chest, stomach and lower back. Remember to breathe deeply and exhale slowly as you release the tension in your stomach. (*Note:* If you have lower back pain, proceed cautiously with the tensing of your back muscles. Contract the muscles as much as you can, but do not strain or overdo it.)

a. Focus on your chest, stomach, and lower back. Tense those areas, lightly pushing your lower back into the bed or chair as you contract your abdominal muscles and shrug your shoulders. Hold the tension until you begin to feel a slight cramping, burning sensation.

b. Now relax, feeling the muscles go limp. Feel the warming blood flow through your lower back, stomach, and chest. Notice the contrast between how these areas felt when they were tense, and what they feel like now.

c. Repeat this procedure twice more. Remember to do relaxed and natural breathing.

For the next two to three days, focus on your shoulder, neck, face, and head muscles. Pay special attention to the facial muscles, since they are extremely sensitive to stress and anxiety. You may be tensing the powerful muscles in your jaw all day without realizing it! Follow this script:

a. Focus first on your shoulder muscles. Do a "shoulder shrug" by raising your shoulders as close to your ears as possible. Hold it. Feel the knots begin to form in the trapezius muscles and back of your neck. Now relax your shoulder muscles. Feel the difference when they are at rest and smooth, rather than creeping up toward your head.

b. Now turn your attention to your head. Wrinkle your forehead as tight as you can. Now relax and smooth it out. Let yourself imagine your entire forehead and scalp becoming smooth and at rest. Now frown and notice the strain spreading throughout your forehead. Let go. Allow your brow to become smooth again. Now close your eyes and squint them tightly closed. Feel the tension. Relax your eyes. Let them remain closed gently and comfortably. Now clench your jaw, bite hard, and notice the tension throughout your jaw. Relax your jaw. When your jaw is relaxed, your lips will be slightly parted. Let yourself really appreciate the contrast between tension and relaxation. Now press your tongue against the roof of your mouth. Feel the ache in the back of your mouth. Relax. Now press your lips together and purse them into an "O." Relax your lips. Notice that your forehead, scalp, eyes, jaw, tongue, and lips are all relaxed.

Differential Relaxation. Differential relaxation is a variation of progressive muscle relaxation. You tense and relax as you would with PMR, but focus on diagonal muscle groups at the same time. For example, when working with the first and second muscle groups, you tense your *right* arm and hand and *left* leg and foot at the same time. You also release both sides simultaneously. As you tense, you also pay attention to the sides of your body that you are not tensing (your left arm and hand and your right leg and foot).

The purpose of differential relaxation is to introduce you to a slightly more complex exercise that more closely resembles your daily activity. For example, when people drive, they often unconsciously clench their teeth and jaw in response to traffic or the normal tensions of driving. But no one ever wants to relax *all* of his or her body while driving. Of necessity, any driver needs to keep a leg and foot tense and alert on the accelerator pedal. Differential relaxation takes this kind of situation into account and teaches you to tense one part of the body while keeping another relaxed.

As you practice this exercise, be sure to pay attention to the feelings of tension on the tense side *and* the feelings of relaxation on the relaxed side. By holding both awarenesses simultaneously, you are encouraging your brain to develop a capacity for staying alert and relaxed at the same time. This exercise will also help you to adapt other forms of relaxation to your everyday activity.

Remember not to rush through each muscle group while practicing PMR or differential relaxation. Allow yourself the luxury of a full week per muscle group.

You may also find it useful to subvocalize these expressions while releasing your muscle tension:

- Let go of the tension.
- Relax and smooth out the muscles.
- Let the tension dissolve away.
- Let go more and more.

Further Reading

Alman, Brian. *Self-Hypnosis: A Complete Manual for Health and Self-Change.* San Diego, CA: International Health Publications, 1983.

Budzynski, Thomas. *Relaxation Training Program.* Three cassette tapes. Boulder, CO: Biofeedback Systems.

Davis, Martha, Matthew McKay, and Elizabeth Eshelman. *The Relaxation and Stress Reduction Workbook.* Oakland, CA: New Harbinger Publications, 1982.

Swami Rama, Rudolph Ballentine and Alan Hymes. *Science of Breath: A Practical Guide.* Honesdale, PA: The Himalayan International Institute of Yoga Science and Philosophy, 1981.

5

Advanced Stress Management Techniques

Autogenics Training

The word *autogenics* means "self-generated." In the 1930s, two physicians named Johannes Schultz and Wolfgang Luthe found that they could help their patients reduce fatigue and tension by teaching them to generate feelings of heaviness and warmth in their extremities.

Autogenics can be an especially helpful exercise for chronic pain sufferers for several reasons. First, there is no physical activity involved with this exercise—no physical tensing and releasing as there is with progressive muscle relaxation. Particularly when you're hurting a lot, it often feels better to relax passively rather than actively with a physical exercise. Second, the phrases used in autogenics encourage the flow of blood to the extremities. When you brace against pain and hold your muscles in a rigid position, you are actually inhibiting the healing circulation of blood. Autogenics can help to reverse this by allowing your hands and feet to be warmer because of better blood flow, and thus help you feel more overall relaxation.

After you have tried the standard autogenics phrases below and felt your body responding to them, you can make the phrases more specific to your particular pain problem. For example, you might first warm your hands and then move them to your stomach if you have an abdominal disorder. In this way, your hands would be acting like a hot-water bottle. Samantha, a migraine sufferer, often experienced cold hands and feet before she began her stress management and biofeedback training. When she first started training, her finger temperatures measured 72 degrees (normally warm fingers measure in the 90s) and her hands felt cold and clammy. She began to use the autogenic phrases, and then shortened them to create her own "warmth mantra" that she could use anywhere, at any time. This exercise would take her approximately thirty seconds. She would often combine her phrase with the image of sitting on warm rocks in the sun by a stream. After about ten weeks of practice, her finger temperatures rarely dipped below 90 degrees. She also had great success warming her feet—even though the bulk of her training took place in the winter! Samantha found that her headaches decreased from a bad one each week to a minor one each month.

You will focus on the same four muscle groups as you did with progressive muscle relaxation.

1. Hands and arms
2. Feet, calves, thighs, and buttocks

3. Chest, stomach, and lower back
4. Shoulders, neck, throat, face, and head

Spend at least twenty minutes per day on each muscle group and set aside approximately two to three days of practice for each group. Beginners often find it helpful to follow along with a tape at first. You can order a prerecorded tape, or make one yourself by recording the instructions given here (adapted from *The Relaxation Training Program* by Thomas Budzynski).

Begin autogenics by lying down or sitting in a comfortable chair with your head supported. Take several deep breaths, releasing each breath slowly. Let the deep and natural breathing be your cue to begin your relaxation session.

1. Focus on the first muscle group—your right hand and arm. Repeat these phrases to yourself:

    My right hand is heavy.
    My right hand is heavy and warm.
    My right hand is letting go.

    My right arm is heavy.
    My right arm is heavy and warm.
    My right arm is letting go.

    Repeat each set of phrases twice, then move to your left hand and arm.

    My left hand is heavy.
    My left hand is heavy and warm.
    My left hand is letting go.

    My left arm is heavy.
    My left arm is heavy and warm.
    My left arm is letting go.

2. After several days on the first group, move on to the second group: your feet, calves, thighs, and buttocks. Repeat these phrases to yourself:

    My right leg is heavy.
    My right leg is heavy and warm.
    My right leg is letting go.

    My left leg is heavy.
    My left leg is heavy and warm.
    My left leg is letting go.

My right thigh is heavy.
My right thigh is heavy and warm.
My right thigh is letting go.

My left thigh is heavy.
My left thigh is heavy and warm.
My left thigh is letting go.

My buttocks are heavy.
My buttocks are heavy and warm.
My buttocks are letting go.

3. Now move on to the third group: your stomach, chest, and lower back. Focus on each area separately, and repeat these phrases to yourself:

My stomach is heavy.
My stomach is heavy and warm.
My stomach is letting go.

My chest is heavy.
My chest is heavy and warm.
My chest is letting go.

My lower back is heavy.
My lower back is heavy and warm.
My lower back is letting go.

4. Next focus on the fourth group: your shoulders, neck, throat, face, and head. Repeat these phrases to yourself, focusing first on your shoulders, then on your neck and throat, then on your head and face.

My shoulders are heavy.
My shoulders are heavy and warm.
My shoulders are letting go.

My neck and throat are heavy.
My neck and throat are heavy and warm.
My neck and throat are letting go.

My head and face are heavy.
My head and face are heavy and warm.
My head and face are letting go.

As you become comfortable with and adept at using the phrases, you can add additional instructions, such as "My right arm is loose and limp." Remember to check your breathing periodically to make sure that you are breathing deeply, slowly, and regularly.

Autogenics and imagery. Imagery can be used very effectively in combination with your autogenics work. Imagine a warm sun beating down on your hands and arms or the tingling sensation of settling into a warm bath. Some people like to imagine that they are sitting by their cozy fireplace or wood stove in the wintertime. To reinforce heaviness, imagine yourself under layers of comfortable, warm blankets that feel so snug and secure over you that you don't want to move. Or imagine that your arms and legs are like heavy objects that are pleasant to you, such as tree limbs or your Aunt Ethel's fruit cake.

These additional expressions may be used while you repeat the autogenic phrases or at the end of your session. (From *The Relaxation and Stress Reduction Workbook*.)

- I feel quiet.
- My mind is quiet.
- I withdraw my thoughts from the surroundings and I feel serene and still.
- My thoughts are turned inward and I am at ease.
- Deep within my mind, I can visualize and experience myself as relaxed and comfortable and still.
- I feel an inward quietness.

Remember to adopt an attitude of passive concentration while practicing your autogenic techniques. Do not force yourself to concentrate. Rather, *allow* yourself to focus on the exercises. When extraneous thoughts intrude on your concentration, simply allow them to pass through your mind. Eventually, with practice, these thoughts will become less numerous and intrusive.

Imagery

Imagery is one of the most powerful tools you can use to relieve pain. Imagery lets your mind communicate directly with your body, instructing it to heal itself or feel better.

Imagery practices have been used extensively in ancient and modern tribal communities as part of the group's ritual. For example, American Indian medicine men call up the image of a god receiving the pain of a patient in order to reduce illness and discomfort.

You are probably affected by imagery during your daily activity more than you realize. When you think about the traffic you'll have to face on your way home from work, you unconsciously clench your jaw. Then you remember that your spouse is cooking your favorite meal, and you relax a little and think pleasant thoughts in anticipation. But while the imagery that comes up in daily life can be either positive or negative, this section focuses on using positive imagery to give you that extra boost you need to effectively manage your pain.

There are many different ways to use imagery for pain control. Perhaps the simplest is to pick an image that represents your pain, put yourself into a relaxed state, and then imagine the image of your pain changing into a pleasant sensation or disappearing altogether.

Jeanne Achterberg, a psychologist who has worked extensively with imagery and chronic pain conditions, takes two approaches to imagery, using it as a diagnostic tool as well as a therapeutic tool. Dr. Michael Samuels, who works with cancer patients as well as pain patients, uses a similar approach, but he terms his dual imagery work "receptive" and "programmed" visualization.

During a basic diagnostic or receptive imagery session, you relax and allow spontaneous images depicting your pain to spring up in your mind. These images can help to clarify your pain and give you a starting point from which to work. For example, Helen, a migraine sufferer, described her pain image as "hundreds of tiny pins pricking my skin." Harry, who suffers from shoulder pain, imaged a bright yellow-red light burning at the point of his pain.

Therapeutic imagery or programmed visualization is the healing component of imagery. This is where you change the symbol you have selected to represent your pain into a more tolerable, even pleasant visualization. Or you distract yourself away from your pain symbol by replacing it with another pleasant image. Helen imagined the tiny pins regrouping to form a splendid silver crown sitting atop her head. Harry visualized the yellow-red light in his shoulder changing into a cool blue light. Other healing images suggested by Dr. Samuels include making hot areas cool, releasing pressure from tight areas, and bringing blood to areas that need nourishment or cleansing.

Four-Step Imagery

The following four-step process will help you use effective pain relief imagery.

1. Learn to relax deeply by regularly practicing some form of relaxation exercise for at least ten minutes daily. Arrange a conducive setting for relaxation. (If your living room is usually as busy as Grand Central Station, it will probably not be a conducive setting.)

2. After you have relaxed, conjure up an image that represents your pain. You may want to draw a picture of the symbol you choose to help you visualize it. Make the image fit the pain.

3. Now visualize the therapeutic image or process that you have chosen to release your pain. Watch the knotted ropes of your aching muscles go limp and melt

away. Or let the tiny pins grow smaller and smaller until they are simply dots, and watch the dots then disappear altogether, leaving only the color gray.

4. Visualize the positive benefits of your pain control. See yourself coping well, moving freely, smiling, and laughing. See yourself growing stronger and stronger, doing more and more. Create an active and positive image of yourself filled with energy and good health.

As you gain experience, change your images to depict your pain and its release more accurately. Make sure that the approaches you select are appropriate and that your images of success are strong. When Helen first started using imagery, she could only visualize vague color changes. Now, with practice, she can visualize the constriction of individual blood vessels to keep her head from throbbing when she feels a migraine coming on.

Suggested Imagery

The following is a representative sample of images collected from patients. This list is designed to get you started; you will find that the most effective imagery is the kind that you create yourself in your own mind.

Pain Imagery	**Relief Imagery**
For dull ache of tension headache pain:	
Band tightening around head	Band loosening, falling away
Vice gripping head	Vice disintegrating, fading in color
Muscles in head contracted	Muscles loose, limp
For sharp, throbbing vascular headache pain:	
Pins pricking around temples and eyes	Pins becoming tiny dots and disappearing
Pain like a razor's edge	Razor disintegrating or melting
Hot, bright colors	Ice block cooling eyes and temples; snow-covered ground; cool colors
For dull, aching muscular pain:	
Bricks, heavy stones, or weights pressing on muscles	Bricks or stones dissolving, fading, falling away
Knotted ropes	Knots untying; ropes limp or becoming flowing water
For ripping, tearing, burning muscular pain:	
Ripping fabric	Fabric mended and strong

| Flames | Flames dying out or extinguished by water flowing over them; cool wind blowing out flame. |
| Knife cutting | Knife dissolving, cut healing |

For gastro-intestinal discomfort:

Flames in abdominal and chest areas	Flames extinguished by cool water
Acid secretions in abdominal and chest areas	Secretions replaced by healing oxygen with each deep breath
Muscles tight and contracted	Healing blood flowing in to warm and release muscle tension

Relax and allow your own images to flow. Don't be discouraged if you feel stuck and your mind seems blank: if you wait for them, the images will come. You can draw on any dream imagery that you have to serve as a catalyst to your daily, waking imagery. Post this simplified four-step program by your relaxation place to remind you of the structure of your image work.

1. Relax deeply.
2. Image your pain.
3. Image your pain relief.
4. Image the positive benefits.

Biofeedback

Biofeedback is a way for you to monitor your relaxation progress. Under stress, your body tends to contract your skeletal muscle groups, such as your shoulder and jaw muscles. Adrenalin is released into the blood stream, causing the blood vessels in your extremities to constrict, making your hands and feet cold. Your heart beats faster. And you sweat more. Biofeedback provides a measurement of the tension in each of these areas. Electrodes hooked up to biofeedback machines and to parts of your body give you "feedback" about how tensed or relaxed your muscles are, how cold or warm your hands are, how much you sweat, and how fast your heart beats. All of these measurements are indications of your degree of physical relaxation.

Biofeedback can also help you to learn about your own unique response to your pain and stress. Some people automatically clench their teeth in response to pain, while others clench their fists, or hold their breath, or become overly active in an effort to ignore the pain. Samantha found that her hand temperatures reflected her typical response to stress. Whenever she became super-busy (and consequently super-anxious), she noticed that her hands would feel like ice. She calls her hands her "vulnerable place."

Placement of the electrodes varies depending on the pain problem and the preference of the person administering the biofeedback. One school of thought in biofeedback holds that you can relax by focusing on a specific muscle group, while a second school believes that it is possible to focus on overall body relaxation. In the first approach, electrodes may be attached to specific muscle group sites such as the lumbar muscles of the lower back or the trapezius muscles of the shoulders. The frontalis muscles of the forehead are commonly used in the second approach as an electrode site for overall body relaxation. For both schools of thought, the general goal is to reduce your tension levels and replace anxiety with calm. This goal follows from the belief that a reduction in your anxiety level will in turn raise your level of tolerance for pain.

Electrodes placed on your muscle groups measure the muscle's electrical activity. As the muscle contracts, its electrical output increases. The needle on the biofeedback machine accordingly registers at a higher level, and a tone beeps at a louder volume to let you hear that your tension level is increasing. Conversely, as you relax, electrical output is decreased. The needle moves in the other direction, and the beeping sound diminishes to a quieter tone. The machine has no physical effect on you; the needle simply provides you and the therapist with a numerical value for your muscle tension. You use the readings that the machine provides as a guide to release your muscle tension, letting your muscles become limp, heavy, and warm, giving you an overall feeling of calm. Many biofeedback patients have remarked that they had no idea they could carry around so much muscle tension. Patients are surprised and pleased to learn that they can use the feedback of the tone and numbers to release even minute bits of muscle tension.

Electrodes placed on your fingertips tell you three things: (1) the temperature of your fingers, (2) the amount of sweat you produce, and (3) your heartrate. These measurements are all expressions of autonomic activity. As you tense up, the blood flows away from the hands and feet, causing your temperature to decrease. The palms of your hands produce more sweat, and your heart beats faster. A person doing biofeedback training with these measurements learns to increase the flow of blood to the periphery, to indirectly decrease the amount of sweat produced, and to slow down the rate that the heart beats.

Biofeedback can be very helpful for managing all kinds of chronic pain conditions. An important benefit is its ability to teach you to avoid unnecessarily tensing your muscles. You can also learn to isolate your pain, rather than have it spread to other parts of your body via muscle contractions and spasming. Mary Jo, a biofeedback client with a shoulder injury, learned that when she tensed her neck in reaction to the pain in her shoulder, she began to have painful neck muscle spasming as well. With the help of biofeedback, she learned to check herself regularly for unconscious bracing and to position her head and neck differently to avoid neck spasming. Kathy, a chronic tension headache sufferer, learned that she unconsciously clenched her jaw muscles regularly, so that by the end of the day she had a whopping headache. Through biofeedback, she learned to monitor her jaw clenching periodically throughout the day, thereby reducing the intensity of her headaches and sometimes preventing them altogether.

You can learn to provide good blood flow to all parts of your body by combining biofeedback with the heaviness and warmth phrases used in autogenics. This approach can be especially helpful to migraine sufferers like Samantha who have chronically cold hands and feet. Samantha found that raising her hand temperatures whenever she felt tense helped to decrease not only the intense pain of her migraine, but its frequency as well. She went from three to four migraines per month to one minor headache every five to six weeks.

Bob, who had been experiencing a daily combination of migraine and tension headaches for years, used biofeedback and autogenics tapes to learn how sensitive the muscles in his face were. "I've learned to avoid some of the daily buildup of muscular tension during the day. At home I lie outstretched on the floor, turn on an autogenics tape of the ocean, and just let my mind wander—let it drift off into a sort of pleasant daydreaming imagery. This whole process has sensitized me enough to know when I'm tense and when I'm relaxed. Before my daily twenty-minute session, I notice my shoulders becoming tense and riding up towards my neck, my jaws clamped shut, and my breathing getting shallow. After the session, I get up feeling refreshed and energized, and the feeling lasts all the rest of the afternoon. I believe this daily routine breaks my cycle of tension."

Biofeedback training usually lasts from eight to ten weeks, one or two sessions each week, with the sessions lasting approximately one hour. Ask your doctor for a referral to a local practitioner, or write to the following organization for a list of biofeedback resources in your area.

Biofeedback Society of America
10200 West 44th Avenue, #304
Wheat Ridge, CO 80033

Relaxation Enhancers

A *temperature ring* can be particularly helpful when used to augment biofeedback training. Samantha regularly wears a ring that tells her about her temperature fluctuations and signals her to let herself relax when she notices her temperature dropping. The ring has a temperature range of 67 to 94 degrees, with little dots that light up at each point on the range. As a preventative tool, the ring functions as an early warning system: if you notice your temperature dropping, you can use this indication as a cue to take note of your situation. Are you feeling tense? Angry? Are you anticipating your pain? Or are you simply in a cold room? For more information, the FUTUREHEALTH Thermometer Ring brochure can be ordered from FUTUREHEALTH, Inc., Dept. P-100, P.O. Box 947, Bensalem, PA 19020.

Stress dots also provide you with a general idea of your temperature range. You peel the dot from a piece of paper and attach it to your hand. The dot changes color as your hands change from cool to warm. Stress dots can be ordered from Mindbody, Inc., 50 Maple Pl., Manhasset, NY 11030.

There are literally thousands of *cassette tapes* available right now, covering every imaginable pain and stress disorder. You can buy cassettes that use specific relaxation techniques, such as progressive muscle relaxation, or tapes that use a combination of techniques, such as music and self-hypnosis. Ask around for recommendations, borrow your friends' tapes, and experiment with the various possibilities to find the tape or tapes you like.

To get you started, here are some tapes that biofeedback patients have felt were effective.

Cassette Tapes

Relaxation Training Program
Thomas Budzynski, Ph.D.
Biofeedback Systems, Inc.
2736 47th St.
Boulder, Colorado 80301
Three cassettes: Progressive Muscle Relaxation, Autogenics, Stress Management

Relaxation and Stress Reduction Cassette Tapes
Matthew McKay, Ph.D., and Patrick Fanning
New Harbinger Publications
5674 Shattuck Avenue
Oakland, CA 94609
Six cassettes: Breathing and Progressive Muscle Relaxation, Autogenics and Meditation, Body Awareness and Imagery, Thought-Stopping, Self-Hypnosis, and Pain Control

Adventures in Learning
Lee Pulos, Ph.D.
2nd Floor, 1260 Hornby Street
Vancouver, B.C. V6Z 1W2
Over thirty different cassettes covering a wide range of subjects using a choice of single-induction or double-induction techniques

Letting Go of Stress
Emmett Miller, with music by Steven Halperin
Box W
Sanford, CA 94305
One cassette: Progressive Muscle Relaxation, Autogenics, and Visualization

Sounds To Relax by
Syntonic Research, Inc.
Mail Order Department
175 Fifth Ave.
New York, NY 10010
Eight cassettes: Sailing, Ocean Waves, Stream, Crickets, Wind in the Trees, Thunderstorm, Heartbeats, English Meadow

Catalogs

New Harbinger Publications
5674 Shattuck Avenue
Oakland, CA 94609

BMA Audio Cassettes
A Division of Guilford Publications, Inc.
200 Park Avenue South
New York, NY 10003

Soundworks
911 N. Fillmore St.
Arlington, VA 22201

For books as well as tapes:
Quest Bookstore
619 W. Main St.
Charlottesville, VA 22901

Also, see the appendix to this book for advice on preparing your own personalized relaxation tape.

Self-Hypnosis

The feelings that you can get from practicing self-hypnosis are similar to the relaxed, refreshed feelings you get after a light nap, a good night's sleep, or a mediation session. Your body feels warm, heavy, relaxed, and refreshed. Through self-hypnosis, you can also explore ways of productively and positively managing your pain—ways that might not be readily apparent to you in a waking state. But self-hypnosis is unlike sleep in that you remain aware of your experience throughout an hypnotic trance.

The trance phenomenon has been used in various forms for centuries. In ancient Greece, priests used sleep temples to cure illness and disease through dreams and posthypnotic suggestions. An English surgeon named Esdaile, living in India in the early 1800s, performed numerous surgeries on patients under hypnotic analgesia. At the time hypnosis was called a "mesmeric" process, after the Austrian physician Franz Mesmer, who began by using magnets and seances to cure his patients of various emotional and physical ailments. Mesmer later found that he could "mesmerize" a person by simply talking to him or her and giving suggestions. Mesmer paved the way for the continuing use of hypnosis throughout the 19th century for treatment of neuroses and in operating rooms for dramatic surgeries performed with minimal or no anesthesia. But with the advent of anesthetic medications in the operating room, the popularity of hypnosis waned.

Unfortunately, popular books and movies have sensationalized the practice of hypnosis, encouraging the misconception that people under hypnosis can be made to do things against their will. In the original film version of *Dracula*, the Count was able to induce people to carry out his evil wishes by simply fixing a steely gaze on his unfortunate victims. The many movies that have used similar characters have done little to enhance the reputation of hypnosis! The very words "hypnotic trance" and "induction techniques" suggest mysterious goings-on, the presence of some magic spirit invading your soul aided by a power you cannot control.

But in recent years, people have begun to understand that hypnosis is a natural process, a simple shifting of consciousness from a waking state to a subconscious place which can be deeply therapeutic. You have total control over each step in a trance and cannot be made to do anything that you do not want to do. The new information that has appeared has sparked a renewed interest by the medical and psychological professions in using hypnosis and self-hypnosis as part of a wide variety of treatment programs. The healing powers of hypnosis have especially gained momentum in the medical world, where it has proven itself a viable tool for enhancing pain relief.

All hypnosis is essentially self-hypnosis. When hypnosis is practiced in a clinic or hospital, a trained therapist guides you through the steps, which you can then continue to use on your own. And many patients do find it useful to begin hypnosis practice under the guidance of a trained clinician who can introduce the techniques, guide you in their appropriate uses, and motivate you to follow through in your home practice.

You have probably experienced self-hypnosis without realizing it. Recall the last time you took a long drive and found yourself staring at the white lines on the highway. Or remember the times when you have been riveted to your seat during a good movie and have lost all sense of time. Even staring out the window and daydreaming is an example of a light hypnotic trance. In each of these cases, you became totally absorbed in thought and forgot for a period of time to pay attention to your environment. You can train yourself to deepen these trances and use them therapeutically to help manage your pain, much as you can use visualization or biofeedback.

But note that, as with the other relaxation strategies introduced in this and the previous chapter, self-hypnosis should never be used as the sole treatment of a health problem.

Simple Instructions for Self-Hypnosis

A key to inducing an hypnotic trance is to become as relaxed as possible. Relaxation helps you to decrease muscle tension and calm your body in general, so that you can avoid distracting thoughts and feelings and focus entirely on changing your pain sensation.

The following six steps are the major components of a relaxation induction that takes you from awake and alert to a deep trance. These instructions and the sample inductions that follow are adapted from Hadley and Staudacher's book, *Hypnosis for Change*.

Step 1. Beginning the induction. The induction begins by focusing your attention on your breathing and inner sensations. As you do so, your awareness of external surroundings will decrease. By breathing deeply, you become aware of your internal sensations. You introduce your body to relaxation. Your pulse slows, your breathing slows, you begin to withdraw, and you can direct your attention to the suggestions that are given to you.

Step 2. Systematic relaxation of the body. As the induction directs you to concentrate on relaxing every muscle in your body, your mind will also become more relaxed. You will experience an increased awareness of internal functions and an increased receptivity of the senses.

Step 3. Creating imagery of deeper relaxation. The induction's image of drifting down deeper and deeper helps you to enter a deeper trance. Tension in your shoulders is released by an image of weight being lifted from your shoulders. Any difference in your bodily sensations will support the suggestion that a change is taking place. It does not matter whether the direction specified in the induction is upward or downward, so long as the image of rising or descending makes it possible for you to experience a change in your physical feelings.

Step 4. Deepening the trance. To help you deepen your trance or "go down," you count backwards from ten to one. In order to return to full consciousness or "come up," you count forward from one to ten. The induction uses the image of a staircase with ten steps, but you can substitute any image you like in order to enhance the feeling of going down. The image of an elevator descending ten floors is a popular alternative.

At this stage your limbs become limp or stiff. Your attention will have narrowed, and your suggestibility will heighten. The surrounding environment will be closed out.

Step 5. The special place. The special place you choose to imagine will be one that is unique to you and your experience. It can be a place you have actually visited or one that you imagine. The place does not have to be real, or even possible. You can be sitting on a big blue pillow floating on the surface of a quiet sea. You can be stretched out in a hammock suspended in space. You can be in a cave of clouds. Your special place must be one in which you can be alone and it must produce a positive feeling in you. It is in this special place that you will have an increased receptivity to further suggestions. That is, once a peaceful feeling is established, you will be responsive to imagery which reinforces and supports posthypnotic suggestions.

Step 6. Concluding the induction. Before counting "up" from one to ten, a feeling of well-being should be suggested to avoid an abrupt return, which may cause drowsiness or a headache. Upon completion of the induction, you should feel relaxed and refreshed. You may walk around to make sure you are fully alert and congratulate yourself on doing a good job.

Recording Your Induction

Many people find it helpful to tape-record an induction to help guide them through each step. You may choose to record your own voice or the voice of a friend, or to use one of the many available prerecorded hypnotic induction tapes. Here are some suggestions for recording the sample induction that follows.

1. Read the induction aloud several times in order to become familiar and comfortable with its content. When recording, speak slowly and in a monotone, keeping your voice level and your words evenly spaced. You will need to experiment with tone and stress until you are satisfied with the way the induction sounds.

2. When you are comfortable with your voice and the length of time the induction will require, make sure that you have chosen a location free of any sounds that may be picked up by the tape, such as clocks, the television, the telephone, or the doorbell. You will also need to alert your family or roommates. Make sure they understand that you are not to be interrupted and that they are not to make any sounds that can be heard in the location where you will be recording.

3. Put on comfortable clothing and get in a comfortable position. You may want to lie down, sit in a rocking chair, or sit at your desk with your feet up. Whatever your preferred position, make sure it is one that will be comfortable throughout the entire recording session. If you are shifting around or feeling physically uncomfortable, this discomfort will be reflected in the tone and quality of your voice.

Going Down

Take a nice deep breath, close your eyes, and begin to relax. Just think about relaxing every muscle in your body from the top of your head to the tips of your toes. Just begin to relax. And begin to notice how very comfortable your body is beginning to feel. You are supported, so you can just let go and relax. Inhale and exhale. Notice your breathing; notice the rhythm of your breathing and relax your breathing for a moment. Be aware of normal sounds around you. These sounds are unimportant, discard them, whatever you hear from now on will only help to relax you. And as you exhale, release any tension, any stress from any part of your body, mind, and thought; just let that stress go. Just feel any stressful thoughts rushing through your mind, feel them begin to wind down, wind down, wind down, and relax. And begin with letting all the muscles in your face relax, especially your jaw; let your teeth part just a little bit and relax this area. This is a place where tension and stress gather so be sure and relax your jaw and feel that relaxation go into your temples and relax the muscles in your temples and as you think about relaxing these muscles they will relax. Feel them relax and as you relax you'll be able to just drift and float into a deeper and deeper level of total relaxation. You will continue to relax and now let all of the muscles in your forehead relax. Feel those muscles smooth, smooth and relaxed, and rest your eyes. Just imagine your eyelids feeling so comfortable, so heavy, so heavy, so relaxed and now let all of the muscles in the back of your neck and shoulders relax, feel a heavy, heavy weight being lifted off your shoulders and you feel relieved, lighter and more relaxed. And all of the muscles in the back of your neck and shoulders relax, and feel that soothing relaxation go down your back, down, down, down, to the lower part of your back, and those muscles let go and with every breath you inhale just feel your body drifting, floating, down deeper, down deeper, down deeper into total relaxation. Let your muscles go, relaxing more and more. Let all of the muscles in your shoulders, running down your arms to your fingertips, relax. And let your arms feel so heavy, so heavy, so heavy, so comfortable, so relaxed. You may have tingling in your fingertips. That's perfectly fine. You may have warmth in the palms of your hands, and that's fine. And you may feel that you can barely lift your arms, they are so relaxed, they are so heavy, so heavy, so relaxed. And now you inhale once again and relax your chest muscles. And now as you exhale, feel your stomach muscles relax. As you exhale, relax all of the muscles in your stomach, let them go, and all of the muscles in your legs, feel them relax and all of the muscles in your legs, so completely relaxed right to the tips of your toes. Notice how very comfortable your body feels, just drifting and floating, deeper, deeper, deeper relaxed. And as you are relaxing deeper and deeper, imagine a beautiful staircase. There are ten steps, and the steps lead you to a special and peaceful and beautiful place. In a moment you can begin to imagine taking a safe and gentle and easy step down, down, down on the staircase, leading you to a very peaceful, a very special place for you. You can imagine it to be any place you choose, perhaps you would enjoy a beach or ocean with clean, fresh air, or the mountains with a stream; any place is perfectly fine. In a moment I'm going to count backwards from ten to one and you can imagine taking the steps down and as you take each step, feel your body relax, more and more, feel it just drift down, down each step, and relax even deeper, ten, relax even deeper, nine . . . eight . . . seven . . . six . . . five . . . four . . . three . . . two . . . one . . . deeper, deeper, deeper, relaxed. And now imagine a peaceful and special place. You can imagine this special place and perhaps you can even feel it. You are in a [INSERT SPECIAL PLACE]. You are alone and there is no one to disturb you. This is the most peaceful place in the world for you. Imagine yourself there and feel that sense of peace flow through you and sense of well-being and enjoy these positive feelings and keep them with you long after this session is completed, for the rest of this day and evening, tomorrow. Allow these positive feelings to grow stronger and stronger, feeling at peace with a sense of well-being, and each and every time that you choose to do this kind of relaxation you will be able to relax deeper and deeper. Regardless of the stress and tension that may surround your life, you may now remain more at peace, more calm, more relaxed, and allow the tension and stresses to bounce off and away from you, just bounce off and away from you. And these positive feelings will stay with you and grow stronger and stronger throughout the day as you continue to relax deeper and deeper.

Coming Up

Enjoy your special place for another moment and then I will begin to count from one to ten and as I count from one to ten you can begin coming back to full consciousness, and will come back feeling refreshed as if you had a long rest. Come back feeling alert and relaxed. Begin to come back now. One . . . two . . . coming up, three . . . four . . . five . . . six . . . seven . . . eight . . . nine, begin to open your eyes, and ten, open your eyes and come all the way back, feeling great. Very good.

Using a Self-Guided Relaxation Induction

Instead of taping your induction, you may prefer to rely instead on your internal voice and mental imagery. If so, change the "you" to "I" in the previous induction and then silently lead yourself through it, keeping the guidelines of the six basic key steps in mind.

Note that the effectiveness of either a self-guided or a recorded induction will depend on your personal preference. You may want to try the induction both ways to determine which type provides you with the most successful hypnotic experience.

Pain Control Suggestions

Once you have learned to use the relaxation induction to deepen your trance, you will be ready to begin experimenting with inserting specific pain control suggestions.

Dr. Joseph Barber, a leading practitioner of clinical hypnosis, has outlined five techniques for creating pain relief while you are in a trance.

1. *Reduce the pain sensation* (direct diminution). Reduce the feeling of your pain by making the discomfort gradually go away. Imagine turning down the "volume" of your pain as if you were turning a radio dial from unbearably loud to barely a whisper. Or dim the brightness of your pain, or cool the heat of your pain. Refer to the section on imagery in this chapter for other visualization suggestions.

2. *Change the pain sensation* (sensory substitution). Reinterpret your pain sensation by replacing it by another sensation, such as itchiness or tingling. The sensation that you substitute does not necessarily have to be pleasant. This technique has the advantage of allowing you to move gradually from pain to pleasure. Trying to shift abruptly from noxious pain to complete absence of pain can be frustrating and difficult—try substituting a sensation somewhere in between, like coldness or numbness. This technique also allows you to know that the pain is still there, in case you need to pay medical attention to it.

3. *Relocate your pain* (displacement). Put your pain somewhere else in your body. For example, move your abdominal pain from your abdomen to your finger. The

relocation helps you to be less incapacitated by the pain and also lets you choose the new location. Eventually, this technique can teach you to move your pain at will, or even to diminish it entirely.

4. *Numb your pain* (anesthesia). Make your painful area feel numb or tingling, with no pain sensation at all.

5. *Observe your pain* (disassociation). With this technique, you still perceive your pain, but you also see yourself removed from your pain. In other words, you distance yourself from the pain, so that your body remains but your mind goes away on a vacation. The "special place" in the relaxation induction can help you achieve this distance by leading you to your favorite vacation spot or a quiet retreat.

The following are three entire pain control scripts (adapted from Hadley and Staudacher's *Hypnosis for Change*) which incorporate some of Dr. Barber's suggestions.

General Pain Control Induction

Now take pain and give it a shape and a form, take pain and give it a shape and a form, make pain into a tunnel, a tunnel that you can enter and exit, now imagine yourself entering the tunnel. You are entering that tunnel and the intensity of your pain increases for a few seconds. As you begin to walk through the tunnel you can see the light ahead, every step now takes you away from the discomfort, the deeper into the tunnel you go, the less discomfort you feel, the light at the end of the tunnel grows larger and larger and you begin to feel better and better, every step reduces your discomfort, every step heals and strengthens your body, with every step you feel more comfortable, much more comfortable, very comfortable, and as you reach the light you feel relieved of any discomfort, you feel relaxed, stronger, comfortable, from now on each time you enter the tunnel pass through the tunnel, watch the light at the end of the tunnel grow larger, you will be comfortable and as you exit you will grow stronger and stronger, heal, and feel better and better. The tunnel is yours, you control it, and can enter it any time you like, any time at all, and passing through it will always make you feel better.

Induction for Chronic Pain

Focus your attention on the part of the body that causes you discomfort. [INSERT THE BODILY AREA, "your shoulder," "your jaw," ETC.] *Now recognize the pain and relax the muscles surrounding the area, relax the muscles all around that area, completely around the area. Feel these muscles relax and imagine the inflamed, sore area begin to reduce, cool, and heal. The inflamed, sore area will reduce, cool, heal and it will feel comfortable, very comfortable. Now feel the discomfort drain out of the* [INSERT BODILY AREA] *and right out of your body. Feel it drain, drain away, now just imagine a cool sensation, like cool water flowing over your* [INSERT BODILY AREA] *and away. The cool water flows over that area washing away discomfort, washing away discomfort, completely away, and now soothe and relax this area, soothe and relax this area, and now you can begin to feel relief, relaxation, and mobility again. Your [INSERT BODILY AREA] feels normal, healed, relaxed, and mobile. From now on your subconscious will keep your [INSERT BODILY AREA] relaxed and stress-free.*

Induction for Injury, Illness, Disease

Focus your attention on your pain, now imagine your discomfort to be a large, red ball of energy, like the sun. Your discomfort is a large red ball. Now imagine and watch this bright red ball of energy become smaller and smaller, imagine the color of the ball beginning to lighten, beginning to change to a soft pink and reduce, reduce in size, as you watch the ball become smaller and smaller you will feel less and less discomfort. The ball grows smaller and you feel less and less discomfort, you begin to feel better and better, you feel better as you watch the ball become smaller, now watch the pale pink ball become tiny, tiny, smaller and smaller; watch the color change from faint pink to pale blue, it is now becoming a small blue dot, small blue dot, and now just watch it disappear and when it disappears you feel much, much better, you feel better, more comfortable, you feel better, more comfortable, very comfortable. You feel completely comfortable.

Posthypnotic Suggestions and Cues

One of the most important parts of practicing self-hypnosis is to carry over what you have learned in a trance state to your everyday activity. Posthypnotic cues can be words, or images, or even events that trigger a desired response after you have finished your self-hypnosis work. Dr. Brian Alman, who has worked extensively with hypnosis, says that posthypnotic suggestions and cues are a powerful extension of your self-hypnosis work.

For example, assume that you have picked Dr. Barber's relocation technique to practice while under self-hypnosis. You could begin by giving yourself the posthypnotic suggestion that whenever you begin to feel pain, you will automatically place your finger on the spot that hurts. As you become practiced at self-hypnosis, you can suggest to yourself that the pain will flow out of your body and into your finger. Eventually you can train yourself to transfer the pain from your finger to another part of your body.

You can make use of another kind of posthypnotic cue by fixing your gaze on something while inducing your hypnotic trance. This can be a familiar object that you see regularly, such as the face of a watch, or a chair. Whenever you see that object, you will associate with it your feelings of relaxation and calm almost immediately. (You will find that eventually even the relaxation tapes you use and the recorder you play them on will elicit relaxed feelings.) Pick an object in your home or office that you know will remind you of the pain-relief work you do under trance.

Obstacles to Self-Hypnosis

When you have a great deal of pain, it is often very difficult to even think about relaxing or distracting yourself from your discomfort. Dr. Alman provides two suggestions for dealing with this problem.

(1) Pick a time when the pain has subsided a bit to practice self-hypnosis. Dr. Alman suggests that a good time might be when you are in a whirlpool, having heat therapy, or under cold packs. The brief moments when you have even the tiniest bit of pain relief can be expanded to longer and longer stretches of time as you become more practiced with self-hypnosis.

(2) Use your pain as a focus for your trance. If you are experiencing all-encompassing pain and are not able to distract yourself from it, then turn all of your attention to it. Examine it carefully. Assign images to it. As you focus totally on your pain, and nothing else, you will find you have greater control over it and will be able to change it to less noxious images.

A young girl named Maggie was practicing biofeedback and self-hypnosis for debilitating menstrual cramps. Before she started the program, her mother had taken her to the emergency room at the local hospital each month for a shot of demerol to control the pain. While practicing self-hypnosis, she discovered that she could focus on each of her cramps. She imagined each cramp as a wave, crashing up on the shore, and then subsiding back into the sea. Maggie loved the ocean dearly, so this was actually a very pleasant image for her. Eventually the sea would grow calm. And when Maggie awoke from her trance, her cramps would be gone. Besides feeling proud of her accomplishment, she had no further need for the emergency room's services.

Further Reading

Imagery

Achterberg, Jeanne. *Imagery in Healing*. Boston, MA: New Science Library, 1985.

Davis, Martha, Elizabeth Eshelman, and Matthew McKay. *The Relaxation and Stress Reduction Workbook*. Oakland, CA: New Harbinger Publications, 1982.

Self-Hypnosis

Alman, Brian. *Self-Hypnosis: a Complete Manual for Health and Self-Change*. San Diego, CA: International Health Publications, 1983.

Bowers, K.S. *Hypnosis for the Seriously Curious*. New York: Norton, 1983.

DeBetz, Barbara, and Gerard Sunnen. *A Primer of Clinical Hypnosis*. Littleton, MA: PSG Publishing Co., 1985.

Hadley, J. and C. Staudacher. *Hypnosis for Change*. Oakland, CA: New Harbinger Publications, 1985.

Holzman, Arnold, and Dennis Turk. *Pain Management: a Handbook of Psychological Treatment Approaches*. New York: Pergamon Press, 1986.

6

Psychological Techniques for Managing Chronic Pain

The earlier chapters of this book have shown you how to practice pain control by physically exercising and reducing your stress levels. In terms of levels or stages of pain control, you have been learning to manage your body's *initial* responses to pain — muscle contraction and arousal levels. By dealing with these responses effectively, you have overcome the first obstacles to getting better.

Perhaps you've already identified the obstacle that remains — an integral part of yourself that can make or break any endeavor. That part is your mind — your ability to accept new ideas, to change old personal myths, to examine your attitudes and beliefs, and to peer into the part of you that forms your reflex reactions to the challenge of pain. Bringing your mind over to your side of the healing process is the final stage of pain management.

Consider Jean's case. She carefully followed her exercise and stress management regimen for back pain, but during the whole process she was also giving herself messages that were sabotaging her efforts. When she examined these messages with her counselor, she realized that she was telling herself that she was a weak person for succumbing to the pain in the first place, and that she had better get back to her old self as quickly as possible. The rushed deadline demanded by the second part of this message was an unrealistic goal — when she couldn't meet it, she had her physical pain *and* the painful feelings of letting herself down. The guilt she heaped on herself for having pain to begin with only increased her anxiety levels, making it that much harder for her to cope and to follow her program. In counseling, Jean was able to identify perfectionistic tendencies like these in many areas of her life which played a part in her pain response. Eventually she learned to slow down, give herself some time and space, and talk back to the inner voice that kept pushing her so hard.

The crucial fact is that your mind can block effective coping. Maybe you have reached a plateau and feel stuck in progressing further with your healing exercises. Or maybe you have trouble concentrating on your stress management techniques. Or you may feel that your family situation or lifestyle doesn't reinforce your new coping behaviors. Whatever your situation, if you feel you have gone as far as you can with pain control and can't seem to go any further, the next two chapters will be helpful to you.

This chapter is divided into two major subject areas: coping with your negative thinking and stress inoculation. Chapter seven covers assertively dealing with your situation, handling conflicts that arise around your pain, and decreasing your resistance to getting better. Read the section on negative thinking first, because it is a foundation for understanding the remaining four subjects and it will help you make the most of the other sections.

Negative Thinking

It is easy to indulge in negative thinking when you have chronic pain. Your pain drags on, and a part of your reaction to that situation comes in the form of thoughts and feelings of fear and frustration. These negative thoughts can be so automatic that you may not be aware of how frequently they occur and how debilitating they are. You need to take the time now to examine your negative thinking and understand its effect on your ability to manage your pain.

Negative thoughts have the effect of *increasing* your anxiety and pain. This is so because they focus on catastrophe and resentment, creating a reality where the worst seems bound to happen and you are the helpless victim. Your body reacts by tensing with fear and anger. As your body tightens, your pain increases.

Right now try to recall some of your typical negative thoughts. See if they sound like any of these:

- I have no control over my pain.
- I'll never get better.
- This is going to get worse and worse until I go crazy.
- This should never have happened to me.
- I should have gotten better quicker than this.
- I'll never work again.
- He or she can never really understand this pain.
- I'll never be able to enjoy life again.
- It's all my (job's, boss's, doctor's, family's, spouse's) fault that I'm in this mess.
- It's all *my* fault that I'm in this mess.
- I'm headed for a lifetime of pain.

Do any of these statements sound familiar to you? Note that these are only a few of an infinite variety of pain-related messages. You may have identified others of your own that are unique to your situation.

Dr. Aaron Beck, a major researcher in the field of cognitive therapy, describes negative thoughts as part of a "downward spiral" of depressed thinking. Once you get started, the momentum of your negative thoughts continues to carry you down and down, unless you do something to break out of the pattern.

Dr. Albert Ellis is one of the original developers of the field of cognitive psychology. He argues that your thoughts *create* your emotions, and that your perception of a situation literally determines your reactions to it. What you think becomes what you feel. Through cognitive restructuring you can learn to change the negative internal monologue that fuels your anxiety, depression, and anger, and inevitably makes your pain worse.

A Little Theory

One way to break out of the "downward spiral" of negative thinking is to understand a little theory about the physiological effects of negative thinking.

Your brain takes in and processes messages and emotions simultaneously. The part of the brain responsible for messages, or thoughts, is the *cerebral cortex*, the center of higher learning and cognition. The part responsible for emotions is an area called the *limbic structures*. It was once thought that these two parts operated independently of each other, but scientific theory now supports the belief that there is a great deal of neuronal interaction between all parts of the brain. Between the cortex and the limbic structures, messages flow freely back and forth through the *hypothalamus*, a pea-sized gland at the base of the brain. The hypothalamus is sometimes referred to as the brain's "central clearing house" because it is responsible for sending and receiving messages from brain to body and back again. The hypothalamus regulates the pituitary gland, which in turn activates certain stress hormones, such as adrenalin. You know from reading the chapter on basic stress management what happens to your body when the autonomic nervous system and adrenalin are kicking up.

So the cortex represents thoughts, and the limbic structures represent feelings, with the hypothalamus acting as mediator. Here's an example of a mind-body interaction: The pain message travels up the spinal cord through the hypothalamus. You think, "I hate this pain," and you feel angry and depressed. Then you think, "What if I never get well?" which causes you to feel afraid. The fear sends out a stress alarm via the hypothalamus, which in turn constricts your muscles in anticipation. The tight muscles fatigue and cramp, causing you more pain.

Because of this simultaneous processing, it is sometimes difficult to separate out which comes first—your negative thoughts, your negative feelings, or the pain. But it is safe to say that whenever you think negative thoughts about your pain, you will probably have a resulting negative physical reaction. Conversely, whenever you feel physical pain, you will probably think negative thoughts about it, setting off a vicious cycle, unless you take steps to reverse this reaction.

Consider Sally's case. Sally's boss has a deadline to meet, and Sally finds herself at the word processor furiously typing away. She skips lunch and breaks in order to try to get it all done. She feels her back strain from the buildup of pressure and sitting in a rigid position. She clenches her teeth against the pain and thinks:

1. "My boss should have planned ahead better."
2. "If I ignore the pain, I can get this done now and relax later."
3. "My back is killing me—I shouldn't have been so foolish that day at the gym when I showed off and tried to lift all that weight."

4. "I can't afford to go slowly or take a break because my boss might think I can't do the job."

By the end of the day, Sally has not only an aching back, but also a pounding tension headache from gritting her teeth all day. She arrives home exhausted and collapses into bed.

Sally could have managed this situation better by controlling some of her negative thinking. Here's a different way to think about each one of those statements above:

1. "Yes, it would have been nice if my boss had planned ahead better, but he didn't. My getting upset about that doesn't help me get through this work. I can manage this."
2. "If I stretch and relax in short intervals throughout the day, the pain won't be so bad later."
3. "For this hassle, I'll reward myself by stretching and doing an easy workout at the gym after work, or I'll relax in the sauna/jacuzzi."
4. "Back injuries and strains happen to many people. My boss won't think less of me for not having a back problem. We both know that I'm a good typist; I'll show him that I can get the work done even better by relaxing and stretching as I do it."

What was your reaction to this second set of statements? Did you feel a sense of relief that Sally did not have to lock herself into a mindset that only leads to frustration and hopeless thinking? When you have pain, how do you typically think?

Getting to know your negative thinking. Take one week to jot down all the thoughts that occur to you concerning your pain. Note when and where these thoughts occur. Take an observer's stance while writing down your thoughts. In other words, try not to censor or debate your thoughts; simply write down all that come to you, whether they're about yourself or others. Remember that it takes practice to become familiar with your brand of negative thinking. Automatic thinking is lightning fast; if you can identify only a few thoughts in a week, that's fine. In time, you'll become more adept at catching your automatic thoughts.

When the week is over, look back over your list. Compare the thoughts you wrote down to the following characteristics of typical negative thinking. Which of the following do you do most often?

Eight Styles of Negative Thinking

1. Blaming. You make someone or something else responsible for your pain. "My lousy boss is to blame for my job accident." "My family demands so much from me, I can't afford the time or money to take care of this pain." Blaming is a natural outgrowth of being tired, frustrated, and angry. But blaming only makes a situation worse, since you are not taking responsibility for what is happening to you, but rather expecting others to take the responsibility.

Some people go too far in the other direction and focus *all* the blame entirely on themselves. "It's *all my fault* that this happened to me." If you continually put yourself down in this way, the insidious nature of self-blame can lead to lethargy and depression. This self-defeating stance can also serve as an excuse for inactivity. "Since I'm such a stupid person, getting better is hopeless. So why should I try?"

2. Shoulds. Albert Ellis states that "should" statements are one of the cornerstones of irrational thinking. The words *should, must,* or *ought* appear regularly in chronic-pain negative thinking. Shoulds are usually a put down, implying that you were stupid, foolish, or weak for not living up to some standard. "I *should* have thought of good body mechanics before I lifted that box." "I *shouldn't* have been in such a hurry when I slipped on the ice." "If only I hadn't been wearing those high heels—I *shouldn't* be such a slave to fashion." "I *should* keep up with all my responsibilities, pain or no pain." "I *shouldn't* react to pain like this."

Should statements can sound a lot like blaming. You are admonishing yourself for not being perfect. But shoulds can also apply to others. You create a set of expectations for other people's performance that you *expect* will be met. "My spouse *should* provide consistent support and sympathy when I hurt."

3. Polarized Thinking. Everything is either black or white, good or bad. There is no gray area in the middle for improvement. Chronic pain sufferers are often tempted to think, "If I'm not better by such and such a date, then that's it—either this program won't work for me or else I've failed." Polarized thinking assumes that things must go perfectly or else. If you have a pain relapse, then the program you're using is no good or the relapse is a sure sign of ineptness.

This thinking can also be directed towards others, particularly medical professionals. "If they can't cure me, then they are useless." People attempting a pain management program for the first time can easily fall into this line of thinking by demanding rapid and total recovery instead of expecting a slow process of building pain control. Small steps toward feeling better are meaningless to these people, because progress is acknowledged only when they feel completely well.

This thinking leads to damaging overgeneralizations. You have *one* relaxation session where you are unable to decrease your pain, and you assume that you'll *never* be able to decrease your pain. Overgeneralizations are often couched in terms of absolute statements; cue words are *all, every, none, never, always, everybody,* and *nobody.* Absolute statements tend to limit your options and ignore any positive data that supports your efforts to change.

4. Catastrophizing. People who engage in this kind of thinking react to life situations by imagining the worst possible outcome and then reacting to their fear-provoking scenario as if it will surely come true. "I know that the only option left open to me is to have surgery. I'm sure I'll be laid up for months. What if the operation is a failure?" "What if" statements characterize this thinking, and greatly add to anxiety levels. "What if my pain *never* gets better, and I have to live like an invalid for the rest of my life? What if my spouse leaves me? What if I am unable to work?"

5. Control Fallacies. Some chronic pain sufferers see themselves as "externally controlled" by others, such as the medical profession. By assigning a doctor or a clinic total power over their fate, they make themselves helpless victims of their pain and of the system. In effect they absolve themselves of any responsibility. Others may see themselves as powerless to change a dysfunctional family situation. "My spouse doesn't think I need to see a counselor for my pain, so I can't come to the session."

On the other hand, people who see themselves as "internally controlled" believe that they have complete responsibility for everything and everyone. "Everyone depends on me. The family will fall apart if I don't recover quickly from this mess." These people assume all of the responsibility, rather than allowing other family members to share some of the load. Some pain sufferers suspect they could be completely well—if only they wanted to enough. "Maybe I don't want to get better, that's why this goes on so long."

6. Emotional Reasoning. This line of thinking assumes that what you feel *must* be true. If you feel guilty about needing time to heal, then taking the time must be wrong and needing the time must be your fault. If you're frightened that the pain will never stop, then you *believe* it will never stop. If you feel grief at the thought that you'll never run again, then you must be right—you won't run again. You let your feelings rule your reasoning ability. While it's usually helpful to get in touch with your feelings, *what* you feel may be quite unrealistic. The strength of the feeling creates conviction, but things may later seem very different as the emotional storm dies down.

7. Filtering. Some people have a tendency to see their pain through tunnel vision, filtering out any potential positive aspects. These people make things worse than they are by focusing only on the pain and nothing else. Ted could not appreciate his spouse's genuine efforts at caring and support because he was so wrapped up in his pain. He failed to enjoy any aspect of a very nurturing relationship.

The process of filtering can also be very selective. You may choose to remember only those things which support your angry feelings, thus pulling your negative memories out of context and isolating you from positive experiences. What you fear can be magnified to the point that it fills your awareness to the exclusion of everything else. Ruth was so obsessed with the possibility of another back attack that she filtered out her doctor's advice on prevention and exercise.

8. Entitlement Fallacy. People often feel that they are "entitled" to a pain-free existence. They believe they shouldn't have to suffer pain or loss. They feel cheated. Life is being unfair. John felt that it was totally unacceptable that he couldn't play tennis after his injury. He felt that his athletic abilities had been "stolen" from him. His sense of entitlement and outrage kept him from considering new sports to replace his old one.

People who harbor the entitlement fallacy feel that the luxury of ignoring or taking their bodies for granted is theirs by right. And if they lose some capacity due to chronic pain, they feel that their life is horribly diminished.

All of these eight thinking styles are related to each other. In fact, if you have a tendency towards one line of thinking, you will probably catch yourself doing several of the others. While the categories are a helpful way of showing how negative thinking works, don't be surprised if you have trouble labelling your own thoughts, since the lines between styles can blur. It's also quite possible to bombard yourself with a number of negative thoughts all at once in a lightening-fast mental shorthand. Be patient with yourself and allow yourself to become familiar with these styles gradually.

Replacing Negative Thoughts

There are three ways of approaching the task of replacing your negative thoughts.

Step 1: Thought Stopping

This behavioral approach focuses on stopping your negative thoughts cold. You simply devise a list of quick responses that you can use to replace your negative and unproductive thoughts. You don't spend any time wondering *why* you do the negative thinking that you do—you simply choose positive thoughts and commit yourself to use them as soon as you notice yourself regressing into your characteristic negative thinking. Here are some suggestions to get you started.

Copy the list below or cut it out and put it next to your sink, refrigerator, word processor, or desk or the dashboard of your car—somewhere you will see it regularly. Breathe deeply first, and then say:

- I can cope
- Relax. I can manage the pain.
- I have managed this situation before. I can do it again.
- I am learning new coping skills everyday.
- I am not a bad person because I have this pain.
- The pain comes and goes. I know how to take care of it.
- No one thinks less of me because I have this pain.
- I am a good worker.
- I am a loving person.
- The pain comes in waves. Soon it will start to abate.

Add positive thoughts of our own:

_____

_____

_____

You can also substitute angry rebuttal statements for the negative thoughts. These are called *howitzer mantras*. The more angry and hostile you make your howitzer mantra, the better. Note that a few well-placed expletives will add conviction and force to your rebuttal. Here are some examples.

- Stop this negative shit.
- Shut up with the negative stuff.
- Stop this garbage.
- To hell with this catastrophic crap.
- Screw this blaming baloney.
- No more of this helpless stuff.

Add your own howitzer mantras:

_____

_____

_____

Step 2: The ABCD Model

This model, developed by Ellis, Beck, and others, can be a very useful tool for confronting your negative thinking about pain.

A is the "activating event," or stressor. In this case, let's make it a muscle spasm in your back which keeps you from fulfilling a commitment.

B is your "belief system," or your thoughts and attitudes about the stressful event. For example, you may think, "Now I can't do what I said I would—they'll think I'm weak. I can't do anything anymore."

C is the "consequences" of the activating event (basically your feelings). When you think poorly of yourself (as a result of *B*), you *feel* quilty, frustrated, and depressed.

D is a way to "dispute" and change this sequence of events. You dispute the negative thinking you discover in your belief system which leads to the *consequence* of feeling bad.

Breaking your thoughts and feelings down into this structured format takes some getting used to. But with practice you'll soon be more familiar with your own typical patterns and be able to automatically and rapidly dispute the negative thinking that gets in your way. Focus on your present pain problem and follow these steps:

(A) Write down a recent event that has caused your pain to flare up. Keep your description concise, concentrating on the essential details. Here's what Sally wrote:

"I twisted in my chair while reaching for the phone and felt my back strain."

The fresher the event is in your mind, the easier it will be to identify all your thoughts and feelings about it. Be sure to keep the event pain related.

(B) Skip this step for now, as it will be easier once you have identified your feelings.

(C) Jot down all the feelings you had when the event occurred, without censoring or debating them. A feeling is a word describing your emotions—a sentence that begins with "I think that . . ." is *not* a feeling sentence, but rather a thought or a statement. However, there may be some feelings hidden in the thought statement.

The feelings that Sally remembered were fear, disgust, and disappointment.

(B) Now go back to *B*. List all thoughts that occurred to you when the event happened. Sally identified three thoughts:

1. My back is going out again.
2. I have to take up the slack and answer the phone for the other secretary who's always out sick.
3. I thought my doctor said this wouldn't happen if I exercised regularly.

Go through this *A-B-C* process several times until you feel comfortable with it. Pay attention to your stress levels as you follow the steps. Also note that the event in *A* doesn't actually cause your negative feelings. The thoughts in *B* cause the feelings. *B* is your perception of the event and determines your reaction to it. Negative thoughts and feelings can also create a pain-making feedback loop. The more negative thoughts you have, the more negative feelings you feel. Your feelings of anxiety and depression in turn lead you to start *thinking* about how horribly anxious or depressed you are. And this only serves to intensify your negative feelings.

Move on to *D* when you feel ready to break out of the negative thought cycles you have identified in the first three steps. Focus on *B* in one of your examples. Pick a thought or belief you had that you find particularly upsetting, one that really "gets" you. "Hot" thoughts are often easier to work with because of the wealth of responses they can bring.

To help you dispute and refute your negative thinking, here is a list of specific suggestions for coping with each of the eight negative thinking styles.

1. Blaming. For *self-blame*, remind yourself that you have always made the best choice you could *at that particular point in time*. Based on your awareness at the exact moment of your choice, what you did seemed reasonable and for the best. Now, with the hindsight and the luxury of knowing how things turned out, you blame yourself. But back when you made the choice, there was no way that you could have known the future. You made what seemed *then* the best decision.

- I did the best I could. Blaming is beside the point.
- I've made reasonable choices, based on my awareness at the time.

If you're blaming others, realize that they, too, make the best choices available to them. They do their best, based on their awareness at the time.

- They are doing the best they can.
- They have their own priorities and needs that I can't hope to understand.

2. Should statements. When you catch yourself saying the words "should," "ought," or "must," you are in effect putting yourself or someone else down. You or they are stupid, wrong, and bad for not doing things differently. The fact is that you do it the way you do it and they do it the way they do it because of unique needs, priorities, and values. No amount of anger or self-admonishment will make the situation any better or easier. You and others make the best choice available, based on current awareness. "Should" statements only immobilize you, and contribute to an unrealistic expectation that you and everyone else ought to be perfect.

- I do not have to be perfect.
- Forget all the "ought to be's."
- I may get irritated when other people don't act according to my values, but other people may think differently than I do. They have different needs and values.

3. Polarized thinking. If you persist in thinking in terms of black and white, you leave little room for the gray area of improvement. Any change effort takes time and steady work. If you expect yourself to be magically better overnight, you will be disappointed when you're not and discount your gradual efforts at progress. Watch out for absolute words like *all, every, none,* and *never.* And remember, YOU ALWAYS HAVE OPTIONS.

- I wish I could be completely well, but I certainly have made some progress in certain areas. Even though it doesn't seem like much now, it will add up.
- Sometimes improvement is not obvious at first. I'll give myself some time and patience.

4. Catastrophizing. When you catastrophize, you assume the worst with little or no evidence and require proof beyond a shadow of a doubt for anything positive. The antidote is to start doing the opposite. Require stringent proof that your worst fear will take place. What evidence do you have that it will happen for sure—other than the fear itself? Is there any reason to believe it might not happen? List the reasons why it might not happen: "This never happened before." "I have better coping skills now than when I first got ill." When catastrophic thoughts arise, firmly remind yourself that this is "what if" thinking without any *definite proof.* Ask yourself, in all honesty, what is the percentage chance that your *worst* fears will come true. Is there a 5 percent chance? A 10 percent chance? A .01 percent chance? Try to make a realistic assessment.

- I have no proof of this.
- There are good reasons why this probably won't happen.
- I'll find a way to cope with whatever happens.
- How can I cope right now?

5. Control fallacies. Whenever you catch yourself saying that "Dr. so and so" knows best, change it to "So and so has experience in that area, and so do I." Do not discount your own experience. You have power and responsibility over your fate. All final decisions are yours. To cope with helplessness, ask yourself what areas of life you do control. List them. Make sure you include your power to say no, to ask for more information, to get another opinion, and to explore alternative treatment avenues. Also be sure to list your areas of control with your family and work.

If you feel overly responsible for everyone around you, list *their* areas of control, choices, and options. Make this list as thorough as possible.

- I am not a helpless victim.
- I have power over my situation to steadily change and improve it.
- I do not have to be totally in control of my own and others' actions at all times. They are not helpless victims. Adults and even children can make their own choices.

6. Emotional reasoning. When you are in the thick of your feelings, it is difficult to reason objectively. And you don't have to. Take some time to feel bad and ventilate your feelings, but put a time limit on your catharsis. Then, move on to a problem-solving stage where you don't let your feelings rule your decision-making ability. Feelings are good and healthy, but not always useful in problem solving.

- I will let myself feel (scared, angry, sad) right now, but I know these feelings don't really give me an accurate picture of my situation.
- When I calm down and relax a little bit, I'll assess my (situation, problem, decision) again.

See the section on stress inoculation for more suggested coping thoughts.

7. Filtering. If you find yourself focusing entirely on the negative aspects of your pain, you need to deliberately shift focus. First, place your attention on coping strategies rather than obsessing about the problem itself. Avoid magnifying your problem. Second, focus on the positive aspects of your situation. Avoid the phrase "I can't stand it."

- I can get used to and cope with almost anything.
- I have skills, resources, and friends. Look how much they have supported me and helped me cope already!

- What is there to celebrate, enjoy, or look forward to right now? (Then make sure you come up with something for all three.)

8. Entitlement fallacy. To dispute this fallacy, you'll need to challenge the notion that you have a right to a totally pain-free existence. You are not *entitled* to anything except taxes and death. No one said that life would be fair. The key is, what do you do *after* you have been struck by trauma, injury, pain? Do you bitterly resent how life has cheated you, or do you accept your pain and sadness and move on to functioning as well and happily as you can? Anger won't help. Creative coping helps. Looking for new ways to get meaning and pleasure helps. Thinking of *what you can still do* helps.

- My life has not been totally diminished because I have this problem.
- I can replace my losses with new things to do. (Start listing them right now.)

Sally's Case

Sally picked the thought "my back is going out again" to work on. Her related feeling was fear. She identified other thoughts that were associated with her fearful feeling, such as "It'll be just as bad as before . . . I'll be laid up again for months . . . My boss won't like me." When she finished searching for all her thoughts relating to fear and "my back is going out again," Sally reviewed the list of eight negative thinking styles and identified elements of catastrophizing, polarized thinking, and even a few "shoulds" in her initial thoughts. Sally realized that she might not actually have to be laid up for months—she was expecting the worst case to happen (catastrophizing). She was telling herself she should be perfect for the boss (a should statement); if she wasn't perfect, he wouldn't like her (polarized thinking). She also realized that when she felt fear, she immediately jumped to the conclusion that all her fearful thoughts were absolutely true (emotional reasoning). With these fallacies identified, here's how Sally disputed "my back is going out again."

Is there any real proof for this fear? Yes, some, because my back went out once before. Is there any reason to believe it won't happen? Right now in this particular situation the pain is not severe, and there's no evidence that my back will be as bad and go out like it did before. And I've had numerous back strains since my first injury, and I've managed to get through each of them without any major problems.

Since the injury, I've been exercising and practicing stress management regularly. I know how to take care of my back in the long run, and I know what to do right now to make sure the pain doesn't get worse—relax, stretch, slow down.

Here's how Sally put it all together in the *ABCD* format:

A	B	C	D
Activating event (stressor)	Belief system (thoughts)	Consequences (feelings)	Disputing
Backpain while typing this afternoon	*Oh no, my back is going out again.* *It'll be as bad as before.* *I'll never be able to do this job right.* *I'll never work again.* *It's all my fault for not doing my exercises.* *My boss should be better organized so I don't get stuck like this.*	*Fear* *Anxiety* *Anger* *Frustration*	*I'm expecting the worst (catastrophizing).* *Even though I'm anxious, that doesn't mean I should jump to conclusions (emotional reasoning).* *My boss doesn't always work like I think he should (should statement).* *Don't worry—it'll take time to do my exercises and get through this (supportive).*

Here's another example of disputing. Seth always seems to get migraines when he finally gets a chance to relax. Sure enough, day one of his vacation he feels prodromal signs.

A	B	C	D
Activating event (stressor)	Belief system (thoughts)	Consequences (feelings)	Disputing
First day of vacation and felt migraine coming on—	*I know I'll get a full blown headache.* *It'll ruin my whole vacation.* *Nobody will have any fun.* *I shouldn't have taken a vacation.* *I'll never get rid of these headaches.*	*Depression* *Frustration* *Lethargy* *Anxiety*	*It's alright—this happens sometimes when I change my routine.* *I've been working very hard and I deserve this vacation.* *I'll practice my relaxation and see if I can limit this headache. It's worked before, it can work again.* *It won't ruin the whole vacation.* *I'm slowly and surely bringing these headaches under control.*

Spend at least twenty minutes each day practicing this model for a period of several weeks. Share it with a friend. With practice, the process will become second nature, and you won't have to write your reactions down—you'll be able to internally identify and dispute your negative thoughts.

Step 3: Analyzing Your Thoughts

You have determined some of the immediate thoughts associated with your pain and have tried several coping tools. Now is the time to dig a little deeper in analyzing your thought patterns and how they relate to your pain situation.

Let's look at Sally again. As an avid downhill skier, she prepares herself for the winter season by stretching and strengthening her back muscles regularly. After the first couple of runs, her whole body aches with fatigue and she feels a familiar twinge in her back. But she is exhilarated by the crisp air, the white snow, and the excitement of the run. She says to herself, "I'm not going to stop now—how often do I get to ski on such great powder? And anyway, the lift tickets are too expensive to waste." She knows she'll have the pleasure of the hot tub at the end of the day to soothe her aching muscles.

A week later Sally wakes up in the morning before work with a stuffy, runny nose and a scratchy throat. She doesn't feel particularly bad, but calls in sick anyway because she feels like she needs a day off. And besides, she doesn't want to risk infecting her co-workers.

These two pain situations are very different. In the first, Sally suppresses a lot of pain for the pleasure of skiing. In the second, her pain is not as great, but gets magnified for other reasons. The point here isn't to decide whether Sally was right to risk her back on the slope or wrong to take advantage of her sick leave, but rather to show that you *can* make important choices about your pain.

This step was saved as the last because it is often the most difficult one to take. It requires a certain degree of honesty from you, and a nondefensive assessment of the choices that you make about your pain. Take time to think about the various situations you've been in where your pain was a factor. Honestly ask yourself if there was a time when you knew you needed, for whatever reason, to magnify your pain. Look for any ways you might have been rewarded for staying focused on your pain. Keep a log of when your pain gets worse and see what activities (or would-be activities) coincide with these fluctuations. Does your pain change how people relate to you? Does it increase your experience of being cared for, or of getting support? Does it help you to avoid unpleasant tasks or stressful events?

If you feel comfortable doing so, talk this issue over with a trusted friend or family member. But don't judge yourself or feel guilty for the choices you have made. Your awareness is simply a learning tool to help you cope. And acknowledging that you may have sometimes chosen to use your pain may help you to control it more effectively.

Stress Inoculation

Fighting negative thinking is not the complete answer for dealing with your emotional pain. If you work hard at confronting distortions, you may reduce the amount of negative thinking that you do by fifty, sixty, or even eighty percent. But some residual amount will inevitably slip through. Furthermore, some of your negative thinking occurs at a level far below your conscious awareness. You simply can't catch the thoughts, because they are too lightning swift or too buried for you to recognize them. Sometimes the thoughts are in the form of images that seem to rise unbidden (you see yourself in a wheelchair, you imagine a muscle ripping). Sometimes the thoughts have no words—you just *know* that something bad will happen.

You can use stress inoculation (a technique developed by Donald Meichenbaum) when some of your hard-to-catch negative thoughts have precipitated an anxious, angry, or depressive reaction. Stress inoculation helps you cope with waves of strong, painful emotion; it helps you make it through without being overwhelmed, even when you are faced with overwhelming feelings. Here's how it works.

1. Self-monitoring. You must learn to recognize the early signs of a strong emotional reaction. Catching the wave of fear, anger, or sadness early is a key to successful coping. Treat your first awareness of a painful feeling, particularly one that seems to be gathering steam, as a red flag warning you to initiate the stress inoculation procedure.

2. Self-instruction. The core of stress inoculation is a process of talking to yourself through the pain. In practice, this means developing a list of coping statements that will keep you calmer during waves of painful emotion. The coping statements that you will create for yourself will be in the form of short, pithy commands that remind you of adaptive ways to deal with your stressful feelings.

When you're feeling anxious, angry, or sad, the first thing you need to do is to rid your body of excess tension. So your first coping statements should focus on breathing and relaxing the areas of your body that characteristically hold tension. Here are some examples:

- Breathe deeply now, full relaxing breaths.
- Breathe deeply and relax the diaphragm.
- Tension is a sign to cope. Relax now!
- Is there tension in my shoulders?
- I can breathe away that tension. Let go of it!

Now try to write several statements of your own. Make sure you include the specifics of *where* and *how* you feel tension most. Include any relaxing activities that you know you can do in a few minutes. For example:

- I'll settle down in the Barcalounger and read some Perry Mason for a while.

- I'll do my nails and forget this baloney.
- I'll take a hot bath and listen to some Brahms.

The second set of instructional statements you will write will help you to cope with the feeling itself. The emphasis here is on getting through it, riding it out. Here are some examples:

- Don't let negative thoughts creep in.
- If I don't feed it with negative thoughts, this feeling will begin to dissipate by the time I get home.
- This is just a wave of pain that I will get through.
- I've survived this before. The wave passes in a while.
- I'll ride it out and I'll be OK.
- There's an end to it.
- I'll reserve a half an hour to feel this way, and then carry on.
- I can distract myself by balancing my checkbook (or doing some task, or calling someone, or jogging, and so on).

As with the relaxation reminders, you should adapt or rewrite any of these to suit yourself. Or use the statements as models to create coping instructions tailored to your unique situation.

Your third set of instructional statements will help you use the skill of *accepting and distancing*. These statements are reminders to pull back from the painful feeling and see it in perspective. You have entered a brief emotional storm, and it will be over in a while. Accept that you'll feel bad for a time, but know also that the wave will pass and the anxiety, anger, or sadness will recede. Here are examples:

- I'm doing my best to cope, and I'll just have to feel this way for a little while.
- I can step back and see the wave, I can get through it.
- I feel the anxiety (or anger, or sadness), but another part of me is watching me go through this from a distance.
- I can float by the worst of this and not be too touched by the feelings.
- I can accept these feelings because I'm doing my best.
- Pull back and see this for what it is—a brief emotional storm that will be over in a while

3. Talking yourself through. Make a list of the coping statements that you think will be most effective. Keep them with you so they can be used as reminders to cope when you experience stressful feelings. Be your own coach. Talk yourself through the trauma. The goal is to keep a part of yourself separated from the pain, a detached observer.

Remember that emotional pain distorts your sense of reality. Everything seems very black. The pain seems eternal. It's hard to imagine ever feeling better. That's why you need the coach, the detached observer to remind you that the wave will pass. Soon enough you begin to relax or get distracted. The emotion begins to burn itself out.

Harry's Case

Harry had been struggling with irritable bowel syndrome for more than five years. When the cramping flared up, he typically slipped into catastrophic thinking: "This is getting worse . . . How will I keep working? . . . Maybe I have cancer . . . I can't enjoy anything feeling like this." With the help of a therapist, Harry began to exert more and more control over his catastrophic thoughts. And he had fewer episodes of anxious rumination about his health. But there were still times when he felt overwhelmed by a sense of dread. The future seemed filled with pain, and he felt incapable of dealing with it.

Harry's therapist suggested stress inoculation to help him cope wih these surges of anxiety. Together they made this list of coping statements.

- Breathe deeply and relax the diaphragm.
- Let go of tension in the stomach, let it be fat and relaxed.
- I'll put the headphones on and listen to some Bruce Springsteen.
- This is just a wave of pain, it never lasts more than an hour.
- There's an end to it, I can survive one hour.
- I can float by the worst of this and not be done in.
- When I step back, I can see it's a wave and I'll feel better soon.

Harry modified and added to this list as he went along. He found that some coping statements worked better than others. And some didn't work at all. After carrying the list and using the technique for about two weeks, Harry reported that he felt less stress during his anxiety episodes. "It's like I'm detached, I can see the whole process from a distance. I just watch it gradually fade out."

Further Reading

Beck, Aaron. *Cognitive Therapy and the Emotional Disorders*. Connecticut: International Universities Press, 1976.

Consciousness and Self-Regulation. ed. Gary Schwartz and David Shapiro. Vol. 1. New York: Plenum Press, 1976.

Davis, Martha, Matthew McKay, and Elizabeth Eshelman. *The Relaxation and Stress Reduction Workbook*. Oakland, CA: New Harbinger Publications, 1982.

Lazarus, Richard, and Susan Folkman. *Stress, Appraisal, and Coping*. New York: Springer Publishing, 1984.

McKay, Matthew, Martha Davis, and Patrick Fanning. *Thoughts and Feelings*. Oakland, CA: New Harbinger Publications, 1981.

Pain Management: a Handbook of Psychological Treatment Approaches. ed. Arnold Holzman and Dennis Turk. New York: Pergamon Press, 1986.

7

Dealing With Others

Assertiveness

As a chronic pain sufferer, you have probably encountered situations that required you to say no to a request to do something that you knew would aggravate your pain. Did you feel guilty when you said no? Did you put yourself down for having the pain in the first place? Did you blame the other person for being rude and trying to embarrass you? Or did you pat yourself on the back for avoiding a potential problem by saying no?

Arthur felt guilty about not doing his share of the car pooling in the mornings. But his back bothered him so much that it was an effort even to get into the car, much less drive around in it. He didn't think that the other parents in the car pool would understand, so he made up excuses about his unreliable car.

When she found herself in a similar situation, Kathleen realized that driving long distances on her job would put her on the disabled list permanently. This realization gave her the confidence to request a meeting with her boss to work out an amicable solution.

Arthur is engaging in passive, avoidant behavior. Kathleen is being assertive. Are the differences obvious to you? If not, perhaps you need to examine your assertive or nonassertive behavior and its interplay with your pain. Learning to deal assertively with all of the situations that your pain disrupts can make a big difference in how well you cope.

People who show relatively little assertive behavior do not believe that they have a right to their feelings, beliefs, or opinions.

Consider these statements:

Do you:	*Or do you:*
1. Think that you should always take other people's advice seriously, especially doctors and health care professionals who take time out of their busy schedules just for you?	Have a right to ignore the advice of others?
2. Think that you should always respect the views of others, especially if they are in a position of authority?	Have a right to have your own opinions and convictions?

3. Think that it is selfish to put your needs before others' needs?	Have a right to put yourself first, sometimes?
4. Think you shouldn't take up others' valuable time with your problems?	Have a right to ask for help or emotional support?
5. Think you should always try to be logical, consistent, and in control?	Have a right to make mistakes, change your mind, or decide on a different course of action?
6. Think that you always have the right to say and do exactly what you feel?	Realize that sometimes you can and need to hear the other person out and can initially keep your opinions to yourself?

Statements one through four on the left can lead to passive behavior. If you behave *passively,* you let others push you around, do not stand up for yourself, and do what you are told, regardless of how you feel about it.

Passivity and chronic pain are a deadly combination. If you always do exactly what the doctor tells you to do, even though you've had previous experience to the contrary, then you are throwing away your own hard-won and tested knowledge and replacing it with a feeble dependency on someone else's supposedly greater insight. Or if your boss demands the same amount of work from you, and you know that it will make your neck pain worse and you do it anyway, then you are behaving passively.

Statements 5 and 6 on the left lead to aggressive behavior. If you behave *aggressively,* you tend to blame, threaten, and accuse people without regard for their feelings. Aggressive people are likely to attack when they don't get their way. They are so intent on being "right" that they often don't hear what others are saying.

Aggression and chronic pain are a dangerous combination. If you are angry because you have chronic pain and then blame your boss for your misfortune, you are likely to behave aggressively and risk your job. If you expect your doctor to cure you and then lash out at the "incompetence" when he or she disappoints you, you are behaving aggressively. You risk alienating a person who may be able to help you.

All of the statements on the right are assertive statements. Assertive behavior involves direct statements and actions regarding your feelings, thoughts, and wishes. You stand up for your own rights and take into account the rights and feelings of others. You listen attentively and let other people know that you have heard them. You are open to negotiation and compromise, but not at the expense of your own rights and dignity. You can make direct requests and direct refusals. You can deal effectively with criticism, without becoming hostile or defensive.

Assertive behavior helps you deal effectively with chronic pain. If you feel that you are not getting adequate advice or service from a health care professional, then you have a right to ask questions and make requests, or to ignore that person's advice and look elsewhere. But if passivity or guilt keep you from making choices like these, then you will have a hard time getting to the problem-solving stage of taking care of your own pain situation.

Problems at home are also made easier by assertiveness. Howard believed that he was primarily responsible for doing all the home repair and maintenance on top of a demanding job. The nature of his arthritis pain made this an unrealistic expectation, but he had trouble asking his family for help. Learning new assertive skills enabled him to request a family conference for the purpose of making changes in work distribution. To his surprise, his family was more than willing to help with some of his tasks.

Identifying Your Style

Reflect on events of the past week where you felt that you responded passively or aggressively. Identify one situation where you can remember the interactions as clearly as possible. Then add other recent events.

Event:	The other person said:	You said:
_____	_____	_____
_____	_____	_____
_____	_____	_____
_____	_____	_____
_____	_____	_____

Can you identify a typical pattern in your responses or interactions? To help in assessing your behavior, refer to the following lists for passive, assertive, and aggressive behavioral clues.

Passive: Moving away from the situation

Verbal clues:
Profuse apologizing, rambling, or beating around the bush. Using words or phrases such as "Um . . ." "Well . . ." "You know . . ." "Never mind . . ." "It's not really important . . ." "Don't bother . . ." "Maybe . . ." "I guess . . ." "Don't you think . . ."

Nonverbal clues:
Slouched posture; downcast, averted or tearful eyes; nervous gestures; soft, unsteady, weak, whining, hesitant, pleading, or giggly tone of voice.

Assertive: Balancing Power

Verbal clues:
Clear, direct, honest, respectful, empathic (feeling) statements; nonblaming language. Using sentences that start with "I want . . ." "I think . . ." "I feel . . ." "Let us . . ." "How can we resolve this?"

Nonverbal clues:
Listens well to others; stands upright and comfortably; uses a strong, well-modulated voice; maintains good eye contact.

Aggressive: Moving Against

Verbal clues:
Blaming, accusing, or threatening others; using putdowns, sarcasm, evaluative comments, or sexist or racist terms. Using phrases such as "You'd better . . ." "You should . . ." "You must be kidding . . ." "You better watch out if you don't . . ." "That's bad . . ."

Nonverbal clues:
Shows of strength; a raised, snickering, or haughty tone of voice; cold, detached looks; a rigid or rejecting posture; dominating gestures (finger pointing, pounding table, or intruding into other's personal space).

You'll find it helpful to practice your new behavior with a spouse, friend, or counselor who you know will provide you with helpful feedback. Try out the assertive responses and note the results. You should be able to reach a problem-solving stage more quickly than you did when you used your old passive or aggressive responses. When you're ready, try out your new assertive behavior with your doctor or health care professional. Explain to them that you are practicing dealing more assertively with your pain situations.

Here are specific guidelines for turning your old patterns of passive or aggressive behavior into assertive requests.

Behavior	*Description*
Maintain eye contact and position your body squarely toward others.	Look the other person in the eye *most* of the time. Do not stare fixedly. Lean forward and use hand gestures to maintain his or her attention.
Speak firmly and positively, and loudly enough to be heard easily.	Avoid mumbling, whining, speaking shrilly, or yelling. Avoid dropping your voice at end of sentence.
Use clear, concise speech. Ask directly for what you want or say clearly what	Avoid numerous repetitions and qualifiers such as "maybe" or "I guess."

you *don't* want.	Avoid undoing statements such as "I shouldn't ask, but . . ."
Keep your nonverbal behavior congruent with the content of your statement.	Don't smile placatingly when refusing or disagreeing. Don't wring your hands when requesting. Avoid a rigid face when expressing warmth or praise.
Listen.	Repeat the point that the other person made, clarify, or say something that shows you are hearing him or her.
Maintain a posture and attitude of equality.	Avoid apologetic statements or a tone which belittles yourself or your ideas. Avoid accusing statements or a tone of sarcasm or ridicule. Be respectful of yourself and others.
Take the initiative.	Don't let others choose for you. Take the lead with "I have a suggestion . . ." or "In my opinion . . ."

When you have said what you wanted to say, stop talking.

Rick has chronic pain from an old whiplash, which can be exacerbated by stress. He knew that certain situations caused his pain condition to flare up, but he had trouble saying no to some of those situations. He remembered one occasion when he had agreed to go to a particularly gruesome horror movie, knowing full well that his shoulder and neck symptoms would get worse. But he felt too embarrassed to say no, and was afraid that his friend wouldn't ask him out again.

When he talked this situation out with his counselor, Rick realized that he could handle the situation assertively without feeling embarrassed. He explained to his friend that he made a point of not going to those kind of movies because they stressed him out, and instead set up a date to see another movie he'd been looking forward to. His friend readily agreed, and Rick felt pleased that he had learned to take care of himself.

Rita had always been told that the "doctor knows best," and so she dutifully took all of the medication that he prescribed for her jaw pain. When she realized that the Valium she was taking was an addictive tranquilizer and that she was beginning to need more and more of it to control her tension, she asked her doctor to refer her to a pain specialist. When the doctor said that he could make the referral but that all she really needed was to take a different tranquilizer, she politely said no. She explained that she was not the kind of person who functioned well on drugs, and that she needed to work with a doctor and counselor who could help her get off the Valium and rely on drug-free resources.

Harry was in a similar situation. Everytime he had a vascular headache, he would run off to the emergency room at the local hospital and get a shot of Demerol, a highly potent and addictive pain killer. In this case, Harry's family physician urged him to seek out pain clinic treatment. But Harry kept thinking that the headaches would go away and that each trip to the hospital would be the last. And anyway, it was easier and more convenient to take a powerful shot which instantly eased the pain than to drive to another town for weekly visits to the pain clinic. Harry didn't realize it, but his dependence on the pain shots was growing, and this drastic remedy was doing little to give him any real control over his pain. When his wife urged him to try other options, he would respond with an aggressive retort such as "You don't know what this feels like." She responded assertively, not because she blamed or judged her husband, but because the way he was handling the pain made her feel anxious and fearful for him. She made it clear that while she could not promise to put herself at his disposal every time he needed to go to the emergency room, she would be glad to arrange her schedule so that she could accompany him to the pain clinic once a week. Her concern and the reasonableness of her offer finally got through to her husband, and he agreed to try out the pain management program.

Assertiveness and Anger

Being angry is a natural byproduct of having chronic pain. There is a lot to be angry about. Your health and well-being have been taken from you, and that loss alone is enough to make anyone furious. It can also be aggravating to find that other people don't always understand what you are going through. At times even your family can seem indifferent. Maybe your doctor wants you to see a psychologist for your pain, and you feel angry because you imagine that he thinks your pain is all in your head. On top of being angry, you hurt, and your angry outbursts only make the pain worse.

The problem is not that you're angry. The problem is that you allow the anger to build up inside of you to the point that you have unproductive and damaging outbursts that interfere with coping. Why can't you let your anger out before you explode? What makes you keep it in?

Many, many people have problems expressing their anger. You may have been given lots of messages as a child that you were supposed to be nice, kind, and sweet — and that angry emotions were not tolerated. One client, who feared expressing her anger, recalled being sent to her room as a little girl after she lashed out at her mother. The message was "don't talk back." So she quickly learned to bottle up her anger in an effort to be a good child and avoid punishment. Years later she realized that the same message had been carried over to other situations in her life, and that her immediate reaction was often to hide her anger rather than learn to deal with it in assertive ways. When she hurt her back lifting groceries out of the trunk of her car, and the painful spasms stayed with her for months at a time, she felt that her only recourse was to keep her anger and frustration inside. If she let it out for even a minute she would be a "bad" person. But the more tightly she held her anger in, the more frequent were her blowups at her family.

With counseling, she realized that her mother's old message about anger was no longer useful. She had the power to exercise other options in her life. She could let her feelings and needs be known in assertive ways that didn't undermine her relationships.

The point here is not to debate *why* you were given the messages you were—not to analyze your mother's personality, or your father's temperament. Your task is to accept the fact that you were given messages, discover how these rules about conflict affect your pain control skills, throw out the unhelpful rules, and replace them with new, productive, and effective strategies for conflict resolution.

Dr. Hendler, in *Coping With Chronic Pain*, says that productive ventilation of anger can be both a therapeutic release of tension and a sign of a healthy attitudinal change. It is unnatural for a person to remain smooth, calm, and unaffected by a chronic pain situation. But expressing your anger doesn't mean that you rage and "dump" your feelings. Instead of venting your feelings in thermonuclear outbursts, you can learn to turn your anger into a motivational tool that will give you a charge of energy and control. And aggressive angry outbursts can have some very negative consequences:

- Outbursts of anger can alienate and isolate you from others. You put people on the defensive by judging, blaming, and accusing them.
- Outbursts can raise, rather than relieve your anxiety levels.
- Aggressive anger can be an obstacle to problem solving. Afterwards, the problem still remains; now you have your anger *and* your problem.

Assertive handling of anger, which is the basis for effective conflict management, uses the following six steps:

Guidelines for Handling Anger Assertively

1. Do you really feel angry enough to want and need to work on the problem that caused your anger? Take a deep breath and listen to yourself for a minute. When Emma had a back spasm, her husband ignored her efforts to discuss how to reorganize the housework. She realized that she was angry and that the issue would not go away—she needed to deal with it. Betty's husband had a busy day and forgot to pick up the laundry. Betty thought about her annoyance and let it go.

2. Pick an appropriate discussion time. If possible, arrange a time beforehand and describe the situation that you need to discuss. State the problem in a neutral manner. While cooking dinner, Emma asked her husband if later on that night they could set aside time to discuss the housework. She knew that he would be more relaxed then than he was right after he got home from work.

3. Avoid blaming, judging, and accusing the other person. Your blame-offensive will only breed a defensive counterattack. Emma accused her husband of being a lazy slob and the main reason that the house was always a mess. He responded by telling her that she'd always been a lousy housekeeper and continued to ignore her requests for change.

4. Make "I" statements about how you feel. Say "I'm feeling frustrated" rather than "You and your stupidity make me feel fed up." "I" statements rarely put people on the defensive, since they are statements of your own feelings rather than accusations regarding the other person's behavior. Feelings are not as debatable as behavior.

> *Emma:* I'm feeling frustrated and a little angry. My back pain makes it impossible for me to do all the things I used to do. Things are piling up around the house. I don't know how long this situation will continue, but the pain seems to be lessening now that I'm doing my exercises regularly.

5. Say what you need. Make your needs clear and very specific. Don't say that you want the other person to "be more considerate" (in some unspecified way at some unspecified time). Instead, ask for help at a specific time or with a specific problem. Don't ask for the other person to feel differently ("Stop being so cold."); instead, ask for different behavior ("Could we talk for a while before putting on the TV?").

> *Emma:* I'd like to work out an agreeable housework solution with you so that in the meantime the dirt doesn't pile up. If you do the vacuuming and laundry, I'll still cook and dust and sort the clothes.

6. Allow the person you're talking to time to respond. Practice good listening skills when they respond: look at them when they talk, don't interrupt until they say they are finished, and acknowledge that you heard what they said (even though you may not agree with what they said). Here's what Emma's husband said and her response:

> *Husband:* I feel frustrated, too. Not only is the housework piling up, but my boss is pressuring me to meet that deadline ahead of time. I've been preoccupied with my job.
> *Emma (acknowledging his situation):* This is a tough time for both of us, since we're both under pressure.
> *Husband:* I guess I'm willing to go along with your plan if we can let things slide a little this week.

By listening to each other, Emma and her husband worked through her anger, which could have erupted into a screaming match and left the dirty house still sitting there. Instead, they were able to get to the problem-solving stage and reach an amicable agreement.

At first this process may seem stilted or unnatural to you, but you'll find that it becomes easier and more natural with practice. Talking this way is really a form of mutual respect and courtesy that can extend beyond your relationship to your family to become a valuable communication skill with friends and co-workers as well. But it is especially important to communicate well within the family during critical times of stress to insure that the family continues to work together.

Chronic pain is a stressor that can tear a family apart, or at least put a dent in how well it functions. When one family member is down and unable to work or perform his or her typical housework duties, the family's harmony is upset. Adjusting to a temporary or a long-term change requires patience and flexibility on the part of each family member. It is natural that tensions build up and erupt while members adjust. During these times, you and your family must be able to talk to each other. What hope will you have of accommodating the demands that chronic pain can make if you shut each other out in anger and fear?

Remember that anger is a healthy and natural sign of adjusting to change. But how you express your anger is the key. Handling your anger assertively can bring you closer to your loved ones, rather than isolate you from them. Your physical suffering has already set you apart, and the lonely times it brings you are hard enough. Anything you do to encourage intimacy will help you to endure the pain.

Resisting Change

Resistance can be defined as all those behaviors in a system that are obstacles to success. Your system includes you, your family, and the agency or institution that you are using for treatment. Overcoming resistance can be a tricky problem, since resistance takes on many forms that can initially confuse and frustrate both you and your health care professional.

Here are some typical resistant behaviors that you may find yourself doing:

- Being chronically late for appointments or not showing up
- Making repeated excuses for not accomplishing assigned tasks
- Expressing continued confusion about the tasks you are to do and your purpose in being at the clinic or treatment center
- Being excessively passive (such as by expecting others to do everything for you)
- Forgetting to take medications on an appropriate schedule
- Blaming everyone else but yourself

Resistant behaviors in your family may include these:

- Blaming all of the family's problems on the pain itself
- Denying any associated problems in the family that result from pain (such as increased stress at home)

- Making statements such as "There's nothing really wrong here" or "If only someone could find a cure, then our lives would be back in order and the way they used to be"
- Being unsupportive of the pain sufferer's attempts to comply with medical or psychological interventions

Part of your family's unsupportiveness may be demonstrated by family members not involving themselves in any way in your healing exercises. Ted's progress in his biofeedback program was slow and unproductive, partly because of family demands that prevented him from finding quiet time at home to practice his relaxation training. When he finally discussed this situation with his family, he learned that his children thought he had to practice because he was "crazy." He had them listen to and try out the tapes, and their resulting understanding helped to increase his success with the exercises significantly.

If you read through these behaviors and find yourself getting upset or feeling that the description is an unsympathetic or inaccurate picture of your situation, please realize that RESISTANCE IS A NATURAL PART OF ANY EFFORT TO CHANGE. It is OK for you to experience some resistance. After all, you *are* being asked to change your habits, attitudes, and behaviors, and who wouldn't feel at least some resistance to such an enormous demand? In their book *Mastering Resistance*, Carol Anderson and Susan Stewart explain that people often seek therapy in response to changes that they do not like or have not adjusted to. If a person must adjust to something new (such as living with chronic pain and its limitations) and is having trouble doing so, it is natural for that person to resist doctors' and others' efforts to change things even more.

Many people *perceive* that seeking help for pain means that they have to give up all control and independence. Most people also have a natural tendency to resist being influenced, and the implication that they cannot solve their own problems may lead them to resist the interventions of a health care professional. A fear that they might be labeled "crazy" or told that their pain is "all in their head" can encourage feelings of hostility and defensiveness.

Accepting change and adopting new ideas can be scary, especially when you may not have accepted your chronic pain situation in the first place. So it is natural to feel upset, particularly if you feel that you've been passed from doctor to doctor, and perhaps finally referred to a psychologist or psychiatrist. When you do feel yourself becoming angry and resistant, your first step should be to realize and accept that these are natural reactions. You're in a difficult situation, and your anger and resistance are simply an attempt to maintain control over yourself and your environment.

Your second step is to accept the fact that you have a chronic condition and that you'll have to make some necessary adjustments to help you live as fully as possible.

The last step is for you to take responsibility for your recovery. You are in control. You are the *only one* who can control your pain. To take control, you will have to adhere to your exercise regime faithfully, make your appointments, take your medications properly, block your negative thinking, and so on. You will have to find the time to practice new skills and the strength to carry on, even when a voice inside tells you that it's hopeless and that nothing will work.

Yes, it's natural to resist. You have been disappointed by doctors and tried things that didn't pan out. You are tired of hurting. But let me assure you that the self-regulation strategies outlined in this book (and practiced in pain control clinics all over the country) do work. You need to give the process your time *and commitment.*

For the Health Care Professional: Decreasing Resistant Behaviors

Resistance can be one of the most difficult obstacles for a health care professional to overcome. What looks like anger and hostility when you first meet a patient can actually be a mask for feelings of intimidation, low self-esteem, and resistance to change. How you handle those first few sessions in a pain management program can be critical in determining whether a patient will attempt to work with you or continue on with his or her doctor-shopping odyssey.

In an article in the journal *Professional Psychology,* Dr. Doug DeGood outlines the following steps for a health care professional to take in diffusing the anger and hostility characteristic of resistance.

1. *Attempt to immediately diffuse a patient's fears about the work you will do with him or her.* Directly address the problem by saying, "You may have some concerns about being sent to talk with me." Reassure the patient that chronic physical problems inevitably produce changes in one's life, and that coping with those changes will be the focus of your concern.

2. *If emotional issues are present, avoid premature efforts to "psychologize" the patient's symptoms.* Any psychological interventions are likely to be rejected unless you have taken the time to establish your credibility as a professional who understands the person's medical problems. DeGood emphasizes that good rapport building with medical patients requires allowing them to relate to you via their physical complaints.

3. *Try to shape adequate beliefs rather than challenge your patients' misconceptions.* Patients often cling to a belief in a specific "cure" or other myth about their physical condition. Particularly important to pain management programs is the quite common belief that a disorder must be less than legitimate if it can be in any way self-regulated. Try to help patients expand their beliefs, rather than challenge them directly. Help patients move away from focusing on a specific corrective procedure toward a broader rehabilitation plan.

4. *Present self-regulation strategies (or other psychological/behavioral interventions) in a positive fashion, rather than as last resort options.* Patients will be more likely to comply with a program if they are convinced that it is a treatment of choice rather than a desperation move. When the medical options have been exhausted, doctors all too often communicate their frustration with a patient. Subsequent attempts

to introduce self-regulation strategies may be received by the patient with minimal expectations and equal frustration.

5. *Require the patient to make a meaningful commitment to a self-regulation program.* This requires patients to understand that they must choose whether to actively participate. Adherence to home practice schedules, self-monitoring, and physical exercise and activity are sabotaged when patients feel coerced into participation. You may need to suggest that patients wait "until they are more ready," especially if there are drug addiction problems or underlying psychopathology.

6. *Foster realistic expectations by specifying feasible outcome goals.* Encourage patients to take a broader perspective than the expectation of a "quick fix" from a self-regulation program. Help them understand that they can anticipate only gradual improvement, with fluctuations—but that the long-term benefits will outweigh by far the lack of instant gratification. Explain that the skills they learn will last a lifetime, regardless of their pain condition.

7. *Integrate self-regulation strategies with other medical treatment.* Clarify the value of ongoing medical interventions as part of a patient's recovery process. Do not encourage patients to abandon other efforts, since this may set up the behavioral treatment for potential failure. Conversely, if inappropriate medication use is a problem, help the patient understand that over-reliance on medication will only sabotage the benefits of self-regulation.

8. *Whenever possible, include a spouse or other significant persons in discussion of self-regulation strategies.* Self-regulation programs can be confusing to family members. It is important to enlist their understanding and support early on in order to help reinforce learning. Family dynamics that encourage passivity, helplessness, and other problems cannot be dealt with in one or two sessions, but their presence may signal you to encourage family therapy in conjunction with the self-regulation program.

Further Reading

Anderson, Carol, and Susan Stewart. *Mastering Resistance: A Practical Guide to Family Therapy.* New York: Guilford Press, 1983.

DeGood, Douglas, Ph.D. "Reducing Medical Patients' Reluctance to Participate in Psychological Therapies: The Initial Session." *Professional Psychology* (1983).

Meichenbaum, Donald. *Cognitive Behavior Modification.* New York: Plenum Press, 1977.

8

Medications for Chronic Pain

by Gregg A. Korbon, M.D.

As a chronic pain sufferer, you know just how important the right pain reliever can be. If you are lucky, something as simple as aspirin may be all you need to function properly. But many, if not most, chronic pain sufferers are not so lucky. They experience the frustration of trying drug after drug and receive only minimal pain relief—or, at worst, dangerous side effects.

Bob was no stranger to the problems of multiple drug use. He had suffered from chronic headaches for years, and as he got older his migraines worsened and developed into tension headaches as well. Over the years, an allergist, opthalmologist, and a neurologist had each prescribed special medication for his condition. By the time he decided to consult a pain clinic, his pill-taking regime consisted of three to four Percodan a day, supplemented by Talwin and Tylenol with codeine. He was so agitated, he could hardly sit still at his first visit.

"I had always been a believer in pills—if something's not working right, take a pill. When I came to the clinic, I knew I was taking too many different kinds of pills. I didn't consciously decide to do that—it was just something I wandered into. And the pills had become a source of anxiety for me because I knew that I was becoming addicted to them. But I still had the pain, and I found it increasingly more difficult to separate the pain out from my need to take drugs. When I found myself worrying about where I was going to get my next prescription, I realized that I was developing a drug dependency and had to do something about it. My drugs would be like a martini at the end of the day—I couldn't wait to get home to have one and get some relief from the stress and pain of the day. I also began to have some memory problems and would get confused about the order of things, two major clues that alerted me to my drug problem. I was feeling desperate and scared by the time I got to the pain clinic."

Bob's story is an example of what happens to many people who search for pain relief. His story also has a happy ending, which I'll describe to you later on in this chapter. But first, I want to give you some information that will help you avoid "wandering into" a similar situation. You'll need to know what kinds of medications are commonly prescribed for chronic pain, which can be most helpful, and which to

Dr. Korbon is Assistant Professor of Anesthesiology and Attending Physician at the University of Virginia Pain Management Center, Charlottesville, Virginia.

avoid. You'll also learn the typical problems associated with addiction, as well as a sensible plan for combining drug therapy with other therapies. This will all help to make you a more informed consumer of medications, so that you can ask the appropriate questions of your doctor and make sure that you are avoiding the problems of drug abuse.

The Search for a Perfect Drug

Medicine's search for a perfect pain reliever has evolved over centuries of trial and error and careful experimentation. For ages this search was only a dream, and it wasn't until a small plant growing somewhere in the Middle East was tasted by an early man who had some painful condition, possibly a toothache, that this dream began to become a reality. The plant was the opium poppy. The word *opium* comes from the Greek name for juice, in this case the poppy juice that the plant probably developed to discourage animals from eating its seed pods. The collection of chemicals found in opium, about twenty in all, cause a variety of unpleasant side effects, including nausea, vomiting, sleepiness, constipation, and respiratory depression. Few animals or people would care for this concoction—unless they happen to be suffering from pain. Two of the twenty chemicals in opium, morphine and codeine, are still the strongest pain relievers known.

Morphine was named after Morpheus, the Greek god of dreams, because the drug's sedative (sleep-producing) effects are quite profound. When morphine was first purified from opium in the early 1800s, the process was found to decrease opium's unwanted side effects and increase its analgesic (pain-killing) effects, making morphine a useful drug in surgery. However, patients must be anesthetized with large doses of morphine before operations can be performed. In this situation, patients have to be on a respirator, because they will stop breathing on their own long before they receive a dose large enough to cause total unconsciousness. This kind of respiratory depression is one of the two major problems with this drug. The other is addiction.

The search for the perfect drug, one which provides pain relief with no significant side effects, continues to this day. Heroin, a rapidly acting derivative of morphine, was said to be nonaddicting when it was first introduced. The same was said for Demerol, another powerful and addicting drug. The same claims are made for new drugs introduced every year. Unfortunately, the only drugs that have these properties are aspirin and acetaminophen (best known as the brand name Tylenol). But while they are nonaddictive, these two drugs provide only mild analgesia.

Let's examine the specific differences between the various classes of pain relievers.

Narcotics

Narcotics are by far the most powerful pain killers—so powerful, in fact, that any amount of pain can be controlled with them. But they are NOT appropriate for the therapy of noncancerous chronic pain. Once addicted, an individual will experience *withdrawal* (painful, flu-like symptoms that occur a few days after not taking the narcotic). Along with the problems of addiction, the user will also feel a need for ever-increasing doses to get the same effect. In other words, a user's *tolerance* to the drug increases, making the drug less effective. As the addict takes larger and larger doses, the potential for serious effects on the brain (sedation, loss of sex drive, and so on) increases.

It is almost always inadvisable to take narcotic medications for a chronic pain condition. Because the pain lasts over many weeks or months, it is just a matter of time before you become addicted. Addiction to Darvon, codeine, Demerol, Percodan, and other narcotics is a *major* problem for sufferers of chronic pain in this country. Like Bob, you end up with two problems: pain and an often stubborn addiction that can greatly influence the course of your life.

For a list of the most commonly prescribed narcotics and a new class of modified narcotics (agonists-antagonists), see table 8.1.

Nonnarcotic Analgesics

In contrast, these drugs have less devastating side effects. They are *not* addicting, they do not exhibit tolerance, and they do not cause serious effects on the brain such as sleepiness or respiratory depression. Usually, their only bothersome side effect is the stomach irritation that they cause, and acetaminophen (Tylenol) seldom has even that effect. They are, however, only effective for mild amounts of pain. As pain level increases, other medications are often added, including antidepressants, anticonvulsants, and, often inappropriately, tranquilizers.

Nonnarcotic analgesics fall into two categories (see table 8.2). First is the acetaminophen class of drugs (best known as the brand name Tylenol), which are mild analgesics and good for reducing fevers. But they have *no* use in conditions like arthritis, because they have no anti-inflammatory actions (the ability to soothe irritated tissue). Acetaminophen is marketed under many names and in combination with other drugs. Any time you read the label on a nonprescription drug and see the name acetaminophen, that is probably the component of the drug which is doing all the pain killing.

The second category of nonnarcotic analgesics is the nonsteroidal anti-inflammatory drugs (NSAIDs, for short). These aspirin-like drugs are mild analgesics, good for reducing fevers, and very useful in conditions like arthritis because they reduce inflammation. (Steroids are also used to reduce inflammation, but they have little use in chronic pain except in the very worst cases of rheumatoid arthritis.)

The trade-off for the anti-inflammatory effects of the NSAIDs is that they often upset the stomach, can cause ulcers, and in a few rare cases may interfere with the ability of the blood to clot, causing a tendency to bleed. New NSAIDs are coming out every day, each with slightly different effects. Some are slightly better pain killers than aspirin, some need to be taken less often, some have less harmful effects on the stomach, and some cause more serious side effects such as liver or kidney damage. The names of some of the more common NSAIDs and their significant differences from aspirin are shown in table 8.2.

The mode of action of the nonnarcotic analgesic appears to be completely different from that of the narcotics. The narcotics work directly on the brain, where they act like endorphins, the brain's own natural painkillers. The nonnarcotics work away from the brain, in the periphery of the body. The NSAIDs probably block the formation of pain-producing chemicals (such as prostaglandins) at the point of injury. The existence of these different mechanisms is sometimes exploited by combining narcotic and nonnarcotic drugs together, a mixture which creates an addictive effect. But this type of prescription is only for conditions of severe pain where addiction is not a concern (a dying cancer patient, for example).

Antidepressants

Many persons with chronic pain are depressed—that is, they have a loss of energy, feel hopeless and helpless, get little enjoyment from life, sleep in an irregular pattern, and often have crying spells. Depression is a natural response to chronic pain and its disturbance of normal activities. The close connection between the two conditions is shown by the fact that about half of all patients with depression also have a chronic pain complaint—a complaint which often disappears when the depression goes away. The brain chemical serotonin seems to be involved in both mechanisms, as well as in the regulation of sleep. This common chemistry makes it no surprise that both chronic pain and depression are also associated with difficulty sleeping. You have probably noticed that your underlying pain condition seems to hurt you more when you get behind in your sleep.

Since the common chemical problem often found in depression, chronic pain, and sleep disturbance is a lowering of the amount of serotonin in the brain, antidepressants are often useful in treating all three conditions. These drugs allow serotonin levels to return to normal, enhance sleep, help relieve depression, and decrease pain. Their major side effect of sedation is directly related to their sleep-restoring ability. Sedation usually becomes less of a problem after taking antidepressants for a few weeks. Other common side effects include a dry mouth, blurred vision, dizziness, constipation, and difficulty urinating (particularly in older males). New antidepressants with fewer side effects are coming out, but the sedative effect appears to be necessary in order to get the desired actions of analgesia and relief of depression. It should be noted that antidepressants do not begin to work until you have been taking them for at least one to two weeks. Some individuals will continue to obtain an increasing benefit for up to two months. The lesson here is that you need to give these drugs enough time to work.

Table 8.3 shows the characteristics of the various antidepressants. Usually, your doctor will try these drugs for a two-month trial period and continue them for several more months if they seem useful. Since the antidepressants are not addicting, they may be continued indefinitely if the side effects are not bothersome. The dosages needed to obtain improved sleep and pain relief seem to be less than that required to treat a significant depression. As a result, the side effects of the lower dosages used to treat chronic pain are relatively less troublesome. As some patients experience transient sleep disturbance after abruptly stopping antidepressants, you should taper off of your prescription over a two-week period.

Anticonvulsants

These drugs were developed to prevent seizures in epileptic individuals. They act by increasing the firing threshold for nerves traveling to, from, and through the brain. In other words, they have a calming influence on the electrical activity of the nervous system, although they are not very sedating to the patient. Some types of chronic pain due to nerve damage, either from injury or disease (shingles, diabetes, and so on), are associated with abnormal nerve firing patterns. By calming these abnormal nerves, patients often experience considerable pain relief. In addition, many other types of chronic pain not associated with known nerve abnormalities can also benefit from this class of drugs. The reasons for this effect of the anticonvulsants is not clear, although it is thought that some of the drug's calming effect may act preferentially upon the nerves of the pain conducting pathways. Regardless of the mechanism, these drugs are usually worth a try for most pain conditions. Since they only take a few days to achieve their maximum benefit, an adequate trial of different dosages can be performed over a few weeks.

The anticonvulsants are shown in table 8.4. The side effects of this class of drugs are more severe than the antidepressants and include liver and bone marrow damage. Prolonged use of these drugs should therefore be done only under the care of a physician, who should regularly draw blood samples to guard against the development of these serious problems. It is reassuring to know that many thousands of patients take these drugs over their entire lives without serious toxicity.

Major Tranquilizers (Antipsychotics)

This class of medication was developed to eliminate the use of straightjackets from insane asylums. To a large extent they have been successful, and most of the severely mentally ill inmates of our nation's institutions now sit sedately without causing trouble. The antipsychotic properties of these drugs also allow many patients who would otherwise need to be institutionalized to function in a relatively normal fashion.

But how can this type of drug help chronic pain? Once again, we don't know. It must be presumed that the pain pathways are preferentially "tranquilized," and there is some evidence that these medications are useful in relieving chronic pain, although my personal experience has been disappointing.

The most common drugs in this class are shown in table 8.5. Unwanted side effects range from the most common ones of an unpleasant drugged feeling, dry mouth, blurred vision, constipation, and urinary retention, to less common but more serious ones like movement disorders (which may be permanent even after discontinuing the drug). Other problems include liver and bone marrow damage. Despite this impressive list of side effects, some patients do appear to benefit from these drugs. Like all patients taking prescription drugs, these individuals should take their major tranquilizers under the care of a physician.

Minor Tranquilizers (Anti-Anxiety Drugs)

Stress is increasingly recognized as an important cause of many medical problems, particularly in the field of chronic pain management. Pills and alcohol to help us relax have achieved enormous popularity in our society. Valium (diazepam) belongs to this class of drug, and until a few years ago it was the most commonly prescribed medication for anxiety and stress. Librium (chlordiazepoxide) is a member of this group, along with an ever increasing list of others, which are shown, in necessarily abbreviated fashion, in table 8.6. It is interesting to note that the medication which recently surpassed Valium in popularity is a drug used for the treatment of ulcer disease (cimetidine).

There are few uses for this class of drug in the management of chronic pain. After long-term use, these drugs are addicting, cause sleep disturbance, and tend to depress the patient. Since most chronic pain patients already have a tendency towards depression, this type of drug is better avoided. Other unwanted effects include drowsiness, decreased memory, impaired coordination, and fatigue. Some tranquilizers are said to have muscle relaxant properties, and are therefore used in the treatment of muscle cramps and spasm. But this claim is true only to a limited extent; since these drugs act by relaxing the brain as much as the muscles, they are better used only for short periods of time for the treatment of acute injuries. You should turn to more appropriate methods to relax chronically tight muscles.

Detoxification

If you have been taking either a narcotic or a minor tranquilizer for several months, you should know that this is the approximate length of time it takes to become addicted. If you are addicted, what can you do about it?

This type of addiction is a common problem, and treatment resources are widely available. Most cases of drug addiction caused by a physician's prescription can be treated by slowly tapering the dose of medication over a few weeks. If any withdrawal symptoms occur, they are usually minor. Of course, the process should be carried out under a doctor's supervision. A few individuals who have been taking large doses of addicting drugs over a long period may require admission to a hospital for more careful detoxification requiring several weeks to months. Physicians who manage this sort of therapy are usually psychiatrists. If you feel that you need this type of treatment, ask your personal physician to refer you to an appropriate detoxification center.

Effective Medication Use

The effects of the many drugs we have discussed are often additive. Aspirin may relieve 20 percent of your pain. Adding an antidepressant may drop your pain level by another 20 percent, so that you end up with only 60 percent of your pain to deal with. This may be a much more manageable level for you, one that allows you to resume many of the activities that will enable you to abandon a chronic pain lifestyle.

Any time you are taking a drug prescribed by a doctor and have problems with it or do not think that it is working, you should contact your doctor before discontinuing it. You and your doctor are partners in managing your pain. If you approach your recovery process with an attitude of teamwork, then you'll be able to work out the "fine tuning" of dosages and schedules that effective drug therapy requires. The key component is good communication between you and your doctor.

Earlier chapters have detailed the differences between acute and chronic pain. Simply stated, the appropriate use of drugs is much different for acute pain than for chronic pain. The treatment of a broken leg involves the use of lots of narcotics, tranquilizers, and minimal activity until the problem is diagnosed and treated. The cost of a few weeks of drugged existence while lying in bed is slight. The potential for addiction is negligible. The likelihood of total resolution of pain is high.

The opposite is true with chronic pain. Your ability to function is impaired. You probably cannot perform a job that requires heavy labor, and may need to consider going back to school to be retrained for a job which requires a higher skill level. Little likelihood exists that the underlying condition will be cured. In other words, the last thing you need is to be on drugs that further impair your ability to do any of these things, such as think clearly and make decisions. You definitely need to avoid drugs that cause addiction and depression. A drug regimen of nonnarcotic analgesics, antidepressants, and perhaps a trial of anticonvulsants, if indicated, can help you regain control of your pain and of your life.

Bob was able to do just that. He carefully followed his doctor's orders in the pain clinic to gradually taper off all of his medications over a period of a month. During that time, he began relaxation training, biofeedback, and psychological counseling. With regular stress management and a strong will to succeed, he was highly successful in eliminating medication from his life. He says that "the daily grinding pain I used to have has all but disappeared, and I've only had one migraine in six months—and that one felt minor by comparison. For others suffering with chronic pain, my advice is to keep an open mind to these techniques and try them out, even though you may not fully understand how or why they work."

You can drug yourself into insensibility, but there are better, more effective ways to deal with the stress of chronic pain. For Bob, biofeedback, counseling, and a sensible detoxification schedule worked. For others, the best program may be a combination of antidepressants, aspirin, and hypnosis. Whatever your choice, know that you need to be well-informed about the drugs you are taking. The various physical and psychological modalities offered by a comprehensive pain management center are designed to increase your physical and mental capabilities and help you live within the limitations of your condition. If you are motivated enough, appropriate medications can help you bridge the gap between disability and a rewarding lifestyle.

Suggested Reading

Gilman, A.G., L.S. Goodman, T.W. Rall, and F. Murad. *The Pharmacological Basis of Therapeutics.* 7th ed. New York: Macmillan, 1985, pp. 491–530, 674–715.

Wall, P.D., and R. Melzack. *Textbook of Pain.* London: Churchill Davidson, 1984, pp. 505–540.

TABLE 8.1

Narcotic Analgesics

Name (brand names(s))	Equianalgesics* oral dose (mg)	Usual oral starting dose (mg)	Duration of action (hrs)	Comments
morphine	30	10	4–6	Available as slow release tablets (MS Contin)
codeine	100	32	4–6	Often given in combination with aspirin or acetaminophen
propoxyphene (Darvon)	150	65	4–6	65 mg usually maximum dose given
acetylmorphine (Heroin)	30	10	4–5	Illegal in U.S.
hydromorphone (Dilaudid)	4	2	4–6	
levorphanol (Levodromoran)	2	2	4–6	
meperidine (Demerol)	150	50	3–4	Poor choice for long term use as it causes brain stimulation
methadone (Dolophine)	10	5	8–12	

Mixed Agonist-Antagonist Drugs

(Will reverse the effect of narcotics. May precipitate withdrawal in narcotic addicts.)

Name (brand names(s))	Equianalgesics* oral dose (mg)	Usual oral starting dose (mg)	Duration of action (hrs)	Comments
pentazocine (Talwin)	90	25	4–6	Available only in combination with aspirin; may cause confusion

*The dose which gives the analgesic effect of morphine 5 mg intramuscularly (a moderate dose)

TABLE 8.1 (con't.)

Mixed Agonist-Antagonist Drugs

Name (brand name(s))	Equianalgesics oral dose (mg)	Usual oral starting dose (mg)	Duration of action (hrs)	Comments
nalbuphine (Nubain)	not available orally			
butorphanol (Stadol)	not available orally			

TABLE 8.2

Nonnarcotic Analgesics

Name (brand name(s))	Oral dose (mg)	Duration of action (hrs)	Comments
acetaminophen (Tylenol, Panadol, etc.)	650	4–6	Used in combination with many other drugs; no anti-inflammatory effect

Nonsteroidal Anti-Inflammatory Drugs

Name (brand name(s))	Oral dose (mg)	Duration of action (hrs)	Comments
aspirin (Bufferin, Ascriptin, etc.)	650	4–6	Used in combination with many other drugs; by far the cheapest of the NSAIDs
sulindac (Clinoril)	150–200	12	
diflunisal (Dolobid)	250–500	12	
piroxicam (Feldene)	10–20	24	
indomethacin (Indocin)	25–50	8	Available in slow release capsules (Indocin SR)
ibuprofen (Motrin, Rufen, Advil, Nuprin)	200–400	4–6	
fenoprofen (Nalfon)	200–300	4–6	
naproxen (Naprosyn)	250–375	12	
tolmetin (Tolectin)	400	8	

TABLE 8.3

Antidepressant Medications

Name (brand name(s))	Oral dose (mg)	Duration of action (hrs)	Comments
amitriptyline (Elavil, Amitril, Endep)	75–200	24	Most sedating

TABLE 8.3 (con't.)

Antidepressant Medications

Name (brand name(s))	Oral dose (mg)	Duration of action (hrs)	Comments
amoxapine (Asendin)	100–300	24	
desipramine (Norpramin)	100–200	24	
doxepin (Adaprin, Sinequan)	75–300	24	
imipramine (Tofranil)	75–200	24	
maprotiline (Ludiomil)	75–150	24	May have a faster onset of action
protriptyline (Vivactyl)	45–160	8	
trazodone (Desyrel)	150–400	8	Least side effects
trimipramine (Surmontil)	75–200	24	

TABLE 8.4

Anticonvulsants

Name	Oral dose (mg)	Duration of action (hrs)	Comments
Depakene	250–500	8	May cause liver damage
Dilantin	100–200	8–12	
Tegretol	100–500	12	May cause bone marrow damage

TABLE 8.5

Major Tranquilizers (Antipsychotics)

Name	Oral dose (mg)	Duration of action (hrs)	Comments
Haldol	0.5–2	12	
Mellaril	50–100	8	
Navane	2–5	8	
Prolixin	1–5	8	
Stelazine	1–2	12	
Taractan	10–50	8	

TABLE 8.5 (con't.)

Major Tranquilizers (Antipsychotics)

Name	Oral dose (mg)	Duration of action (hrs)	Comments
Thorazine	10–25	8	
Triavil	Various dosage combinations	8	Combination of Prolixin and amitriptyline (antidepressant)

TABLE 8.6

Minor Tranquilizers (Anti-Anxiety Drugs)

Name	Oral dose (mg)	Duration of action (hrs)	Comments
Ativan	2–3	12	
Centrax	15–30	12	
Librium	5–20	8	
Limbitrol	Various dosage combinations	8	Combination of Librium and amitriptyline (antidepressant)
Serax	10–20	8	
Tranzene	15–30	12	
Valium	2–10	12	
Xanax	0.25–1	8	Also has antidepressant effects

9

Back and Neck Pain

The most common of all chronic musculoskeletal pains is back pain. Some studies show that the lower back area, known as the lumbar region, accounts for 50 percent of all reported pain, with the neck area accounting for another 20 percent. In terms of time lost at work, this total of 70 percent of all chronic pain disorders is second only to respiratory infections such as colds and sore throats.

It is safe to say that back and neck pain is really a problem for all ages. A surprisingly large number of injuries occur in young people, aged 20 to 30. A partial explanation may be that people fresh out of school may have been relatively active through their school years, but have graduated to take up full-time sedentary work. Their muscles lose some of their tone and flexibility and become more injury prone.

The greatest concentration of injuries occurs in the 30 to 40 age range, as people continue to do their normal activities and as the aging process begins to show. Aging takes its toll on the spine, as you will see in the explanation of back and neck anatomy later in this chapter. This chapter focuses on this middle group by introducing sound principles and practices to prevent the muscular sprains and strains most common in back and neck pain before the inflammation and deterioration so common to older ages set in.

Back pain and injury is not a problem endemic to one specific type or group of people. You can have back problems if you work all day at a manual labor job, or you can have them if you sit all day at a desk. Though it is hard to predict exactly when, where, and who will get an attack of back pain, there are some common factors predisposing you to this problem.

- Poor posture
- Poor body mechanics
- Overweight
- Weak, inflexible muscles
- Stress

Your spine is a complex interweaving of muscles, tendons, ligaments, joints, discs, and cartilage—and no two spines are exactly alike. This is why it is so difficult to prescribe just the right exercises for your individual problem—and why it is so important for you to understand how your spine works. Only then can you know which measures to take to regain as much mobility as possible and help prevent further injury. This chapter is designed to explain the basics of back and neck pain and examine the current methods of treatment and prevention.

For purposes of organizing the vast amount of available information, back and neck pain can be divided into the following categories:

1. Infections
2. Inflammations
3. Metabolic disorders
4. Neoplasms
5. Referred pain
6. Trauma and mechanical problems

In this chapter we will primarily be examining the sixth category. Mechanical problems make up the bulk of all low back and neck disorders, such as muscle sprains, strains, and herniated discs. Traumatic back injuries are primarily made up of fractures and other acute problems. The other categories on the list are beyond the scope of this chapter. Back problems secondary to arthritis are examined more closely in chapter twelve.

Anatomy of the Back and Neck

In his book *Goodbye Back Ache*, Dr. David Imrie explains that the spinal column is the body's principal scaffolding, providing both strength and stability along with movement and flexibility to your body. The bones in the spinal column are attached to and connect the muscles, tendons, and ligaments that permit the body's movement. The spinal column also houses the spinal cord, the vital nerve cable that links the brain to all other parts of the body.

All of the major areas of the spine are made up of box-shaped building blocks called *vertebrae*. In medical terms, the first of those is the *cervical* or neck area, which supports the head and neck and allows them to move right and left. Since these vertebrae only have to support the weight of your head, they are smaller, flatter, and more delicate. The *thoracic* or chest area includes the vertebrae that are part of the rib cage's protection of the heart and lungs. These vertebrae are fairly immobile and are larger than the cervical vertebrae, since they have to support the weight of your arms and shoulders. The *lumbar* or lower-back section contains vertebrae that are larger and heavier than the vertebrae above it. This is because they bear the most weight and allow forward and backward bending motion (see diagram 9.1). The *sacral* vertebrae are actually formed into a very large bone at the base of the spinal cord, which is immobile, wedged in between the two hipbones. The *coccyx*, below the sacrum, is a series of small vertebra which together with the rest of the pelvic bones supports the powerful buttocks muscles. The areas that we will focus on are the neck and lumber regions of the spine. The spine's flexibility and mobility in these areas combine with the alignment and pressures upon the vertebrae to contribute to defects and fractures.

DIAGRAM 9.1
The Spinal Column

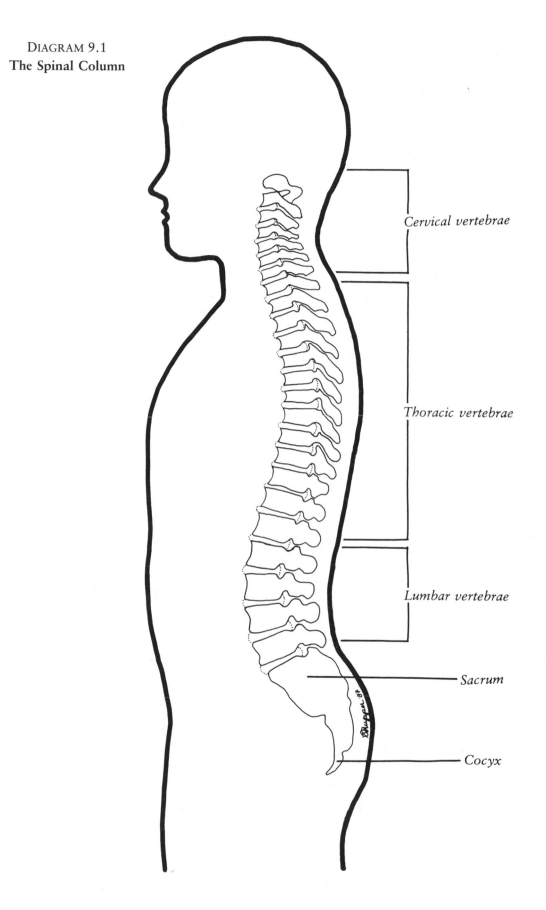

Cervical vertebrae

Thoracic vertebrae

Lumbar vertebrae

Sacrum

Cocyx

DIAGRAM 9.2

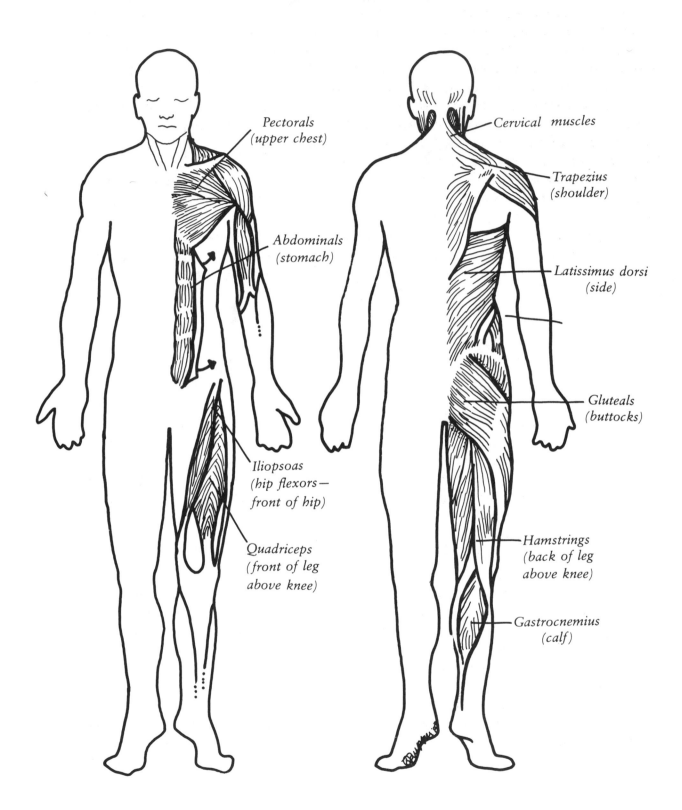

Pectorals
(upper chest)

Abdominals
(stomach)

Iliopsoas
(hip flexors—
front of hip)

Quadriceps
(front of leg
above knee)

Cervical muscles

Trapezius
(shoulder)

Latissimus dorsi
(side)

Gluteals
(buttocks)

Hamstrings
(back of leg
above knee)

Gastrocnemius
(calf)

A healthy back normally curves in four places: at the cervical region, the thoracic region, the lumbar region, and the sacral region. (The overall shape that these four curves make is sometimes called the "double S" curve.) Poor posture, obesity, and muscle spasming can flatten out or exaggerate most of these curves, causing pain and dysfunction. Exercise, good posture, and proper lifting techniques can strengthen the surrounding muscles and ligaments and restore these curves to a healthy position.

A healthy spine has pressure evenly distributed throughout its curves. This means that all of the muscle groups up and down the spine are working together in a balanced fashion, and no one muscle group is doing more than its share of work. In an unbalanced spine, one or more muscle groups may be taking up the slack for an injured, unconditioned, or deficient group, causing the harder-working muscles to fatigue and weaken and be more injury-prone. When you compensate for your chronic pain by holding your injured muscles immobile for a long time, you are shifting weight, pressure, and work onto the other muscle groups. This is why an evenly balanced exercise program is very important to restore your body to its preinjury balance.

Diagram 9.2 shows the major muscle groups important to proper exercise for management of back, shoulder, and neck pain.

Vertebrae and Discs

The approximately 33 vertebrae that form the spinal column are the building blocks of the spine. They are cube shaped with bony protrusions that you can feel when you run your fingers up and down your spine. The bony protrusions, called the *spinous processes*, have connecting ligaments that interlock each vertebra and allow for a certain amount of bending and twisting motion. These bony protrusions help to form a canal that houses the spinal cord.

Ligaments are tough elastic bands that reinforce the joints and help to hold the vertebrae together. The muscles help to hold the spine upright and allow for forward (flexion), backward (extension), and twisting (rotation) movements.

Between each vertebra lies another structure called a *disc.* The disc contains a gelatinous substance called the "nucleus pulposus." This jellylike fluid, together with the bony vertebra and outer cartilagenous disc, act like a shock absorber in a car. When pressure is applied (such as from lifting), the fluid is compressed; it springs back to its original shape when the pressure is released. Without this spongelike effect of the disc fluid, the vertebrae would grind together and eventually deteriorate.

The disc gel can cause pain by leaking or bulging out and pressing against the nerves located along the spinal column. You may hear this condition referred to as a herniated disc, ruptured disc, slipped disc, bulging disc, prolapsed disc, or a protruding disc. All of these terms mean roughly the same thing—a tear or deterioration of the wall surrounding the disc, which allows some of the fluid to bulge out or rupture and escape. But the term "slipped disc" is inaccurate, since the disc rarely actually slips out of place. (Sometimes the vertebra can have a crack or defect in it that causes it to slip away from the vertebra below it, but this is a separate condition known as *spondylolisthesis* that is not covered here.)

The discs most likely to herniate are those in the cervical and lumbar regions. When a disc bulges or fluid escapes and puts pressure on the nerve roots that become the *sciatic nerve* (a very large, thick nerve going out of the pelvis below the sacrum and down both legs), the pressure against the nerve roots causes a type of pain known as "sciatica." This shooting pain alters the signals sent by the nerves, which may then cause numbness and weakness in your legs. If the disc bulges against the nerve roots in the neck area, you will often feel pain and experience numbness and weakness in your arms.

Sometimes bone spurs or scar tissue can also press against the nerve roots, causing altered mobility and sharp pain. Spurs can be thought of like calluses on hands—they may be an attempt on the part of the body or bone to heal or stabilize itself. Scar tissue may be a result of previous surgery and is often not detected on X-rays. Bone spurs can be removed by surgery.

Before we discuss treatment of back disorders, let's examine the currently available diagnostic tests, so that when you're sent for a CAT scan or an EMG you'll know what kind of test is meant.

Diagnostic Tests

X-rays are films of the back and neck taken to rule out diseases, inflammation, abscesses, and other bone disorders. Muscle spasm and soft tissue damage such as swelling, both very common causes of back pain, do not show up on X-rays. *Myelography* is a special kind of X-ray test where a contrast dye is injected into the spinal fluid space to assess soft tissue damage around the spinal cord or nerve roots. This test requires you to stay in bed for several hours afterward to prevent headaches. It is usually performed before any surgical intervention. A *discography* is a process similar to myelography, where the injected dye demonstrates the integrity of the disc. A *CAT scan*, or Computerized Axial Tomography, is a type of X-ray scanning procedure that enables your doctor to see more closely and in much greater detail any soft tissue damage. The word "axial" means that the view is shown in layers, much like a sliced loaf of bread. The computerization of this process is what gives the CAT scan its much greater resolution.

Electromyography (EMG) is a test where a very thin needle-type electrode is inserted into the muscle to electrically measure the nerve and muscle integrity and the muscle's ability to contract or relax, thereby assessing any damage to the muscle's ability to function. Electrode insertion can cause some discomfort.

Several other newer tests that are not yet widely used also use imaging techniques. *Magnetic resonance imaging* (MRI) uses an electromagnetic field to stimulate the nuclei in cellular tissue, which in turn emit radio signals that are transformed into a picture of the problem area. *Thermography* determines "thermal imbalance" in tissue and bone by measuring the amount of heat radiated from the problem areas and translating that heat into electronic signals that form images. Both tests are noninvasive and without risk and can be especially beneficial as an adjunct to other diagnostic tests. Check with your doctor about the effectiveness and availability of these tests in your area.

Medical Treatments for Back and Neck Pain

Surgery

There are only two situations that clearly require immediate surgical intervention for back and neck pain: (1) if there is a mass lesion (a tumor or ruptured disc) pressing upon the major nerve roots or spinal cord, and (2) if there is spinal cord or nerve-root compression from a fracture or other major instability from injury. The following are the most commonly performed surgeries for these conditions.

Laminectomy. The surgeon cuts through the lamina (part of the bony ring surrounding the spinal cord or nerve roots) in order to remove the herniated disc.

Discectomy. Discectomy for a herniated or ruptured disc is considered following unsuccessful conservative treatment (bed rest, traction, medications) for one to four months. A partial laminectomy provides access to the disc, which is removed. The success rate is 40 to 80 percent, based on the patient's circumstances. Repeated disc surgeries are significantly less successful.

Spinal fusion. Fusions are sometimes performed for spinal instability, or in order to stabilize the spine following a discectomy. Vertebrae are "welded together" by bone grafts, which are small or sometimes larger pieces of bone that can be placed between the vertebrae to allow the bone to heal as a single piece. This type of surgery is done if injury or disease has resulted in instability of the spine, or in order to stabilize or straighten the abnormal curves of scoliosis.

Chemonucleosis. In 1982, the FDA approved the use of Chymopapain, which is a substance injected into the disc space to dissolve the problem disc. Chymopapain is derived from the papaya plant and is related to the active substance in meat tenderizer. The advantage of this process is that it does not require an incision and is less traumatic to your back than surgery.

Medication

In the acute stages of back or neck pain when muscles are spasming and mobility is severely hampered, some narcotic medications are extremely useful for helping you to rest and relax. Examples of these are Darvon, Percodan, and others listed in table 8.1 of chapter eight. But if the pain still hasn't abated after several weeks, the dangers of becoming addicted to these drugs outweigh their initial benefits. In order to avoid addiction, which can become a problem far greater than the pain itself, you need to take steps to discontinue narcotic use and begin safer, healthier treatments with nonnarcotic analgesics such as aspirin and anti-inflammatory drugs, gentle exercise, and relaxation training. If you suffer from depression to an extent that it hampers your recovery, some physicians will prescribe Elavil, a nonaddictive antidepressant, to help you get started. The minor tranquilizers are definitely NOT indicated for relief of chronic back and neck pain. These drugs may relieve some anxiety associated with your pain in the short run, but in the long run they can cause more problems by lowering your pain threshold and causing addiction. Refer to chapter eight for more information on appropriate medications for chronic back and neck pain.

Nerve Blocks

Local anesthetic nerve blocks and trigger-point injections are used to interrupt the pain-spasm-pain cycle, which can prolong your pain sensation by keeping you tense and anxious. These blocks can help relieve postural stress and allow you to participate in gentle exercise, relaxation techniques, and other rehabilitative treatments. One safe and effective type of nerve block is a *steroid injection* into the *epidural space* surrounding the spinal cord and nerves. Epidural steroid therapy is especially helpful for sciatica, the leg pain secondary to disc disease. Another newer type of block, less common but apparently as safe, is a *facet joint injection*. *Trigger-point injections* place a local anesthetic at the actual site of pain or at the referred pain site to block the nerve impulses carrying the pain message. All three of these blocks can be extremely useful for at least temporarily alleviating chronic back and neck pain. All are most useful when combined with exercise and other resources from a pain management center. You should not look to nerve blocks for your only treatment for pain, but regard them as part of a comprehensive treatment program.

Other Physical Treatments

Other more conservative forms of treatment that your doctor may prescribe for you are *braces*. These are form-fitting jackets that look like corsets that help support and immobilize the spine. *Neck braces* hold the chin at a level or slightly lowered position and also support the neck muscles and cervical area.

Traction is used to straighten and stretch the soft tissue around the facet joints in order to straighten the spine. This may be helpful for pulling the vertebrae slightly apart to allow a herniated disc in the back and neck to heal.

TENS and other electrical stimulation devices can perform a very useful function by providing an alternate tingling sensation to the pain. (See chapter two for a more thorough explanation of TENS.) *Point stimulation*, a newer form of electrical stimulation, may work similarly to acupuncture in providing pain relief. All forms of electrical stimulation can be placed at trigger points or at the site of pain.

Heat can be applied in several different ways. Hot towels or heating pads applied directly to the pain site or hot baths can increase blood flow and soothe tensed and spasming muscles. *Diathermy* stimulates deep muscle heat by means of an electric current applied lightly to the surface of the skin. *Ultrasound* also elevates tissue temperature by penetrating deeply into the muscle with high-frequency sound waves.

Popular heat-generating devices are two hands! *Massage* can be an excellent way to warm and relax a tight muscle by stimulating increased blood flow to the area. But if you or your massage therapist press too firmly on a spasming muscle, the spasm can get worse. Try a hot bath or heating pad first. Any time you feel a sharp pain when using massage, back off. See chapter two for more information on massage.

Sometimes back and neck pain sufferers find relief for acute and chronic pain by using the services of a *chiropractor*. A doctor of chiropractic is a highly trained health care professional who uses *spinal manipulation* or *adjustment* to correct spinal misalignment caused by disease and injury. A chiropractor works on each specific vertebra, manually moving one segment at a time to bend, twist, or stretch the vertebral joint, helping to reposition it. When there is nerve-root compression, as with a herniated disc, chiropractors will determine this condition first through a series of diagnostic tests (such as X-rays, CAT scans, or straight leg raises) before they attempt to manipulate your spine. If nerve-root compression is present, they may elect other forms of treatment, such as traction tables or other traction devices.

Chiropractors employ a wide variety of treatments to alleviate pain. As with physical therapists, osteopaths, and athletic trainers, they may elect to use electrical stimulation techniques, acupuncture, or massage, and they will work closely with your regular general practitioner to monitor your medication and diet. Chiropractors are also aware of the importance of regular exercise and will often prescribe back and neck flexibility, strength, and range of motion exercises to supplement regular treatment.

Research has not yet provided conclusive evidence for the effectiveness of chiropractic treatment. Ask your doctor or friends for a recommendation to a reputable chiropractor in your area. Carefully discuss your back or neck problem with your doctor and chiropractor before you begin any treatment. Manipulation can make some problems worse, such as fracture of a vertebra resulting from the brittle bones of osteoporosis.

What You Can Do

Back Exercise

Consult any two people and you will get different advice about what kind of exercise to do for your back. Some say that doing the type of exercise that requires only backward bending (extension) is the best to do; others say bending forward (flexion) is the best. But most experts do seem to agree on one thing—that a certain amount of exercise is critical in rehabilitating your back. As discussed in chapter three, stretching and strengthening your muscles help to increase their ability to absorb shock and strain and to decrease muscle spasming. As your muscles become stronger and more flexible, the chance that you will sustain another injury diminishes. And if the stress in your life registers directly in your back, strong, flexible muscles will be better able to withstand potential spasming from tension.

If you have a disc problem, you can still use many of the exercises that are good for back strains or sprains—with the exception of specific exercises that are flagged both here and in chapter three. Even though a bulging disc poses a special set of problems, the muscles surrounding and supporting the spine are still prone to tension and spasming from the pain and stress of the disc problem. This means you need to keep stretching and strengthening the abdominal and back muscles to protect your vulnerable disc area.

You will need to check with your doctor before beginning to exercise. A physical therapist, exercise physiologist, or athletic trainer can also provide expert assistance. Your therapist or trainer will look at the normal "S" curves in your back, your posture, walk, flexibility, strength, and endurance before they suggest specific exercises to correct any spinal imbalance. This may mean that you do a combination of extension and flexion exercises, supplemented by TENS, traction, or whirlpool. This combination of exercise and devices will change as you gain strength and flexibility or as the pain subsides.

A sensible approach to exercise is to start out gradually with passive, gentle stretches and work up to more active, strenuous exercises. Some experts suggest that you start out on the bed or floor, move up to standing exercises, and finally go on to activities that offer cardiovascular exercise as well as gentle resistance. The following sets of exercises present a typical program of this kind.

Stretching and gentle strengthening. First, increase your flexibility by doing *non*-weight-bearing exercises. This means that you stretch only those muscles that need it and avoid putting unnecessary and dangerous body weight pressure on your spine. Complete the following three exercises on your floor or bed for a minimum of fifteen minutes per day for two to three weeks or until pain subsides.

1. *Lower back flattener (pelvic tilt).* This exercise is a gentle strengthener of abdominal and buttocks muscles. See chapter three, exercise V.1, for full instructions. Do at least three times per day to start.

2. *Hip flexor stretch.* This is a gentle stretch of lower back and hip muscles. See chapter three, exercise I.3, for full instructions. Do NOT attempt the advanced flexor stretch at this point.

3. *Double knee to chest.* This exercise is a more complete stretch of lower back and hip muscles. With your hands laced under your knees, pull both knees to your chest, keeping your lower back flat on the floor or bed. Hold for twenty seconds. Repeat three times.

Sitting and rotation. Now you can progress to more active exercises. Add the three exercises below to the first group of exercises and set aside a minimum of fifteen minutes per day for them for several weeks. *Note:* Rotation may put added pressure and strain on your back if you have a disc problem. Check with your doctor first to see if these are appropriate exercises for you.

1. *Abdominal curls (curl-ups).* An excellent exercise for stomach strengthening and relieving back strain. See chapter three, exercise V.2, for complete instructions. Start with curl-ups. Try curl-backs when you feel comfortable and stronger during the curl-up exercise.

2. *Advanced hip flexor stretch.* This is an excellent lower back stretch and abdominal strengthening exercise. See chapter three, exercise I.3, for full instructions. Be certain to do the *advanced* stretch where you raise your head and shoulders slightly toward your bent knee.

3. *Lower back stretch and roll.* A good exercise for relieving back strain. See chapter three, exercise II.2, for full instructions.

Standing and extension exercises. Now you can add two extension exercises and one standing exercise, the side stretch. *Note:* These three exercises may be problematic for people with disc injury or disease, because the backward-bending and side-bending motion narrows the disc space even further and pinches the already protruding disc material, causing more pain. Check with your doctor, therapist, or trainer before attempting these exercises.

NOT FOR DISC PROBLEMS UNTIL MEDICALLY APPROVED.

1. *Press-ups.* This is a good lower back stretch. See chapter three, exercise II.3 for full instructions. Keep your elbows bent when you first do this exercise. Only after you are comfortable doing press-ups with elbows bent should you attempt the advanced press-ups.

2. *The mad cat.* A good exercise for lower back tension. Kneel on all fours with your back straight. Inhale and round your back, tightening your abdominal and gluteus muscles simultaneously. Then, slowly exhale and arch your back, pointing your head and tailbone toward the ceiling. Return to straight back position. Repeat three to four times.

3. *Side stretch.* Keeping both knees bent slightly, extend both arms overhead. Grasp your right hand with your left hand and slowly bend to the left, pulling your right arm over your head and feeling the stretch on the side of your body. Hold for twenty seconds. Repeat three times each side.

Cardiovascular exercises. Last, you can add gentle cardiovascular exercises, such as walking or swimming, to all three groups of exercises. Make sure that you spend at least five to ten minutes warming up before you do your activity and cooling down after you finish. Otherwise you may reinjure yourself because your muscles are "cold." You can use the stretches and strengtheners above for this purpose.

Do your exercises regularly at home, once or twice a day as needed for at least fifteen minutes each session. If you feel more pain at the end of a particular set of exercises than you did at the beginning, or if you feel more pain the next day, then you need to stop the exercise and consult with your doctor, therapist, or trainer. Remember that you will feel some discomfort as your muscles become stronger and more flexible, but you'll usually be able to distinguish between your pain and the normal discomfort of exercise. You may find that you need to try out several different types of exercise before you find a group that suits you. Once you find a group that helps you feel stronger, more flexible, and more pain free, do those exercises regularly. Your rewards will be great in the long run.

Again, keep in mind that you should be thoroughly examined by your doctor before beginning any exercise program. If possible, get additional guidance from a physical therapist, physiatrist, exercise physiologist, or certified athletic trainer to determine the best exercises for your individual injury, lifestyle, and physical condition.

Neck Exercise

Neck pain is primarily due to overstretching of the muscles, ligaments, and other soft tissue surrounding the cervical vertebrae. Overstretching and injury may be caused by sudden strain on the neck from jerking or collision when playing sports or from whiplash, when the head is abruptly thrown forward and backward (also known as flexion-extension injury).

If a cervical disc loses its ability to absorb shock and bulges and presses against the spinal nerve, it can cause pain and dysfunction similar to disc problems in the lower back. It can also cause referred pain down the arm, much like sciatica in the leg.

Bad posture is the main culprit for neck pain, however. If the lower back is allowed to slouch and the head juts forward, the normal cervical curve is flattened, putting a strain on all the muscles supporting the head. If bad posture becomes a habit, as it is when you sleep in a bad position for your neck or slouch when you sit at work, then you are likely to be prone to "cricks" in the neck or sore, spasming neck and upper shoulder muscles by the end of the day.

When sleeping, be sure not to prop your head up on too many pillows, as this will continue to jut your head forward throughout the night. If you sleep on your stomach, this tends to thrust your head into a hypercurve backward which strains the delicate vertebral bodies. Sleep in the fetal position, as shown in chapter three, or sleep with a cervical pillow placed in the hollow of your neck. A lumbar roll is also useful to restore proper posture and protect your neck when sitting or driving. When used regularly and in combination with exercise, both the cervical pillow and the lumbar roll can help to maintain your spine's normal curves in the lumbar and cervical regions.

The following exercises are stretches and gentle strengtheners for the neck.

1. *Yes-no-maybe.* See chapter three, exercise III.4, for full instructions.

2. *Advanced neck stretches*. These are good for spasming and tightness in the trapezius muscle. See chapter three, exercise III.5, for full instructions.

3. *Shoulder shrugs*. See chapter three, exercise III.6, for complete instructions.

4. *Neck strengthener*. See chapter three, exercise III.7, for full instructions.

5. *Gentle resistance neck exercise*. Using a towel and giving moderate resistance, roll your head from side to side.

Proper Lifting

Many back injuries result from improper lifting. And lifting the simplest, most harmless-looking object can be the cause of a terrific backache. If your back and stomach muscles are out of condition to begin with, or if you are under a lot of stress and your muscles are tight, then a simple twisting motion such as reaching for the phone or picking up a magazine can throw a weak back into spasm.

Common scenarios for sprains, strains, or tears while lifting or reaching are reaching for an object on a shelf that's too high, twisting suddenly, lifting any object that's too far away from you, pulling something heavy, picking up small children, being pregnant, or doing nearly anything when you're feeling tense and anxious. That about covers it!

The principal rule of good body mechanics is LET YOUR POWERFUL LEG MUSCLES CARRY THE LOAD. Your quadriceps and hamstrings are larger and stronger than your weaker back muscles; let them do the work. Other rules to remember are:

- Maintain a broad base of support by keeping your feet apart for stability.
- Bend your knees; don't bend at the waist.
- Tighten your stomach muscles to help support the spine.

- Hold the load close to your body.
- Keep your back upright and avoid twisting.
- Push, don't pull.
- Get help.

Stress Management for Back and Necks

As you probably know, stress can register directly in your back or neck. This is why relaxation and visualization techniques are a perfect component to your regular exercise and medical treatment program. Some relaxation exercises work particularly well with physical exercise. Try doing deep breathing five or six times as part of your daily workout, warm-up, and cool-down. Warm-up breathing will prepare you emotionally and mentally for your exercise, as well as help relax tight muscles. When combined with stretching, cool-down breathing will help you slow down after your workout and keep your muscles limber.

If you are unable to take a break at your desk and your neck or back is aching, stretch it out by doing some of the stretches mentioned in this chapter and chapter three. Focus on a quick image or word that is relaxing to you, such as the sensation of the sun warming your back or neck, or the words "calm" or "relax." When I am tense I quickly conjure up the image of myself sitting on a bleached-white sailboat on a dark blue sea, wind whipping through my hair. Works every time.

One relaxation technique that you may NOT find helpful at first is progressive muscle relaxation. This technique involves tensing and relaxing the muscles, and contracting a spasmed or injured muscle may not feel very good and may perhaps contribute to more pain. You can see for yourself, but do go easy at first. Please refer to chapters four and five for more ideas about relaxation techniques.

Remember that there are always negative thoughts lurking about, ready to pounce on and sabotage your best efforts and intentions. You may say to yourself, "Give up—it's hopeless. I'll never get better." This kind of thinking is self-defeating, and if you indulge in it regularly, you will have a more difficult time making progress. Refer to chapter six for more ideas on controlling your negative thoughts.

Finally, respect your limits. Learn to say no to tasks and activities that you know will aggravate your back or neck pain. Don't be embarrassed about asking for help when you need it. Think about proper lifting techniques before you move something. Avoid twisting and sharp movements. Plan ahead. Take care of yourself!

Further Reading

Chronic Low Back Pain. ed. Michael Stanton-Hicks and Robert Boas. New York: Raven Press, 1982.

Del Pozo, Cal. *The Back Book*. New York: Arbor House/Priam Books, 1983.

Evaluation and Treatment of Chronic Pain. ed. Gerald Aronoff. Baltimore: Urban and Schwarzenberg, 1985.

Goleman, Daniel, and Tara Bennett-Goleman. *The Relaxed Body Book.* New York: Doubleday, 1986.

Imrie, David. *Goodbye Back Ache.* Toronto: Prentice-Hall/Newcastle Publishing, 1983.

Management of Low Back Pain. ed. Harold Carron and Robert McLaughlin. Boston: John Wright PSG, 1982.

McKenzie, Robin. *Treat Your Own Back.* Waikanae, New Zealand: Spinal Publications, 1980.

_____. *Treat Your Own Neck.* Lower Hutt, New Zealand: Spinal Publications, 1983.

Steinman, Marion. *Back-Care.* New York: Random House, 1984.

White, Augustus. *Your Aching Back.* New York: Bantam Books, 1983.

Williams, Paul. *Low Back and Neck Pain.* Springfield, IL: Charles Thomas, 1974.

10

Headaches

by Douglas DeGood, Ph.D.

There is ample evidence that headache is the pain condition most responsive to the types of self-regulation techniques described in this book. This may not come as a surprise to you, since headache is the one chronic pain condition that most of us link with everyday emotional tension or stress. You may also already know that headaches are a most peculiar type of pain disorder in that they are usually *benign*—that is, not symptomatic of serious lasting tissue damage. This benign status makes it much easier for doctors to casually dismiss headache complaints than it is for the headache sufferer to dismiss the symptom.

If most headaches are in fact not associated with lasting tissue damage, can it be concluded that headaches are "imaginary" psychological events without any actual physical basis? The answer is clearly no. In fact, very real physical events can be involved in a headache, such as allergic reactions or hormonal variations. And stress, however defined, does not magically transform itself into a headache. To the contrary, there is a considerable degree of bodily involvement in the transformation process. In vulnerable individuals, stress affects nerves, muscles, and blood vessels in the head, neck, and upper torso in such a way that these structures give rise to the pain of the headache. And the emotional reaction provoked by stress can in turn affect the normal functioning of your head, neck, and shoulder muscles.

There are also a few noteworthy exceptions to the general benign status of headaches. Headaches can stem from a traumatic injury to the head or neck or they may accompany a number of illnesses, some of which can be serious. And finally, headaches are one of the most common symptoms of tissue damage from tumors or strokes. Anyone who develops headaches for the first time or experiences a new pattern of headache symptoms should be medically evaluated prior to beginning any treatment plan.

Physical Mechanisms of Tension and Migraine Headaches

Tension Headaches

It has been estimated that 25 to 50 percent of the population suffer at least occasionally from tension headaches. In fact, tension headaches may be the most

---

Dr. DeGood is Director of Psychology of the University of Virginia Pain Management Center, Charlottesville, Virginia.

prevalent pain disorder of our contemporary age, possibly as a symptom of the stress of modern life.

You may be confused by the multiple meanings of the word "tension." To some the word may imply the emotional arousal caused by the major and minor hassles of daily life. To others the term refers specifically to the mechanical contraction of muscles in the region of the head and neck that result in a tension headache. While both meanings are appropriate, in the present discussion we will consider primarily the second use. Thus, for our purposes, the terms "tension" and "muscular contraction" headache are used synonymously.

Tension headaches usually include most of these characteristics:

1. The pain is gradual in onset.
2. The pain is highly variable in duration.
3. The pain is experienced as tightness or pressure around the head.
4. The pain is constant, rather than throbbing.
5. The pain is bilateral (affecting both sides of the head), often beginning in the upper neck (occipital area) and working forward.
6. The pain often becomes worse over the course of the day, especially on stress-filled days.

Excessive tension and spasm of the muscles controlling the jaw are often suspected to play a major role in chronic tension headaches. While this muscle tension may be emotional in origin, it can also be due to poor tooth alignment or other dental problems. (See chapter eleven on TMJ.)

The pain of the tension headache may come from several sources. First, muscles in the shoulders, neck, and head become fatigued and irritated. Just imagine how painful your jaw and neck muscles would become from gritting your teeth hour after hour. Second, these same muscles can eventually become *ischemic* (that is, suffer from inadequate flow of blood), adding to the pain. Third, tensed muscles can put pressure on nerves and blood vessels, pinching them between the skull and the surrounding bands of muscle fibers, causing a secondary source of pain sensation. This secondary pain can feel like a burning, throbbing sensation, on top of the characteristic dull ache of the tension headache.

Migraine (or Vascular) Headache

A migraine headache is the best known of the vascular headaches—those headaches that arise from blood vessels, both intra- and extracranially. Vascular headaches are much less common than tension headaches. Two out of three sufferers are female, a fact that suggests a possible hormonal link. Most vascular headaches, and especially migraines, cannot be ignored. The pain is so intense that it can overwhelm your ability to attend to and concentrate on even routine activities. The chronic migraine sufferer will almost always eventually seek medical assistance.

A classic migraine is the outcome of a complex process involving the neurochemical regulation of blood vessels in the head and neck. The somatic process begins with constriction of these arteries and arterioles. Emotional stress or excitement may trigger the process, although stress need not be the exclusive precipitant. Hormonal changes, temperature changes, and food, drink, and drug reactions are also common triggers. The vasoconstriction causes localized ischemia (obstruction of blood supply) in the brain, which in turn appears to be responsible for the *prodomal warning aura* (changes in vision, tingling or weakness of the limbs, dizziness, or faintness) which can precede a migraine attack. The vasoconstriction also stimulates the production of counterregulatory neurochemicals intended to maintain adequate blood flow and thus proper nutrition in the cells of your brain. When this corrective effort is too vigorous and overshoots the normal target level, it produces a "rebound" vaso*dilation*. This excessive dilation and the subsequent swelling of certain blood vessels, especially around the temples, forehead, and eyes, stimulates stretching in the vessel walls, which in turn is thought to produce the pain sensation.

Migraine headaches usually include the following characteristics:

1. The pain is preceded by prodomal signs.
2. The pain is unilateral (on one side of the head), often focused in one temple or behind or above one of the eyes.
3. The pain is often accompanied by nausea and vomiting.
4. The pain can sometimes be prevented with vasoconstricting drugs.

Actually only 10 to 15 percent of migraine headaches fit the classic pattern described above. More frequent are vascular headaches that are not preceded by prodomal signs and are not distinctively unilateral in nature. This pattern is referred to as a "common," as opposed to a "classic" migraine. Although immensely uncomfortable, the pain of the common migraine is usually not quite as severe as that of the classic migraine.

Still another vascular headache pattern is the so-called cluster headache. These intense vascular headaches are very brief in duration (often about 20 minutes). They may occur with great frequency over a period of several days or weeks, and then disappear for several months before returning again.

Chronic headache sufferers may actually experience symptoms of both tension and vascular headaches. Symptoms characteristic of either headache type may occur simultaneously or sequentially.

Stressors, Stress, and Personality Factors in Headache

Stressors that can bring on headaches are those occurrences in your daily life that cause emotional stress. These may vary from the mundane hassles of completing your daily schedule to deeply distressing personal losses and disappointments. In this context, the term "stress" refers to your physical and emotional reactions to stressors.

The word "personality" simply means the unique ways you feel, think, and act. This includes your characteristic response to stressors—and how you respond to stressors may play a role in your susceptibility to headache. Some people develop effective coping skills that serve to reduce or limit the negative emotional impact of stressors. Others acquire maladaptive reactions. Good coping skills reduce the liklihood that a particular stress will become chronic, and it is the chronic, seemingly unsolvable problems in life that are likely to result in serious headache symptoms.

At least equal in importance to difference in coping skills are individual physiological differences in your body's response to emotional stress. The natural physical response to any increase in stress is an increase in muscle activation, along with an increased production of neurochemicals. These neuroactive substances stimulate the nervous system, resulting in widespread changes such as an increase in heart rate, blood pressure, respiration rate, sweating, and dilation of bronchial air space. They also stimulate constriction of blood vessels near the skin surface and in the gut, accompanied by a corresponding increase in blood flow to the brain and large muscles. All of these changes prepare your body for action and are often referred to as "fight or flight" responses.

Physical responses to stress vary considerably from person to person. Some people will demonstrate a specific cranial blood vessel response that leads to migraines, while others may display a more generalized vasoconstriction that puts them at risk for developing hypertension. Muscular reactions for one person may occur predominantly in the jaw, for another in the neck, and for still another in the back. Thus the same degree of stress may result in a migraine headache for one person, in a tension headache for another, or in low back pain for another. Whether these individual differences are primarily genetic in origin or are gradually acquired is often not clear. But especially with migraine headaches (which are known to have a strong familial inheritance pattern) genetic predisposition is without doubt an essential ingredient.

The only definite conclusion we can draw concerning the role of personality traits in headaches is that it is difficult to sort out personality traits from objective stressors and purely physiological predispositions. A tendency to have headaches certainly does not constitute sufficient proof that an individual has inadequate personality skills for coping with the stresses of living. In fact, many chronic headache patients are highly successful individuals. Many are energetic achievers and leaders with unusual personality resources. Whether or not their personalities are any different from those who are not prone to headaches is not really very important. What is important is that if you have the particular physiological response to stress that leads to headaches, then you do need to be concerned about your ability to reduce your stress reactions—certainly more so than someone who has not inherited or acquired this particular response pattern.

Drug Treatment

The first line of treatment for chronic headaches is usually medication. Aspirin and other mild analgesics can be quite effective in controlling tension headaches, and a number of vaso-regulating substances can be useful with vascular headaches. Powerful pain killers like the narcotic analgesics can be used to manage the headache pain as long as the headaches occur only occasionally.

If one begins to have several headaches a week and more and more medication is required to manage the pain, problems with tolerance and addiction to medication can develop. Eventually, natural pain tolerance seems to be reduced, and continually increasing drug intake does little to control the pain. Ultimately, a reciprocal relationship between headaches and medication may emerge, especially with the use of narcotic analgesics. While the medication may provide some temporary relief, the headache may actually become conditioned to the level of medication in the bloodstream. Every time the blood level drops, the headache returns with ever-increasing vigor. Thus increasing amounts of medication actually begin to amplify the chronic pain.

A Rationale for the Use of Self-Regulation Techniques

The self-regulation strategies described elsewhere in this workbook (such as biofeedback, self-hypnosis, progressive muscle relaxation, autogenic training, and related mental imagery exercises) are intended to promote general cognitive and physiological relaxation. The rationale for using these strategies to treat tension headaches is quite simple. Using self-regulation skills, you can learn to prevent or reduce the tightness of muscles of the head, neck, and upper torso. It follows that you can use the same skills to prevent, or at least reduce, the pain emanating from these structures.

Acquiring the necessary self-regulation skills can be viewed as a three-part process. First, you develop sensitivity to early signs of increases in your muscle tension. Second, you learn specific self-regulation exercises to counter this muscle tension. Third, you generalize this skill to situations outside the training setting. When you are able to put all these skills together, you can respond to early signs of increases in muscle tension with a relaxation response, and do so even while engaged in other activities.

The rationale for using cognitive and physiological relaxation to counter migraine or other vascular headaches is more complicated than for tension headaches. In fact, relaxation as a counter-headache response may contradict the intuitive experience of many migraine sufferers. Migraine patients often report the paradoxical experience of the onset of a headache during times of low stress—while sleeping, on weekends, or while on vacation. If you are a task-oriented individual who faces frequent deadlines, these paradoxical headaches may occur only after you have completed your tasks and expect to enjoy some recovery time.

The key to understanding this paradoxical migraine pattern is the "rebound" nature of these headaches. The physiological events that accompany emotional stress do not directly cause head pain, but instead are the precursors of a headache. This preheadache stress phase is associated with increases in the release of epinephrine (adrenalin) and corresponding increases in sympathetic activation that may lead to vasoconstriction. In turn, the vasoconstriction leads to localized ischemia in the brain, and in some individuals to the prodomal signs of a forthcoming headache. The ischemic condition will also stimulate homeostatic counterregulatory neurohormonal activity. Once the stress is over and you have the opportunity to relax, this counterregulatory action may be so powerful that it overshoots the mark, causing the opposite vascular response, namely, over-dilation. With over-dilation comes the paradoxical "relaxation" headache.

Given this set of circumstances, the goal of self-regulation training must be to learn to stabilize these vascular extremes by controlling the initial stress-related vasoconstrive response. Much as with the tension headaches, you must learn to recognize the early cognitive and physiological signs of stress and then attempt to gain control over the characteristic autonomic nervous system activation which sets the stage for your eventual rebound headache. Once the dilation headache phase has been reached, it will be too late for you to intervene with a self-control strategy.

Choosing an Appropriate Self-Regulation Strategy. Having read the list of self-regulation strategies, and having read the chapter on relaxation techniques, you may be wondering how to select a strategy that's right for you. The short answer is that everyone is different, and you will have to experiment to see which approach or combination of approaches will give you the best results. Here are some ideas that may help.

If you have chronically tight muscles in your head or neck and feel that you need help to learn to relax, biofeedback may be appropriate. The EMG machine, hooked to the frontalis muscle in your forehead, directly registers the muscle tension in this very sensitive area. With the help of the feedback monitor, you can learn to relax this and other muscle groups that contribute to tension and vasoconstriction at will.

If you prefer to learn to relax on your own, start with a simple technique like progressive muscle relaxation or deep breathing exercises. When you feel competent at these, move on to one of the more comprehensive techniques like self-hypnosis or autogenics. Stick with one of these until you have achieved a reasonable level of mastery. To make relaxation more profound, borrow from some of the imagery techniques. If you have used self-hypnosis or autogenics faithfully for several months with no improvement, try the other technique. Often a person will respond well to one technique and not to another.

Well-established patterns of neurohormonal responses to stress develop and become habitual over many years. Don't expect to alter such patterns easily or rapidly. It may take weeks or even months before you notice significant changes. An early positive sign is any change in the pattern of the headache. Your prodomal signs may be somewhat altered, or the headache itself may occur at a different time of the day than is usually the case. Since positive improvement may be gradual, it is important for you to keep careful records of the intensity, frequency, and duration of your headaches. It's easy to feel discouraged in the midst of a painful attack unless you hold fast to the belief that in spite of the current pain, tomorrow will be better. If the overall frequency of your headaches this month is less than last month, and if your headache diary reveals that the average intensity of your headaches has been steadily declining for several months, then you're doing something right. And if you continue to practice the relaxation exercises daily, you can continue to expect your headache pattern to improve long after your formal self-regulation training has been discontinued.

This chapter's discussion of the origins and control of headaches is of necessity very simplified. But even where headaches are not primarily stress-related, the ability to relax at will is useful. No matter what the cause of their headache is, almost everyone finds the pain more tolerable when both the body as well as the mind are as relaxed as possible.

Further Reading

Andrasik, Frank. "Relaxation and Biofeedback for Chronic Headaches," *Pain Management: A Handbook of Psychological Treatment Approaches*. ed. Arnold D. Holzman and Dennis C. Turk. New York: Pergamon Press, 1986, pp. 213–239.

Bakal, Donald A. *The Psychology of Chronic Headache*. New York: Springer Publishing Company, 1982.

Nigl, Alfred J. *Biofeedback and Behavioral Strategies in Pain Treatment*. Jamaica, New York: Spectrum Publications, 1984.

11

Temporomandibular Disorders

by Richard Gevirtz, Ph.D.

One of the most commonly reported sources of discomfort is pain emanating from the jaw, head, and neck. When this pain is presumed to involve the movement or position of the jaw bone (mandible), it is often referred to as temporomandibular joint dysfunction (TMJ dysfunction). In recent years this single label has been widely used to describe several probably distinct problems and disorders. Other names that you may hear for these problems are:

1. Myofascial pain dysfunction (MPD), which does not refer to the face (as in facial), but to the *fascia* (tissue which surrounds many muscles)
2. Cranial mandibular pain syndrome
3. Mandibular dysfunction or, more rarely, "Costen's syndrome"

At present, few experts agree which of these labels are best suited to describe particular groups of symptoms. But as a general rule, many health professionals are now using two diagnostic categories, based on whether actual damage to the temporomandibular joint seems to have occurred. When this damage is present, the diagnosis of TMJ syndrome is often given. TMJ syndrome also includes the symptom of sharp pain localized to the area in front of the ear. When no obvious joint damage is present, the condition may be diagnosed as MPD. Other characteristic symptoms of MPD include unilateral (one-sided) general pain and pain in a larger area of the head, including the temples, neck, and upper back.

Note that even this apparently logical division into two disorders is somewhat arbitrary. Many cases demonstrate a good deal of overlap, with symptoms from both categories. Many cases of both TMJ syndrome and MPD are also mistaken for muscle contraction and migraine headaches—and many cases of muscle contraction headaches do have a TMJ component. To simplify matters, in this chapter all of these syndromes are referred to as temporomandibular (TM) disorders.

TM disorders are thought to be fairly common. Many researchers have reported joint clicking and popping in 40 to 60 percent of the population. Some 5 to 10 percent of this group usually report having facial pain. Although women constitute 60

Dr. Gevirtz is an Associate Professor at the California School of Professional Psychology in San Diego, and is in private practice with the San Diego Family Institute.

to 80 percent of clinic patients, the incidence in men is probably higher than these clinic figures indicate.

The severity of the disorder varies. Patients report symptoms ranging from mild annoyance with jaw sounds to severe crippling pain and limited jaw function. At its most severe, the disorder can be personally devastating.

This chapter is intended to provide those of you who suffer with TM disorders with an overview of key issues in diagnosing your problem and of the range of treatments available to you. Special emphasis is given to the roles that you can play in managing or eliminating your pain.

Diagnostic Considerations

The symptom that brings most patients into treatment is pain. To help your health care professional make a reasonable diagnosis and treatment plan, you need to pay close attention to the severity, frequency, and location of your pain. Here are some questions to consider.

Diagnostic Self-Evaluation

1. Do you feel a dull ache or a sharp pain or both?
2. Can you point a finger to the spot where it hurts or would you need to use your whole hand to cover the area?
3. Is the pain one-sided or two-sided?
4. Does it hurt in the morning when you wake up?
5. Is the pain affected by eating, chewing, yawning, or talking?
6. Does the pain begin at a mild level in the morning and get worse as the day goes on?
7. Is it better on weekends or vacations?
8. Is it worse on weekends or vacations?
9. Feel all the muscles around your face and neck. Which ones are tender to the touch?
10. If someone rubs your shoulders, does it hurt or feel good?
11. Do you experience sharp shoulder pain?
12. Do you clench your jaw often?
13. Has anyone heard or noticed you grinding your teeth in your sleep?
14. Have you experienced any dizziness?
15. Ask someone to hold your arm and catch it after letting go. Does your arm fall limply or do you have to force it down?

Dental Evaluation. In addition to investigating these pain symptoms, your dentist can examine you to look for clicking and popping of the TM joint, how far you can open your mouth, whether your jaw moves sideways when opening or closing, whether your bite (occlusion) is proper, and whether there is any sign of wear on your back teeth. Excessive wear of teeth or scalloping of the tongue may indicate excessive teeth grinding (called bruxing).

Although a large proportion of the population reports some signs of TM disorders, many people live their entire lives with a few symptoms and experience no serious problems. If your pain is more than occasionally annoying, or if you have to change your eating habits to accommodate it, treatment is probably indicated.

Causes: An Overview

Although specific causes of TM disorders are unknown, most recent research has pointed to a combination of factors rather than a single cause. Sometimes the problem can be caused by a trauma such as a car accident, a blow to the jaw, or a fall, or it may result from dental procedures. If you experience a sharp pain in the jaw area following such an event, contact your dentist or an oral surgeon immediately. You may have damaged the disc (meniscus) that enables your jaw to move freely.

But in most cases, trauma cannot be blamed for the problem, and identifying the cause and its treatment becomes a frustrating, painful, and costly experience for the patient. This situation occurs because several theories of origin are still being researched. Three general causal theories have predominated:

1. Malocclusion
2. Muscular disturbance
3. Psychological disturbance

Malocclusion. For many years, it was believed that a poor bite (malocclusion) was responsible for most TM pain. It was reasoned that pressure from misaligned chewing surfaces caused soft tissues around the jaw to compress, resulting in pain and loss of blood supply. Many professionals still treat patients based on the assumptions of this model. Unfortunately, most research does not support this theory. Certainly, occlusion contributes to TM disorders, but probably in concert with other factors.

Muscular disturbance. Muscular disturbances have also been implicated in TM disorders. Most of the pain that people experience seems to be muscular in origin. This pain may originate directly from the stressed muscle or may be "referred" or shifted to another locale. In addition, the pain may be centered in certain specific spots called "trigger points" (see chapter two). The muscles most often involved are the jaw muscle (massiter), the muscles that help control jaw movement (pteragoids), and the muscles of the front of the temples (anterior temporalis), the upper shoulder (trapezius), the front of the neck (sternocleidomastoid), and other neck muscles.

While evidence is strong for a muscular involvement in TM disorders, it is increasingly recognized that the disturbance should be labeled "neuromuscular," since both the nervous system *and* the muscles work together as a system in creating the problem.

Psychological disturbance. Little evidence exists to support a view that TM patients can simply be labeled hysterical or neurotic. Instead, it is now recognized that a strong "psychophysiological" component is involved in TM disorders. This means that psychological factors such as daily stress create a chronic pattern of muscular disturbance and dysfunctional oral habits in "vulnerable individuals." Thus, a combination of psychological factors (stress, anger, depression) and physiological factors (muscle bracing, clenching, bruxing, tongue thrusting) join together to cause TM disorders.

The systems view. It is vital to use an interdisciplinary perspective when dealing with TM disturbance. Many patients go from practitioner to practitioner looking for help and are given plausible explanations at each stage. A variety of problems may be correctly diagnosed, ranging from poor bite, abnormal jaw movement and function, and oral habits to poor posture, psychological considerations, and functional patterns. But it is only when all the factors are viewed as a system that successful treatment is likely to occur. TM problems clearly represent a variety of disorders, not a single dysfunction. You will need to do your best to keep an open mind in working with your health care professional to diagnose and treat your specific problem.

Treatments

The lengthy catalog of reportedly successful treatments of TM disorders includes (but is not limited to) these approaches:

Structural change therapies
1. Occlusal splints (plastic appliances that change your bite)
2. Mock occlusal splints (plastic appliances that make you aware of your tongue position, teeth, and jaw)
3. Orthodontic work
4. Full mouth reconstruction
5. Equilibration (building up and grinding down uneven biting surfaces)

Surgical or direct medical intervention
1. Joint injections (steroids are injected into joint capsule)
2. Corticosteroids (anti-inflammatory medication)
3. TM joint surgery

Direct muscular intervention
1. Muscular exercises
2. Electrical stimulation (muscles are gently stimulated with mild electrical current)

3. Physical therapy
4. Muscle relaxants
5. Immobilization
6. Trigger point therapy

Pharmacological agents
1. Tranquilizers
2. Muscle relaxants
3. Aspirin
4. Antidepressant drugs
5. Placebo drugs (almost any credible treatment has some short-term effect)

Psychological treatments
1. Biofeedback (daytime and nighttime)
2. Counseling
3. Cognitive restructuring and stress inoculation training
4. Group psychotherapy

In addition to these treatments, which are based on at least some scientific evidence, approaches from virtually every health care modality have been reported as successful.

How can you make a reasoned decision about the treatment that will be best for you with so vast an array of interventions available? The most important factor that you can use is the type of evidence available in support of the treatment.

The weakest basis for a decision is a simple case-study testimonial (John Doe testifies to his successful treatment with grapefruit seeds). Systematic case studies are better, but not definitive. The ideal way to determine the best treatment approach is through controlled studies where the treatment group is compared to a credible placebo or control group. The presence of a control group is crucial, since TM disorders have been shown to improve temporarily with placebos alone, and patients often go through cycles of spontaneous remission.

The most carefully evaluated of the treatments listed above have been the occlusal splints, surgery, and biofeedback procedures. All have been shown to be effective after a fairly long follow-up. But many problems remain in the research and further study is required.

Structural Therapies

Most TM disorder patients have been treated by dentists with one of the structural therapies listed. Several theorists have well-developed explanations for these treatments based on jaw imbalance. But however reasonable these theories may sound, they are not scientifically established and a great deal of controversy still remains. It does appear that conservative interventions, such as the fitting of a flat-plane occlusal splint, do alleviate pain and improve function. Based on these results, the Presidential Conference on the Examination, Diagnosis, and Management of Temporomandibular Disorders recommends initial treatment with *reversible* conservative procedures. This means that before you submit to any procedure which is not reversible (can't be brought back to the way it was), you should seek a second opinion — preferably from a dentist or surgeon with special training in TM disorders.

Surgical or Direct Medical Intervention

Most experts agree that surgery is the treatment of *last* resort. Surgeons have made great progress in pioneering new techniques that make surgery less invasive and more effective. But in many instances you should be able to obtain relief without surgical intervention.

In many patients, X-ray techniques will indicate damage to the miniscus, the disk which cushions and guides the jaw. However, even these cases will often respond to nonsurgical treatment. Furthermore, surgery doesn't always work and can make things worse.

If surgery is recommended, you should get a second opinion. Look for an oral surgeon who collaborates with other health professionals and will try many conservative treatments before surgery.

Injections into the joint can sometimes bring immediate and dramatic relief; but be cautious and do not permit this procedure to be repeated too often. The injection can burn out the disk and create new problems.

If you are dealing with medical personnel who have a broad perspective on TM disorders, you will be adequately informed and cautioned. If you are *not* being "educated" as well as "treated," go elsewhere.

Direct Muscular Interventions

Among physical therapists, a subspecialty has developed which deals specifically with TM disorders. These practitioners use a variety of methods to relax the painful musculature, including ultrasound, TNS (transcutaneous nerve stimulation), sprays, diathermy, massage, postural instructions, advice on oral habits, muscular exercises, and other techniques. Although little data exists on the effectiveness of these procedures, most people familiar with them think that they help, and they rarely do any harm. It is important that the therapist address the disorder as a *neuro*muscular problem, and not merely apply procedures for loosening up tight muscles.

Pharmacological Agents

Appropriate medication can be useful in treating TM disorders in the short run. Non-narcotic analgesics (aspirin, ibuprophen, and so on), anti-inflammatory agents, anti-anxiety drugs (minor tranquilizers) and sometimes antidepressant drugs are used (see chapter 8 for more information about these types of drugs). These medications have been shown to produce positive short-term effects, but unfortunately they do not provide a good long-term solution.

Psychological and Behavioral Treatments

The fact that so many diverse treatments have been shown to be at least partially successful in the treatment of TM disorders lends support to the proposition that something other than physical, structural changes are responsible. All successful therapies seem to have one factor in common: the patient's attention is directed towards the jaw and mouth. In addition, most involve supportive relationships with helping professionals.

There is good evidence that behavioral treatments are successful. Biofeedback is the most researched technique of these approaches. Other forms of behavioral treatment such as cognitive therapy have also produced positive research results.

Rationale for Psychological and Behavioral Treatment of TM Disorders

If we exclude those TM disorders that involve clear trauma, arthritic conditions, growth disorders, or other clear disease processes, a unique pattern emerges. In the remaining disorders, there is an interaction of structural biomechanical, muscular, and neuromuscular factors and oral habits. This interaction is seen even when the TM joint itself shows evidence of "derangement" or dysfunction.

In addition to moving the jaw, supporting the head (which weighs over nine pounds), turning the head, and moving the eyes, lips, and tongue, the muscles of your face, neck, and head also have an automatic bracing response. When a person feels threatened, a braced muscular response for fight or flight is elicited. This response is characterized by tightened neck and shoulder muscles, a clenched jaw, and drawn facial muscles.

Psychological stress is the underlying process that fuels this complex bracing system. When an individual with certain jaw characteristics experiences chronic stress, an overload on the craniomandibular system is created.

This overload can develop in several ways. Excessive daytime jaw clenching can combine with nighttime teeth grinding to produce it. Clenching or bracing, or dysfunctional oral habits such as excessive gum chewing, tongue thrusting, frowning, forced smiling, or jaw thrusting can also contribute to an overload. Highly tensed muscles in the shoulders, neck, or forehead are another part of this assault on the craniomandibular system. Many studies in both laboratory and natural situations have demonstrated that psychological stress leads to hyperactivity in the jaw muscles of TM disordered patients.

When enough of this hyperactivity is created, symptoms appear. These may include muscular pain, jaw pain, or both. Sometimes the pain will be far-reaching, covering any area of the head or neck. In some cases the tension of the jaw muscles will create a ringing in the ears or dizziness. Teeth can show wear from nighttime grinding and become sore. Gums can be affected (periodontal disease). Patients may hear clicking and popping noises in their jaws. This noise is due to either the effect of the discs being deranged in some way or to inhibited jaw movement caused by tight, shortened muscles that no longer allow the jaw to move through its pathway freely.

In all these cases, stress (broadly defined) represents the underlying fuel for the disorders. This probably explains why many studies have found TM disorder patients to be more anxious and to have a more difficult time managing life's stresses. Any factor that prolongs the stress will eventually make symptoms worse.

Finally, it should be remembered that once pain has begun, it represents a major stressor in and of itself.

Psychological and Behavioral Treatment

Be sure that you understand the reasons for your specific symptoms before proceeding with treatment. Go back over the symptoms you listed in the diagnostic section and make sure that you have a clear understanding of what is happening to you. If you are not sure of the source of your symptoms, get help from someone who will take a comprehensive, rather than a narrow perspective.

Behavioral treatments are aimed at breaking the cycle of chronic bracing, clenching, and teeth grinding. This cycle of pain is broken with a number of tools, including biofeedback, cognitive approaches, and stress inoculation training, along with other techniques.

Biofeedback

Biofeedback refers to a variety of techniques that take information from biological systems (like muscles and arteries) and feed back some relevant aspect of this information to the patient. This information seems to allow the patient to make systematic and permanent changes in his or her biological system.

Electromyographic (EMG) biofeedback is the type primarily used with TM disorders. This type of feedback involves information from neuromuscular structures. When the brain instructs groups of muscle fibers to contract (or stop contracting), tiny amounts of electrical activity are produced. With modern electronic systems, this electromyographic activity can be detected and displayed to the patient. These EMG levels are reported in millionths of a volt called microvolts (MV). When the patient becomes aware of this activity, he or she can learn, with training, to change it. Thus EMG biofeedback can be used to retrain chronically tight muscles to relax.

For TM disorders, the jaw, neck, or upper shoulder muscles are used for feedback. An EMG assessment can determine what, if any, dysfunctional muscle activity might be involved. By getting readings from all the muscles in the head and neck area, an experienced practitioner can get a more complete picture of the dynamics and complexities of the problem. Following this assessment, patients are usually trained to let all of their head and neck muscles relax. This muscle relaxation procedure enables patients to eliminate or minimize pain. EMG biofeedback training typically takes five to fifteen sessions to be effective.

Biofeedback is also used to aid in general relaxation training. This may be especially important to eliminate nighttime bruxing and grinding. Along with the EMG feedback, patients also learn to produce a calm, quiet state typical of low sympathetic nervous system (SNS) arousal.

The SNS is the emergency or "fight or flight" system for the body. When the more complex outer shell of the brain perceives any sort of danger or threat, it sends signals to more primitive brain areas to ready the body for the coming emergency. Using both the adrenal glands (set in motion by the pituitary) and the SNS, the body then becomes an efficient machine for fight or flght.

In this process, heart rate or blood pressure increases. Blood is shunted from the skin surface to the muscles (producing cooler hands and feet). Sweat glands begin to work (especially on the palms of the hands), and muscles begin to automatically spring to attention. These and other reactions get the organism ready for the threat. When the threat is a physical one, the body recovers normally after the physical effort is made. But when the threat is embedded in thought patterns or more chronic stimuli, this emergency system can stay on too long. Such a chronic stress reaction can produce TM disorders. In order to adjust the functioning of the SNS and to combat this chronic stress, biofeedback-assisted relaxation training is used. In this instance, sensors from your hands feed back information about sweat gland activity. For most people, a relaxation state will be accompanied by less sweat gland activity in the palms of their hands. This is called an electrodermal response (EDR). Information about the temperature of your hand can be measured by a thermistor, a kind of thermometer. As you become relaxed, blood flows to your skin and to your hands, which then get warmer. Other body functions like heart rate can be measured in similar ways.

The goal of all of these procedures is to insure that you profoundly relax your body for a short period of time each day. Such relaxation interrupts the chronic stress or emergency reaction and enables your body to return to a more natural level of functioning. Although there is not clear agreement on how much time is required for this daily relaxation, most clinicians recommend at least one period of 13 to 18 minutes each day.

It seems important to produce the relaxation in the middle of the most stressful time of day. If we imagine that an individual's typical day looks like the graph in figure 11.1, we might anticipate that problems will occur. This is because the stress levels are chronic. The goal of biofeedback-assisted relaxation training is to produce a pattern such as that shown in figure 11.2. Here, by interrupting the chronic reaction to prolonged stress, physical recovery is possible. In this process, the chain of stress leading to pain leading to additional stress is broken.

FIGURE 11.1

Conceptualization of chronic stress

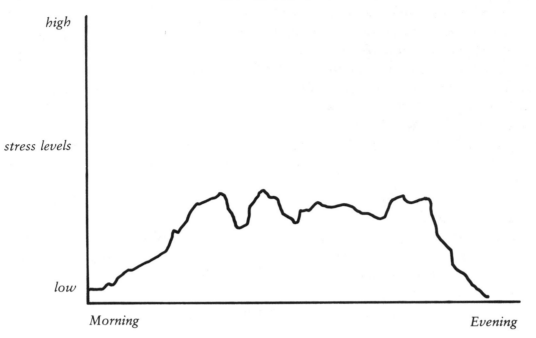

FIGURE 11.2

Using a relaxation period to break up chronic stress

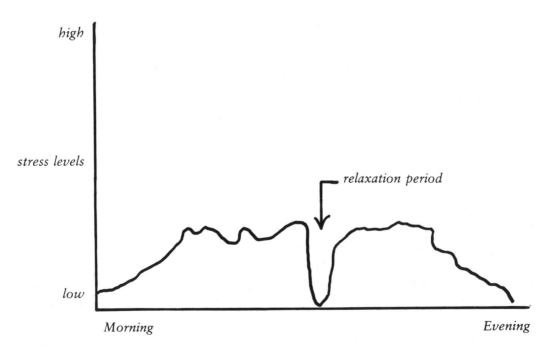

What would happen if you constantly tightened up and then relaxed your arm muscle for an entire day? Some stiffness might well occur, but once the muscle was developed, you could probably keep on doing this same activity all your life with no serious consequence. But suppose you tightened your arm muscle *and kept it tight* for four or five hours, never letting up. Most probably, you would then have a chronically sore arm. In TM disorders, this kind of chronic pain develops in muscles that have been continuously tensed in the face, head, and neck.

Biofeedback-assisted relaxation training is designed to interrupt this pattern. For most people, a simple change of direction in the level of tension once or twice per day produces powerful positive change. Such daytime relaxation training also seems to relieve nighttime bruxing and jaw clenching for many people. Scientific evidence for this result is somewhat sketchy, but the available research does bear out positive clinical observations.

When choosing a health care practitioner for biofeedback treatment, look for appropriate credentials. One safeguard is to choose *certified* practitioners. An independent certifying agency, The Biofeedback Certification Institute of America, (10200 West 44th Avenue, #304, Wheat Ridge, Colorado 80033) is an internationally recognized source of credentials. If you write or call, they will send a list of certified professionals in your area. In addition, the practitioners you select should have special training in treating TM disorders.

Cognitive Influences on TM Disorders

Another set of treatment approaches that have some scientific backing are cognitive therapy interventions. As we have seen, most chronic bracing and clenching is thought to be related to stress in some way. It is also now recognized that most stresses are heavily influenced by personal appraisal or perception. In other words, how you perceive or think about a particular source of stress in your life has a great deal to do with the impact that stress will have on your body. Many practitioners use special techniques to reduce such cognitive or thought-based sources of stress.

Let us apply the principles presented in chapter six to the specific problem of TM pain. If appraisal or perception are the key triggers for chronic stress, then learning to see things differently and process emotions differently may eliminate a major source of the TM disorder.

Negative Thinking. Not only does negative thinking lower the pain threshold (make pain noticeable sooner), but it also may have a direct effect on the facial, head, and neck muscles that perpetuate TM problems.

Kim was quite wrapped up in her own pain and misery and complained about it constantly. When hooked up to EMG feedback, she had difficulty getting her forehead or jaw muscles below 3 microvolts. After some time, I asked her to take a break and chatted with her about her young children. I asked to see pictures. She dug out some snapshots and proudly watched my smile as I admired her beautiful kids. At that moment I pointed out to her that her muscle levels were 1.5 microvolts, far lower than she had been able to achieve with biofeedback alone.

Kim's response is a dramatic demonstration of the direct role of negative thinking in TM disorders. Since the face and head are intimately involved in emotional expression, it is important to pay attention to the thought and feeling components of pain in those areas.

Stress Inoculation. In addition to following the suggestions given for dealing with negative thinking in chapter six, you also need to learn skills for coping with the negative feelings and thoughts that do slip through.

Joyce was a very efficient, perfectionistic, and motivated administrator in a large organization. After a dental procedure, she developed a great deal of pain in her jaw, temples, and upper neck. A combination of biofeedback, splint therapy, and physical therapy worked well for her, but she still had some pain. As she worked on countering her negative thinking, she found that she couldn't seem to shake a problem that occurred at work.

Joyce had been assigned a secretary named Grace who was not really very competent or motivated to become so. Joyce had tried to get a replacement, but the bureaucracy of her organization made this change impossible. In effect, Joyce was constantly bombarded by a need to "grin and bear it." And she was clenching her jaw and "bearing it" a great deal of the time.

Joyce applied the stress inoculation skills described in chapter six. She recognized that the situation was an unavoidable stressor. And she saw that she needed to become more "stoic" in thinking about her work. Maybe it was unfair or inefficient, but life was full of injustice and waste. Her job was to *get over it* as fast as she could. She charted her "Grace" attacks each day. These lasted for hours at first, but gradually she reduced their length to a few minutes. Simultaneously, she reduced her jaw clenching to an acceptable level and consequently got rid of almost all her pain.

Psychological techniques are a key to reducing your sources of chronic stress. Review chapter six again, and if you need help implementing these principles, consult a cognitively oriented psychologist, psychiatrist, or social worker.

Other Psychological Approaches

The earlier sections of this chapter should have made it clear by now that anything that helps reduce chronic stress will help many TM disorder sufferers. Although little research evidence is available to prove it, many people are probably also helped by a variety of counseling, therapy, or skills training approaches. Some promising treatments include grief therapy, Gestalt techniques, assertion training (see chapter seven), self-hypnosis or autogenics training (see chapter five), or traditional psychotherapies.

Lifestyle Changes

Oral habits. The chief culprit here is gum chewing. Almost all dental authorities recommend taking the work load off the jaw joint by eliminating gum or other repetitive chewing habits (including pipe smoking). Moving towards softer foods and smaller bites is also recommended.

Some people are tongue thrusters; that is, they push their tongues against their teeth repeatedly. Just becoming aware of this habit can sometimes lead to change. Some people can also stop clenching their jaw just by paying more attention to that behavior.

Oral health. It is especially important for TM sufferers to maintain good oral hygiene. Key habits here are brushing and flossing teeth regularly.

General lifestyle. A lifestyle that promotes good general health will also help with stress management. This in turn will alleviate or eliminate TM problems. Regular aerobic exercise and cutting down on dietary fats, sugars, and salt are often recommended. Some people report that giving up caffeine helps. Cigarettes are another source of trouble. The nicotine in cigarettes is a stimulant that actually creates more stress. In addition, smokers generally have significantly poorer oral health than nonsmokers do.

Sleep patterns. You may find it helpful to regulate your sleep patterns to make sure that you get adequate amounts of sleep. Setting a regular schedule for bedtime and awakening each day is usually helpful in adjusting sleep patterns. While this advice may sound simplistic, note that such regulated patterns can aid in relieving your TM pain.

TM disorders can be potentially serious and are usually quite complex. Make every effort to inform yourself about your problem by insisting on both education and treatment from your health care professional. If you feel like you are being patronized or babied, find another care giver.

Try to seek out professionals with a multidisciplinary perspective. These are usually dentists who also work with a team of specially trained psychologists, physical therapists, oral surgeons, prosthedontists, orthodontists, ear, nose, and throat specialists, and neurologists. Such a team will have a comprehensive perspective for your specific problem. Avoid anyone who claims to have a fast and easy cure. It may do more harm than good.

You may find that one of the behavioral approaches is effective in treating your TM disorder. Biofeedback and cognitive therapies are two treatments that have been positively evaluated in controlled studies.

Finally, by taking an active role in your treatment and not labeling yourself as helpless, neurotic, hypocondriacal, or hysterical, you can greatly improve your chances of getting better and staying better. Taking charge of your body, with the assistance of appropriate health care professionals, will enable you to understand and manage or eliminate your TM problem most effectively.

Further Reading

Laskin, P., W. Greenfield, E. Gale, J. Rugh, P. Neff, C. Alling, and W. Ayer (eds.). *The President's Conference on Examination, Diagnosis and Management of Temperomandibular Disorders.* Chicago: American Dental Association, 1983.

A self-help guide that emphasizes dental aspects of TM Disorders is:

Gelb, H. *Killing Pain Without Prescription.* New York: Harper and Row, 1980.

12

Arthritis

by Stephen Wegener, Ph.D.

Approximately one person out of seven has some form of arthritis. In fact, almost everyone who lives long enough will develop some joint damage from wear and tear. The condition can be extremely unpredictable, flaring up with no warning or remaining a constant, nagging pain. The word *arthritis* means "inflammation of the joint," referring to the disease's characteristic redness, heat, swelling, and pain. But while it frequently involves some form of inflammation, over 100 different conditions are called arthritis. The first step in developing self-help skills is to learn about your arthritis. Knowledge is power!

Although these diseases have many things in common, each has its own pattern of symptoms and treatments. The two most common types are:

- *Osteoarthritis* (OA, also known as *degenerative joint disease*, or DJD) is the most common form of arthritis. It involves the breakdown of the cartilage around the bone and can lead to bone destruction. While OA is often due to years of wear and tear on the joints, it can also result from the trauma of an injury or an infection. The joints usually affected are the knees, hips, fingers, and back.
- *Rheumatoid arthritis* (RA, also known as *crippling arthritis*) involves inflammation that is so severe it can lead to joint deformity. Persons with RA often feel like they have the flu—they are tired and aching, but also have swelling and pain in one or more joints for several weeks. Often many joints are affected simultaneously. RA is generally considered to be a systemic (or whole-body) illness.

Other types of arthritis that you may hear about or have experience with are systemic lupus erythematosus (SLE), ankylosing spondilytis, bursitis, fibrositis, and gout. These less frequent types share several very important characteristics with OA and RA. Most of these rheumatic diseases are chronic; that is, they often last a long

Dr. Wegener is an Assistant Professor at the Department of Orthopedics and Rehabilitation of the University of Virginia Medical Center, Charlottesville, Virginia.

time or recur frequently throughout life. Most forms have no cure. You can be helped by the health care team and by your own efforts, but you should be skeptical of people or products who offer a quick fix.

The warning signs of arthritis are:

- Swelling in one or more joints
- Early morning stiffness
- Recurring pain or tenderness in any joint
- Inability to move a joint normally
- Unexplained weight loss, fever, or weakness combined with joint pain
- Symptoms like these persisting for more than two weeks

If you have two or more of these signs, you should see a doctor for a diagnosis and to receive proper treatment. It is particularly important for you to know what kind of arthritis you have.

Identifying which joints are most inflamed will help you to communicate with your health care team and plan your self-help program. Use figure 12.1 to mark the joints that are problematic for you.

FIGURE 12.1

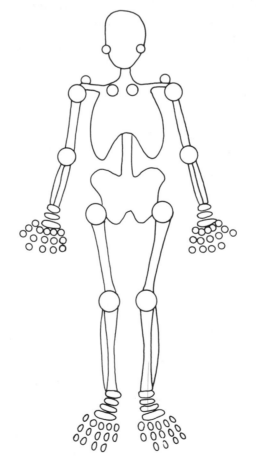

Medical Treatments

Most arthritis specialists recommend a "pyramid approach" for the treatment of the disease. The treatment is progressive, using many different methods and involving the entire treatment team, including its most important member — *you*. You and your health care team start at the bottom of the pyramid with important basic therapies. If your arthritis does not respond, you then move up the pyramid to the next level of treatment. As figure 12.2 demonstrates, the basic self-help approaches are used as the building blocks of arthritis care.

FIGURE 12.2

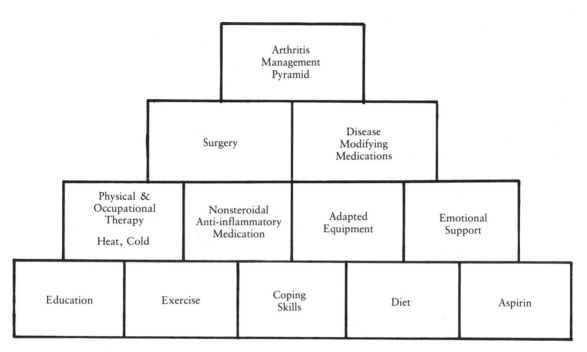

While this chapter will touch briefly on the treatments administered by other members of the health care team, I will devote most of the time to arthritis self-management skills. That's because people who learn self-management skills like exercise, stress reduction, joint protection, and assertiveness report *feeling less pain* even though *their basic condition remains unchanged*. If you begin to feel effective at managing the problem, your subjective experience of pain diminishes.

Medication

The medications prescribed for arthritis are used to treat the pain you experience and the inflammation which leads to that pain. Some medications used are not unique to arthritis and have been described in chapter eight of this book. The arthritis medications which are most commonly used are:

Aspirin. This time-tested medication is used often because it reduces inflammation and pain. It has been shown that a substance called *prostaglandins* contributes to the pain that results from inflammation. Aspirin reduces the amount of prostaglandins produced, leading to a decrease in pain. Your doctor may prescribe large doses of aspirin. Don't be fooled into thinking, "This is only aspirin—how can it help?" Aspirin can be powerful medication if taken appropriately.

Nonsteroidal anti-inflammatory drugs (NSAIDs). These medications are similar to aspirin in that they reduce prostaglandin production and decrease pain. The primary difference is that many people have fewer side effects with NSAIDs than with aspirin. NSAIDs are also more convenient, as you may only need to take them a few times per day. Except for ibuprofen, NSAIDs are available only with a prescription and are more expensive than aspirin.

Corticosteroids (steroids) are strong drugs that quickly reduce inflammation and pain. But even though you may feel better, steroids do not reverse the underlying disease. They may also cause serious side effects such as thinning of the bone, high blood pressure, muscle weakness, or depression. Steroids are used primarily when other efforts have not been successful. You should never change or reduce the amount of steroids you are taking without talking to your doctor.

Disease-modifying drugs attempt to slow the underlying progress of the disease, although how they work is not well understood. This class of drug is used primarily in rheumatoid arthritis. Examples include gold, penicillamine, and anti-malarial and cytotoxic medications.

You need to play a responsible role in using medication to modify your arthritic pain. First, be an active self-manager: know what medications you are on, what the side effects may be, and how often they should be taken. Second, follow the treatment that you have agreed on with your doctor. Missing doses of medicine can increase your pain. Use a worksheet like the one below to keep track of the medication you are taking.

Medication	How many and how often	Side effects
_____	_____	_____
_____	_____	_____
_____	_____	_____
_____	_____	_____
_____	_____	_____

Surgery

Most people who have arthritis will never have surgery. I will not discuss arthritis surgery in detail as every case is individual and needs to be decided by you and your doctor. However, a few points are worth remembering. The primary reasons for surgery are for joint repair, joint replacement, and removal of joint lining (a synovectomy). These surgeries are seldom urgent, so you will have time to consider the decision. Think it over and possibly get multiple opinions. Remember that surgery cannot replace good self-management skills. In fact, you will have better results from surgery if you are in good physical and mental condition. You will also need to plan on a rehabilitation program to maximize your benefits from the operation.

Exercise

The physical benefits of regular exercise—strength, conditioning, and maintenance of range of motion in the joint—are all helpful in managing arthritis pain. Just as important are the benefits of psychological well-being, sense of purpose, and feeling that you are helping to manage your disease that exercise can give. The specific exercises that are best for you depend on the type and severity of your arthritis as well as on your overall physical condition. You and your health care team are the best ones to make a decision regarding the proper exercise for you. Some general guidelines apply to many different patients:

- Range of motion, strengthening, and endurance exercises are all important. A good program will balance all three.
- If you have pain for two or more hours following an exercise, discontinue that particular exercise.
- It is best to exercise when you have the least pain and stiffness and are not tired.
- In general, avoid exercising inflamed joints.
- Begin at a comfortable level for you and stick to your program regularly. A few exercises every day are much better than a "weekend warrior" approach.
- Avoid any exercise that puts extra pressure on an inflamed joint.
- A particularly excellent type of exercise for people with arthritis is swimming. Water exercise, sometimes known as "aquadynamics," involves most of the typical calisthenics you do on land. However, the buoyancy of the water supports your muscles and joints so that you feel lighter, able to move easier, and run less risk of injury than if you were performing the same exercises on land. The water also provides gentle resistance, much like light weights, so that you are strengthening your muscles and improving your endurance while you work out in the water. Check with your local Arthritis Foundation for the location of a water exercise program in your area.

1. *For fingers.* To help increase movement in the joints of the fingers, start with joint 1 at the tip of the finger. Slowly bend with other hand till you reach joint 2. Continue gradually applying pressure through joint 3. You can reverse this process, starting with joint 3 and working up. Do this exercise as many times in the day as feels comfortable, but at least once a day.

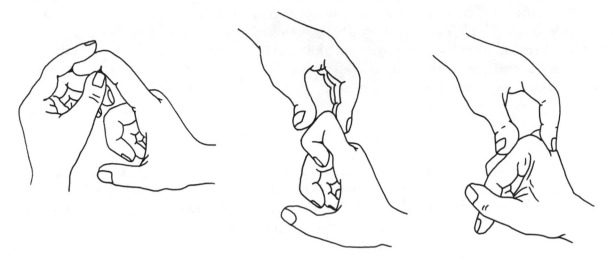

2. *For wrists.* To increase flexibility and movement in the wrists, place palms together with fingers interlaced. Slowly apply pressure by pushing the palms on one side and then the other. Push to the point of discomfort, then just a little bit beyond. Repeat as many times as feels comfortable, but at least once a day.

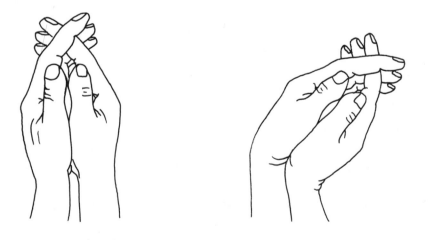

3. *For elbows.* Place palms and fingers together, bringing arms to right shoulder. Now press downwards on a diagonal toward your left knee, straightening both arms. Go slowly and push just a little beyond any discomfort. Repeat on the other side. Repeat as many times as feels comfortable, but at least once a day.

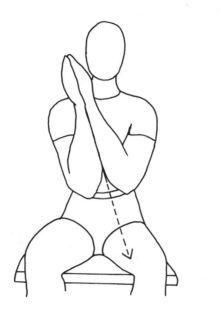
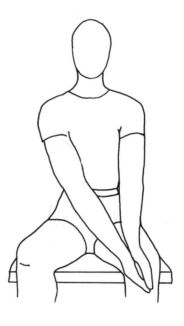

4. *For shoulders.* Clasp your hands behind your neck. Slowly pull your elbows as far back as you can, then bring them forward and touch them together if you can. This exercise rotates your shoulder to help increase movement and also stretches out your chest muscles. Repeat three to five times.

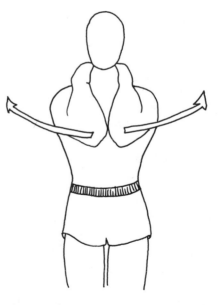

5. *For calves and ankles.*

   (a) Using a stable object such as a table or wall, lean into the object with both hands. Bend your left knee as you lean forward and stretch your right leg behind you, straightening the leg as much as possible. Make sure both feet are pointed straight ahead to get the right stretch. You should feel a good stretch in your calf if your heel is as flat to the floor as possible. Hold 20 seconds. Switch to other side and repeat with left leg.

(b) Now place both legs back together as you lean into the table or wall. Slowly raise up on the balls of your feet and back down, pushing your heels flat to the floor. Repeat ten times. This exercise is excellent for promoting flexibility and movement in the calves and ankles.

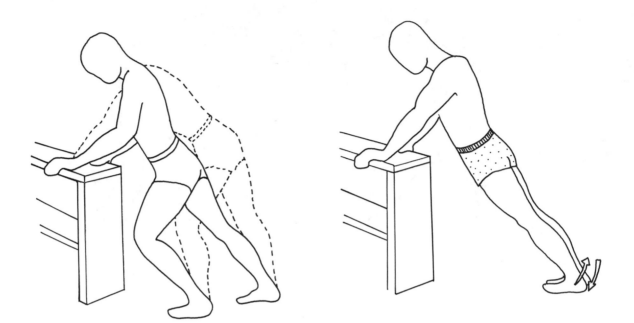

6. Other suggested exercises for the rest of the body. (Please refer to chapter three for a full description of these exercises.) Once you get started, all of the exercises in chapter three are good for promoting overall body strength and flexibility. But for beginning exercisers with arthritis, do the exercises here first because they are low-stress, low-load range of motion exercises (moving the joints through all positions).

a. *Hip flexor stretch* (exercise I.3). Promotes movement and flexibility in the hips as well as a stretch for the lower back. Start with the easier exercise first, lying flat, and work up to the harder exercise where you tuck your chin towards your knee at your chest. As you get better at this exercise you can also straighten the non-chest leg.

b. *Cross leg rotation stretch* (exercise II.1). Good for hip rotation and stretching lower back and sides. Keep shoulders on the floor or bed.

c. *Lower back roll* (exercise II.2). Also good for hip rotation and lower back stretch. Keep shoulders on the floor or bed.

d. *Neck stretches and strengtheners* (exercises III.4 and III.5). Neck rolls are good for promoting flexibility in neck and shoulders. Neck hold promotes strength in muscles in front and back of neck.

Physical and Occupational Therapy

Physical therapists teach you how to perform exercises and help you to carry out exercises that you may not be able to do alone or will need special equipment for. They can also train you to use pain relief methods such as heat and cold treatments or transcutaneous electrical stimulation (TENS). Occupational therapists can teach you ways of protecting your joints and techniques to conserve energy and provide adaptive devices and aids to help with your daily activities. Ask your doctor about the ideas and techniques reviewed below if you feel that they would be helpful.

Heat and Cold. Either of these two pain management techniques may be helpful with arthritis pain and stiffness. For some people with arthritis heat works best, for others cold. You may also want to try a combination of heat and cold. This *contrast bath* involves soaking the inflamed joint in warm water, then in cool water, and then in warm water again. Repeat this cycle every three to five minutes for a total of twenty minutes. Physical and occupational therapists can tell you more about the use of heat and cold.

Joint Protection and Energy Conservation. Taking care of your joints and yourself are key principles in *preventing* arthritis pain. The Arthritis Foundation lists eight principles for protecting your joints and conserving your energy.

1. Respect pain. If you have pain for two or more hours after doing a task, you have done too much.
2. Become aware of your body position. Avoid activities that involve a tight grip or put too much pressure on your fingers.
3. Control your weight.
4. Avoid staying in one position for a long time.
5. Use your largest and strongest joints and muscles for the task. For example, carry your purse on your shoulder or elbow rather than with your hand. Lift with your larger leg muscles rather than your weaker back muscles.
6. Balance activity with rest. Listen to your body's signals.
7. Simplify your work by planning ahead and managing your time.
8. Ask for help.

Transcutaneous Electrical Stimulation (TENS). TENS involves stimulation of the nerves in a painful area by low-level electrical impulses. (See chapter two for more information about TENS.) In arthritis, TENS is most successful in reducing pain if the pain is localized in a specific joint. Be sure to try different positions of the TENS electrodes and different levels of stimulation to see which will be most helpful.

Nonmedical Treatments

Diet. Good nutrition is important for everyone, and particularly important for anyone who has a chronic disease. But note that *no diet or food has been proven to prevent or cure any type of arthritis except gout*. People with gout have to avoid foods that contain high levels of purines such as organ meats, peas, beans, the nightshade family, and others. Other types of arthritis require a balanced diet that includes portions from each one of the four basic food groups: meats, vegetables and fruits, milk products and grains.

Some people have advocated a diet that eliminates red meat among other things, while others are reporting that their arthritis symptoms are secondary to allergies and reactions to toxic substances. If you notice that your symptoms are worse after eating certain foods or staying in certain environments, try eliminating them. Although any beneficial effects of these treatments have not been scientifically proven, you may want to discuss an elimination or rotation diet with your health care team to see if any foods are contributing to your symptoms, especially if you have a history of food allergy.

Use a common sense approach to any diets you hear about. If they totally avoid any of the basic food groups, they may be harmful.

Self-Massage. Massage increases blood flow and brings warmth to the painful area. This technique may be useful for arthritis pain. To perform self-massage, you need only devote some time and patience to it. Some people have found that using a menthol gel provides a comfortably warm or cool sensation that can ease the arthritis pain. (Be certain to remove the gel before using heat, or you may burn yourself.)

The Relaxation Response. Many people with arthritis, along with many scientists, believe that stress can lead to arthritis flare-ups and increased pain. Pain and stress have similar effects on the body. Muscles become tight, breathing becomes faster, and blood flow is restricted. Learning methods to relax can help you combat the pain and stress related to arthritis. Relaxation is more than just sitting back, reading, or watching television. It involves learning ways to calm and control your body and your mind. Relaxation does not come easy if you are in pain or have a chronic disease such as arthritis. It must be practiced like riding a bicycle.

Several methods can be used to develop the relaxation response. These include progressive muscle relaxation (PMR), autogenics training, self-hypnosis, biofeedback, and imagery. Follow the instructions for performing these relaxation exercises given in chapters four and five. Here are a few hints for using these techniques when you have arthritis:

- *Progressive muscle relaxation* can place excessive strain on inflamed joints if done too strenuously. A more passive relaxation method such as autogenic training or imagery may be more helpful. If you choose to use PMR, be sure not to strain your joints excessively.

- *Autogenic training* may be a helpful exercise to begin with, as it will not affect your joints. It also allows you to focus the relaxation on particular parts of your body.
- *Imagery* can be extremely useful when you have hot, inflamed joints. You might picture your pain as a setting sun—hot, red, and bright. As the sun slowly sets in your mind, you feel your pain going down with it. You can picture the sun setting again and again until you feel cool and relaxed.
- *Self-hypnosis* is really just deep relaxation created by focusing your attention internally. See chapter five for instructions and a sample induction that you can adapt to fit your condition. Not everyone has the knack of using hypnosis successfully, so don't be discouraged if it takes some time for you to develop this self-regulation skill.
- *Biofeedback* can help you learn to relax, even if other techniques are difficult for you. With it, you can also develop a reassuring sense of control over your body.

Psychological Treatments

Pain

Do you spend time thinking about the pain you are having from arthritis? How often do you think about it? The amount of time that you spend thinking about your pain has a great deal to do with how much pain you feel. People who concentrate on their pain are more likely to say that their pain is severe than people who think less frequently about it. Here are a few tips to help change your thinking about pain.

- *Do something that takes your mind off the pain and yourself.* Your distraction could be reading, talking to others, watching TV, or seeing a movie. Pick something positive to do that will take your mind off the pain and focus it on something pleasurable or rewarding.
- *If you can't help but think about the pain, try to think about it differently.* Don't think of the feelings as pain, but as your body's message to take a rest break. Try thinking of the arthritis pain as a tingling feeling, not as intense pain. Calling the pain by a different name can sometimes make you feel differently about it. (But don't try to make your mind blank, because this is very hard to do.)
- *Try to put your pain in perspective.* Remind yourself of what you have, instead of what you don't have. Think of what you can do, as opposed to what you can't do. Find a way to use positive thinking to manage your pain.

See chapter six for discussion of psychological techniques you can adapt to your circumstances.

Other Psychological Issues

Depression. It is common for people with a chronic disease to experience depression. Major signs to watch for are sadness, a change in sleep habits, poor appetite, withdrawal from others, and crying spells. If you feel that you are depressed, try using some of these self-help strategies.

- The most effective way to control depression is to control negative thinking (see chapter six) and to cope with feelings of helplessness by learning to ask for what you want (see chapter seven).
- Keep a positive events diary. Each day write down two or three activities that give you pleasure—a call from a friend or family member, a nice meal, a good movie. (Reading this book and trying some of these exercises is a positive event!) When you are depressed you need to remind yourself of the parts of your life that still feel meaningful and rewarding.
- Make a positive comparison. We all compare ourselves to one another; these comparisons can make us feel better or make us feel worse. Look around, and notice how much you still have and how well you are doing, compared to others who are less fortunate.
- Most people who have arthritis find that sharing their experiences and feelings with a support group of others in similar situations makes coping easier. Ask your doctor or contact local arthritis organizations for information about groups in your community.

Sleep problems. Disturbed sleep patterns will contribute an additional burden to your pain. Practicing relaxation techniques at bedtime can often help improve your sleep. Using self-hypnosis or an hypnosis tape is often especially helpful. Ask your doctor for other suggestions to improve your sleep.

Sticking with the program. Managing your arthritis will require you to do many self-care activities—keeping up your medication regimen, exercising, learning about your disease, practicing stress management, and attempting to maintain home, work, and social responsibilities. You may get discouraged and feel that it's just too much to do all of these activities on top of the burden of your arthritis pain. To help yourself cope, set up a daily diary. List the activities that you will do to manage your arthritis pain. Check off each activity that you do each day. For an extra boost, treat yourself to something special each day when you start the program. Once you get started, do something special for yourself for each week that you stick to your program.

Lifestyle Changes

A chronic disease like arthritis requires you to change your life in many specific ways. For some individuals, these changes will touch every aspect of their lives. You'll need to draw on the skills listed in this chapter, as well as others listed elsewhere, including assertiveness (see chapter seven). Keep in mind that you are not alone. Others who have arthritis are also trying to cope with their pain, and a health care team is ready to back you up. You may find additional helpful information in the suggested readings below.

Kate Lorig and James Fries have written an excellent book called *The Arthritis Helpbook,* which provides information on additional exercises and self-help strategies useful for arthritis. For more information you may wish to contact the Arthritis Foundation, which has a national office and local chapters around the country. The local chapter can direct you to doctors and clinics in your area, provide educational materials, and occasionally may be able to help with financial problems. They often provide scheduled activities and volunteer opportunities. The address is:

The Arthritis Foundation
1314 Spring St., N.W.
Atlanta, Georgia 30309
(404) 266-0795

Further Reading

American Medical Association. *Back-Care.* New York: Random House, 1984.

Coping With Arthritis Pain. Atlanta, GA: Arthritis Foundation.

Lorig, Kate, and James Fries. *The Arthritis Helpbook.* Reading, MA: Addison-Wesley Publishing Co., 1986.

Rooney, Theodore, and Patty Ryan Rooney. *The Arthritis Handbook.* New York: Ballantine Books, 1985.

Ziebell, B. *Wellness: An Arthritis Reality.* Dubuque, IA: Kendall/Hunt Publishing.

13

Irritable Bowel Syndrome

by William Stewart, Ph.D.

The incidence of pain in gastrointestinal disorders is quite high, and irritable bowel syndrome (IBS) is no exception. One research survey found that three quarters of those attending a gastrointestinal clinic reported pain symptoms; in roughly one half of these patients the pain was found to be benign but chronic, probably due to IBS. This chapter will describe the commonly observed symptom patterns of irritable bowel syndrome and suggest ways that sufferers can learn to manage the pain and other distress associated with it.

Description of the Problem

Irritable bowel syndrome is thought to be a disorder of the motor activity of the large intestine. The large intestine, or colon, makes up the final 6 of the overall 28 feet of the human digestive system and consists of three distinct segments. The first, known as the cecum, is a pouch that connects the small intestine to the colon. It begins in the lower right quadrant of the abdomen and merges with the *ascending colon* which extends upward toward the liver. The *transverse colon* drapes across the abdomen, toward the left side. Here the large bowel again turns, this time downward toward the pelvis. This final segment, called the *descending colon,* merges into the sigmoid colon with its S-shaped turns and ends at the rectum. The primary functions of the colon are absorption of water from fecal material and storage of feces prior to defecation.

The colon's two movements are the mixing and propulsion of its contents. Mixing is accomplished by large circular or ring-like contractions at discrete points along the colonic tube. The colon's propulsive movements are unlike peristaltic contractions found in other sections of the gastrointestinal tract. These *mass movements* consist of a constrictive contraction at some point, usually somewhere along the transverse or descending colon, followed by a rapid mass constriction of the next short section "downstream" from the first constriction. The contents of the colon are thereby forced toward the rectum en masse. These contractions usually occur only a few times a day, most commonly during the hour following the morning meal.

William Stewart, Ph.D., is an Assistant Professor of Internal Medicine, Division of Gastroenterology, at the University of Virginia Medical Center, Charlottesville, Virginia.

Some basic facts about the types of abdominal pain and the known stimuli for them help to explain the pain involved in IBS. One of the more curious facts about hollow organ or visceral pain is that noxious stimulation that would ordinarily elicit intense pain at the surface of the body rarely produces severe pain when applied to the gut. As described by gastroenterologists and physiologists, the internal digestive organs (or *viscera*) can be cut, torn, or crushed, and the stimulation is seldom even detected. This is so because the nerve endings that transmit pain from the smooth muscle walls of the gut are primarily sensitive to rapid stretching or distention, which is one likely cause of IBS pain. Other significant sources of visceral pain include inflammation of the viscera from bacterial infection or exposure to chemicals, ischemia (the buildup of metabolic waste materials because of poor blood circulation), spasm of the gut's smooth muscle, or stretching of ligaments in the abdominal cavity.

Gastroenterologists and physiologists have identified three types of abdominal pain. *Visceral* pain arises from the organs in the abdomen in response to noxious stimulation. The quality of visceral pain is generally dull and seldom localized to a specific site. However, because the *afferent nerves* that transmit pain signals travel from the affected organ to both sides of the spine, IBS pain is often experienced near the midline of the abdomen. This pain sensation is typically experienced as cramping, burning, or gnawing.

Somatic pain arises from noxious stimulation somewhere on the *parietal peritoneum*, the membrane which lines the walls of the abdominal cavity to form a skinlike sac that holds many of the digestive organs. Like outer skin, the parietal peritoneum is richly supplied with pain nerves. As these nerves are of a different type than those found in the viscera, somatic pain is frequently very sharp and intense and usually is aggravated by movements and coughing. Because the parietal peritoneum's nerves conduct pain sensations directly from it, the sensations are restricted to a limited area, often directly over the area of noxious stimulation.

To complicate matters further, a third type of abdominal pain exists. *Referred pain*, felt in a part of the body distant from the site of the diseased or distressed internal organ, is not an uncommon occurrence. This type of pain exists because of the particular neural wiring of pain fibers in the trunk of the body. Basically, branches of visceral pain fibers join with structurally similar pain fibers from particular regions of the skin at the same terminal-like sites in the spinal cord. When intense pain stimulation in a visceral site sends pain signals to the spinal cord, these signals can in effect "spill over" to the fibers from a relatively remote skin site, creating the feeling that pain is also originating from the skin site. Although the actual site of a referred pain can be on the surface of the body or at another internal organ, referred pain does tend to be restricted to limited areas.

The abdominal pain of irritable bowel syndrome is probably the result of spastic contractions, excessive stretching, and distention from gas and stool in the bowel, or hypersensitivity to otherwise normal stretching and distention. Recent research has shown that spontaneous and stress-induced spasms can occur in the small bowel as well. The type of activity in the gut of the IBS patient probably differs little from that in individuals without the disorder, but IBS patients do react with greater amounts of pain and contractile activity to a range of stimuli, including stress, eating, and distention of the gut wall by balloon inflation (a research procedure). Almy (1978) suggests that the patterns of movement in IBS are indistinguishable from the gut's normal role during emotional arousal, but that the movements may be more prevalent in IBS because of chronic emotional tension.

As there is no known physiological abnormality underlying the disorder, the medical definition of irritable bowel syndrome is simply a description of the symptoms associated with it. While agreement about a set of descriptive symptoms has yet to be reached, research has progressed in attempts to identify symptoms that distinguish the syndrome.

Abdominal pain is the cardinal symptom in at least one variant of irritable bowel disorder. Referred to traditionally as spastic colon, this condition often entails pain associated with alternating constipation and diarrhea. The pain varies considerably in quality and is reported variously by patients to be crampy, dull, vague, burning, aching, and sharp. Pain intensity can also range widely from mild to severe. More often than not, the pain of IBS is located in the lower left quadrant of the abdomen, but most patients experience it at several other locations as well. The pain is characteristically relieved by a bowel movement or sometimes the passing of gas. It is episodic, tending to occur frequently (some experts suggest at least six times in a twelve-month span), and usually lasts at least several weeks per episode.

A second type of IBS has painless diarrhea as its primary symptom. Painless diarrhea is probably a separate disorder since several research surveys taken together suggest that abnormalities in the frequency of bowel movement or whether it typically involves diarrhea or constipation are not that discriminative in irritable bowel syndrome. The data gathered so far suggest that alterations in bowel habits are an intermittent finding in many individuals and in those with irritable bowel syndrome may occur as seldom as 25 percent of the time.

The presence of additional symptoms will help your doctor to clarify a diagnosis of IBS. In addition to abdominal pain, a great many patients with IBS report (1) the sensation of incomplete evacuation during bowel movement; (2) the presence of mucus in their stools; (3) feelings of distension in the abdomen and sometimes visible distension in the abdomen as well; and in at least some patients (4) looser stools or more frequent bowel movements with the onset of episodic abdominal pain.

Your doctor will confirm a diagnosis of IBS by excluding the presence of physical disease through medical examination and testing. The absence of signs of organic disease is a crucial part of diagnosis and should never be overlooked. Loss of greater than 5 percent of body weight in the past year, the presence of blood in the stool (except from local anal lesions), fever, anemia (low red blood cell count), a positive lactose tolerance test (many symptoms of IBS mimic those seen in individuals who cannot digest a common sugar present in milk), evidence of intestinal parasites in a stool culture exam, or the suggestion of inflammatory bowel disease on barium enema are all signs of problems beyond simple IBS. Note that abdominal pain is a cardinal symptom for many serious diseases. If you feel a distressing abdominal pain that you have never experienced before or had medically evaluated, you should consult your doctor for examination immediately.

Ongoing abdominal pain must also be medically evaluated, as it may be a sign of a condition other than IBS. Lower right abdominal pain may occur chronically but recurrently and still be appendicitis, a medical emergency. Other conditions that warrant immediate medical attention and may give rise to frequent, recurrent lower abdominal pain are diverticular disease, inflammatory bowel disease, pelvic disease such as rupture of an ovarian follicle, painful menstruation, and carcinoma of the colon. Other organic diseases that can cause pain in the abdomen or epigastric region include gall bladder disease, peptic ulcer, pancreatic disease, angina, dyspepsia, esophagitis (heartburn), and aortic aneurisms.

Stress and IBS

The role of stress, chronic emotional tension, and ongoing psychological disorders in modifying the function of the gut remains a controversial issue. While the notion that feelings and thoughts influence the normal function of the gut has been a matter of common knowledge since time immemorial, it has received serious scientific attention only recently. Many authorities have reported a relationship between psychological stressors and the onset or worsening of IBS symptoms, and it is estimated that between 50 to 80 percent of IBS patients have reported noticing this relationship themselves. The kinds of psychological stressors often reported by patients with IBS vary considerably, but include worries about work and family; the loss of a parent or spouse through death, divorce, or separation, sometimes accompanied by feelings of unresolved grief; and life changes that demand many social and personal adjustments, such as multiple marriages and separations, multiple jobs, or many changes in residence. Recently, a history of physical or sexual abuse in childhood or in a recent or current marriage has also been found to be associated with chronic abdominal pain conditions such as IBS.

The most common psychological distress symptoms that occur along with IBS include fatigue, low mood, irritability and other symptoms of depression, anxiety, interpersonal sensitivity, and sensitization to the functioning of the body. Studies using psychological tests show that individuals with IBS tend to report less nonspecific psychological distress than found in psychiatric outpatients, but more emotional distress than reported by the average individual. Most authorities agree that irritable bowel syndrome is the gastrointestinal disorder with the most persuasive evidence to suggest that psychological factors play a significant contributory role.

Medical Treatments

Sensible remarks about the medical management of IBS were written by Thompson (1984):

Satisfactory management of the irritable bowel syndrome demands much of the art and science of medicine. It is a common experience that lasting cures are unusual. . . . Thus the physician's duty is to help the patient to understand and cope with his symptoms and to avoid any therapy which might be harmful. (p. 313)

It is clear from the above that better understanding of this disorder will become possible only within a consistent, trusting, and open relationship between you and your doctor, sometimes a tall order in these days of hectic physician and patient schedules. Nevertheless, you can prepare to develop such a relationship by seeking out a physician with whom good rapport is easy to establish, by taking stock of how stressfully you may be running your life, and by recognizing that it is important to assess the role of other factors, including your feelings and the amount of stress that you experience at work and at home. A good physician will be prepared to explain the condition to you and will listen to and calm your fears about whether your symptoms indicate serious conditions such as colitis or cancer.

Few proven medical options are available. Surgery is never an appropriate option for the benign pain of IBS. There is evidence both for and against the value of alterations in diet, primarily in the addition of bran or other bulking substances. Bran is thought to shorten the time it takes for a meal to travel through the intestinal tract and to increase stool bulk, features that some consider useful in patients with constipation and hard stools. As for medication, most patients with IBS do not seem to benefit from trials of antispasmodic drugs, a group of medications that are prescribed to relax the overactive smooth muscle of the colon. However, your doctor may suggest that you try a drug from this group, particularly if you have persistent pain following meals. Anti-anxiety and antidepressant medications are commonly prescribed for the psychological distress symptoms often seen in IBS patients, but these drugs have not yet been shown to have a direct beneficial effect on the symptoms of IBS. You should regard these drugs as supplements to be taken only on a short-term basis. IBS is often a lifelong condition, and there is little to recommend the long-term use of mind-affecting drugs in chronic benign pain conditions.

Psychological Treatments

Whitehead and Schuster's excellent 1985 review shows that stress reactivity, social-family learning factors, and psychological disorder are significant factors that influence the course of IBS in many patients. IBS is a common disorder—occurring in as much as 10 to 15 percent of the adult population—and when that fact is put together with the recognized role of psychological factors and the chronic nature of the syndrome, it is surprising that so little attention has been devoted to developing psychological and self-regulation approaches to its management. Psychological treatment methods have been explored, but additional clinical trials are needed to show that they exceed the improvement usually seen with the simple passage of time. One half to two thirds of untreated patients with IBS report improvement within several months time. Unfortunately, most will also eventually experience a recurrence and exacerbation of their symptoms.

Given that most patients with IBS recognize that psychological stress frequently increases before, during, or after a flare-up of their symptoms, many IBS sufferers could clearly benefit from developing effective stress-management skills. Several options exist and include practicing deep breathing skills or progressive muscle relaxation (see chapter four) or using self-hypnosis or autogenic training (see chapter five).

Learning to relax quickly and deeply can also be accomplished by motivated individuals by listening to audiocassette tapes. But perhaps the best approach is to work closely with a qualified behavior therapist in a chronic pain or stress clinic. In these settings, therapists often use biofeedback to assist patients in learning to recognize and deepen relaxation states. Learning meditation procedures for relaxation and focusing is another potentially beneficial option.

A brief course of personal psychotherapy may be the most effective and lasting approach that you can take. In a recent well-conducted study in Sweden, half of a large sample of IBS patients participated in seven to ten sessions of brief psychotherapy, along with the routine medical management that the other half also received. The work of therapy, adjusted to each individual's needs and personal strengths, consisted of finding new solutions to old problems, recognizing and modifying maladaptive behavior, and learning better styles of coping with stress and emotional tension. Both groups had improved at three months, with the patients who had received therapy showing the most improvement. At a one year follow-up, the therapy patients reported still greater improvement in physical and emotional distress, while the untreated patients, true to the natural course of IBS, had some relapse. It appears that IBS patients can readily make the emotional adjustments that lead to reduced abdominal pain and other gastrointestinal symptoms by briefly involving themselves in problem-resolution psychotherapy. The study suggests that a treatment approach to the whole person, physical and psychological, benefits those IBS patients motivated to explore the role of psychological stress in their disorders. If you consider counseling and psychotherapy for IBS management, your willingness to discuss personal concerns sincerely and candidly is essential.

What You Can Do

If you and your physician have determined that you suffer from irritable bowel syndrome, you can be grateful because the disorder is benign in nature. Nevertheless, yours is a painful, recurrent, and chronic condition. While you are faced with a serious challenge in adapting to the disorder, there is increasing reason to believe that personal adjustments within your control can influence the natural course of the condition for the better. In addition to establishing a cooperative dialogue with your physician, there are several other areas that you can learn to manage.

The first is your attitude. How well you adapt to your condition is ultimately up to you. Optimally, you will come to accept the fact that yours is likely a chronic condition of periodic remissions and worsenings, something that you must learn to live with as well as you can. Frequent complaints about your distress to others will accomplish little.

Second, you can begin to examine your lifestyle and personal relationships for excessive strain and tension. You can learn to better manage stress and emotional strain through regular deep relaxation and other stress management procedures.

Finally, consulting a good, qualified psychotherapist and investing yourself in a brief course of therapy or counseling can lead to greater personal resiliency, stronger coping skills, and better problem-solving skills. In the long run, this kind of personal growth can help you reduce your gut's reactivity to stress.

Further Reading

Almy, T. P. "The Gastrointestinal Tract in Man Under Stress," *Gastrointestinal Disease.* ed. M. H. Sleisenger and J. S. Fordtran. 2nd ed., vol. 1. Philadelphia: Saunders, 1978.

Thompson, W. G., "Progress Report: The Irritable Bowel," *Gut,* XXV (1984), 305–320.

Way, L. W. "Abdominal pain," *Gastrointestinal Disease.* ed. M. H. Sleisenger and J. S. Fordtran. 3rd ed., vol. 1. Philadelphia: Saunders, 1983.

Whitehead, W. E., and M. M. Shuster, eds. *Gastrointestinal Disorders: Behavioral and Physiological Basis for Treatment.* Orlando, FL: Academic, 1985.

14

Neuralgias

by Patricia Wolskee, Ph.D.

The sharp shooting pain of neuralgia characteristically extends along the course of one or more nerves and occurs suddenly with little or no stimulation from injury, infection, or stress. The pain occurs intermittently. Almost any infection or disease that can cause damage to the peripheral nerves may be the genesis of a neuralgic pain potentially worse than the pain of the original injury. This peculiar property makes neuralgic pain especially difficult to understand, endure, and treat.

This chapter will discuss three different types of chronic pain that share common neuralgic traits. They are:

1. Postherpetic neuralgia
2. Trigeminal neuralgia (also known as *tic douloureux*)
3. Reflex sympathetic dystrophy (RSD)

Postherpetic Neuralgia

Postherpetic neuralgia is caused by the herpes zoster virus, an acute viral infection characterized by nerve inflammation and skin eruptions on any part of the body. The attack (also called *shingles*) causes pain which subsides in most patients, although some patients suffer from unremitting pain that may last for years.

The persistent pain of postherpetic neuralgia can be exacerbated by almost any type of stimulation. For instance, your pain may be aggravated by putting a piece of clothing on the affected area, or it may be intensified by other external stimuli such as noise. Emotional upset may also cause an increase of your pain.

The medical treatment of postherpetic neuralgia greatly depends on the stage of the disease. The key element is early treatment—the earlier you receive treatment, the more likely you are to be successfully treated.

Dr. Wolskee is a Clinical Psychologist with the Pain Management Center of the University of Medicine and Dentistry of New Jersey, Newark.

The medication most prescribed for postherpetic neuralgia is a combination of Elavil (amitriptyline, an antidepressant) and Taractan (chlorprothixene, a major tranquilizer). It is not clear why these medications are effective. As with all medications, there can be side effects—those most often seen are morning grogginess or a dry mouth. But since people respond differently to medication, it is important for you to be individually monitored by your physician.

Other medical treatments that are helpful in the treatment of postherpetic neuralgia are transcutaneous electrical stimulation (TENS), sympathetic blocks, and injections of a steroid or local anesthetic into the affected area.

TENS is the electrical stimulation of a nerve by placing electrodes on the surface of the skin. (TENS is described in detail in chapter two.) With postherpetic neuralgia, you will most likely feel a very uncomfortable sensitivity in your skin. If TENS is applied to the sensitive area, you will feel a return of *normal* sensitivity to the area. In their 1974 study, the anatomists Nathan and Wall found TENS to be a useful as well as a noninvasive treatment for patients with postherpetic neuralgia.

If performed in the disease's early phase, sympathetic blocks can be a useful treatment. An anesthetic agent is injected through needles placed in the neck area. This temporarily blocks activity of the sympathetic nervous system in the affected area.

Local injections of a steroid (cortisone) or a local anesthetic (such as xylocaine) usually take place once a week and can be performed in your doctor's office. The side effects of this treatment are minimal, unless you are allergic to cortisone or steroids. As a rule, your doctor will need to determine any allergic predisposition that you may have before this treatment can be administered.

Surgical treatment is not recommended for postherpetic neuralgia as the cutting of nerves may cause loss of sensation and permanent numbness in the area. Also there is no guarantee that surgery will relieve your pain. You may be left with the pain—but now it will be magnified by sensory loss and numbness. If you are asked to consider surgery, weigh these factors before making your decision.

Progressive relaxation, self-hypnosis, autogenics, and imagery can all be useful nonmedical treatments for postherpetic neuralgia. Many times you may find yourself tensing the affected area. By practicing progressive relaxation (see chapter four), you can learn to relieve some of the tension contributing to your pain as well as to halt or lessen any tightening of muscles in the pain area.

Through self-hypnosis, you can use one of many pain-relieving techniques to either filter the pain from your body, a technique that I find useful, or to move the pain to another area of the body. Through autogenics, you can learn to send soothing warmth to the afflicted area by increasing blood flow. Imagery techniques can be used to change your pain sensation to something more pleasant by focusing on relaxing scenes or images. All three techniques are covered in chapter five.

Cognitive restructuring (see chapter six) is a useful psychological treatment technique. Through it, you can learn to think differently about your pain as well as relieve some of the distress and anxiety associated with it.

Trigeminal Neuralgia (Tic Douloureux)

Trigeminal neuralgia is a neuralgic state associated with nerves in your face. The pain may occur spontaneously, but in most cases it is triggered by a stimulus such as eating, talking, washing, brushing teeth, shaving, or exposure to cold winds. Patients describe the pain as a knife-like, jabbing sensation; one of my patients said that it felt like a "lightning bolt" in her face. During the period of a few seconds to a few minutes that the pain lasts, you appear to be stunned; you hold yourself very still and are unable to speak. A pain-free period follows the attack, and the time between attacks varies from hours to days. Periods of remission do occur; these may vary from months to years.

Trigeminal neuralgia occurs mostly in older people, on the right side of the face, and in women more often than men. It is not clear why these differences exist.

Before you begin treatment, you should rule out any other peripheral cause of the pain. Consult a dentist to make sure that dental faults, pulp disease, cysts, or impacted teeth are not contributing factors. An X-ray of your jaw can also be helpful to rule out other causes.

The most effective and widely prescribed medication for trigeminal neuralgia is tegretol (carbamazapine, an anticonvulsant). The drug is usually started on a small dose of 100-200 mg per day and built up to a therapeutic dose that may be as high as 1600 mg given in four divided doses. Side effects that you should be aware of include nausea, dizziness, drowsiness, and, more seriously, aplastic anemia, which is a severe form of anemia resulting from cell production failure in bone marrow. Routine blood work should be done so that your blood levels are carefully monitored. Although tegretol is very effective for the treatment of trigeminal neuralgia, you may develop a tolerance for it—which means that a more invasive treatment could be necessary in the future.

TENS and acupuncture are the two less invasive medical strategies available to you for the treatment of trigeminal neuralgia. Although TENS treatments are not as effective as medication is, some patients have responded to them positively. Weekly acupuncture treatments are effective in the relief of trigeminal neuralgia.

If these less invasive treatments fail, a *gasserian ganglion block* is the next treatment usually considered. In this approach, alcohol is injected into the ganglion, which is the collection of nerve cell bodies. This intervention may leave you with permanent facial numbness and nerve regeneration in the future.

The surgical treatment for trigeminal neuralgia is the decompression (removal of pressure) of the ganglion and cutting of the sensory root. Once again, these procedures may cause numbness. Even if successful, regeneration of the nerve can occur, leaving you with your original discomfort and possibly greater pain.

The nonmedical treatment of trigeminal neuralgia includes relaxation and cognitive behavioral intervention. Due to the intermittent nature of the pain, you may find yourself anticipating your next "attack," and this anticipation generates anxiety. In extreme cases, you may end up avoiding any activities that could possibly bring on an episode of pain (for example, shaving). Relaxation training can help you to deal with these kinds of anticipatory anxiety and stress.

Cognitive behavioral intervention may also help you cope (see chapter six). Think of the kinds of thoughts and feelings that usually occur to you before an attack. Through cognitive behavioral training, you can learn to focus your attention in ways that will help you to abort an attack, rather than letting yourself get caught up in its stressful antecedents. With your thoughts and feelings focused, you can start to intervene early to help decrease the severity of your pain reaction. By involving you in the treatment process, this method also helps to give you a sense of control in dealing with your pain.

Reflex Sympathetic Dystrophy

Although reflex sympathetic dystrophy (RSD) is not classified as a medical neuralgia, it shares common properties with the other neuralgias and so is included in this chapter. Other names for the syndrome include *causalgia* and *sudeks atrophy*.

RSD is an extremely painful condition that usually begins after a trauma such as a crush injury, fracture, or sprain. Its symptoms are burning pain, vasoconstriction, coldness of the affected limb, skin changes, and limited range of movement. The physiology underlying the condition is not clearly understood.

An early diagnosis is very important because successful treatment depends on early intervention.

Diagnosis is based on a physical examination and evaluation by thermography and three-stage bone scan. Treatment is given according to the stage that the patient's condition has reached. The four stages are:

I. Characteristic pain and sympathetic overactivity (sweating). Coldness in the affected area.
II. An extension of stage I, and a limited range of movement.
III. A significant restriction of both active and passive range of movement and dystrophic changes (meaning a lack of adequate nutrition to the tissues via the blood supply).
IV. Presence of a frozen and useless extremity.

Treatment is given according to the stage. In stage I, a series of stellate ganglion blocks is given. Injections of standard analgesics and/or steroids are placed just lateral to the trachea (throat area). The danger involved is the possibility of making contact with the cervical vertebral disc and possible penetration into the epidural space.

In stages II through IV, in addition to the stellate block, a Bier block is administered using reserpine, which depletes serotonin. If you are suffering from high blood pressure, this procedure has an inherent high risk factor that must be taken into account. Sympathetic blocks are also a possible treatment in stages II through IV.

A surgical sympathectomy was used in the past for later stage cases of RSD, but its use is declining because of its lack of effectiveness.

A recent development is the use of a dorsal column stimulator for RSD, a small device surgically inserted into the spine at a location determined by the pain site. Dorsal column stimulation acts like an internal TENS unit that you can regulate yourself. While the mechanism of its use is not clearly understood, it has proven to be an effective pain-relieving alternative for RSD patients.

Another very recent development in the treatment of RSD is the use of an internal infusion pump. During this procedure, a catheter is inserted into your epidural space (between the vertebrae and spinal cord) and a small thermosensitive pump is implanted into your flank. Continuous morphine or local anesthetic is pumped into the epidural space, allowing you to become active in a physical therapy program with minimal pain.

The medical and nonmedical treatments for RSD are best conducted together. If physical therapy is conducted during pain-free periods, the chances of regaining use of a limb are greatly increased. But during periods when you are experiencing an increase in pain, a treatment plan consisting of aggressive (too rigorous) physical therapy is often counterproductive to your long-range needs.

There are a number of very understandable reasons why RSD patients develop psychological problems.

1. Many years pass before you are diagnosed. You begin to become defensive.
2. Remission may occur for long periods of time. Years may pass before you suddenly wake with a recurrence of symptoms. You develop fear and anxiety.
3. You are given false expectations by the treating physician. You are told that you will get better and you see no relief. Discouragement sets in.
4. You are told, "You could have been helped if your condition had been diagnosed earlier." You feel a sense of anger, despair, and frustration.
5. Symptoms develop in more than one limb. You begin to develop anxiety because of fear of additional body involvement.
6. Statistics recently gathered by the RSD association of New Jersey show that 97 out of 100 randomly chosen patients still have the disease after treatment. Left with the disease, you become frustrated, angry, and discouraged.

These many difficulties concerning the diagnosis and treatment of RSD make psychological intervention crucial. Early intervention is the most beneficial, because it can eliminate or counter many reactions to the condition that may otherwise develop. When an early diagnosis is made, psychological intervention can also be strengthened by the development of a working relationship between the physician and the psychologist.

Effective psychological treatments include individual therapy, biofeedback, group therapy, and family therapy.

In individual therapy, success can only be achieved if you are an active participant and not a passive observer during the therapeutic process. You need to be an educated patient (that is, you need to know why physical therapy or exercise will help you). You need to learn skills to manage anxiety and discouragement.

In 1979, a psychologist named Blanchard taught a patient to warm an affected limb by 1 to 1.5°C using thermal biofeedback. Along with the temperature increase came significant pain relief. Biofeedback can also involve you in your treatment and give you some control over your pain.

Group therapy provides a setting where a number of benefits take place:

1. You meet others with a similar disease.
2. You can observe the behaviors and attitudes of others like you.
3. You can see the positive and negative aspects of each other's behaviors.
4. You can reinforce each other's compliance with the appropriate medical treatments.
5. You can set short- and long-term goals and monitor them in the group.
6. You can become educated about RSD and exchange techniques to deal with the pain.

An important psychological intervention that is often overlooked is the inclusion of your family in therapy. Because so little is known about RSD and because of the long period of misdiagnosis that many patients experience, family members often misunderstand the condition or doubt the patient's pain. The goals of family therapy are:

1. Education
2. Support
3. Teaching family members to help you comply with your treatment regimen
4. Teaching them to reinforce use of the affected limb through exercise and daily activity

I strongly feel that your treating physician needs to be psychologically "educated" concerning your psychological treatment. In particular, your doctor should be able to give you realistic expectations about your condition. You can help the process by encouraging communication between your treating physician, your psychologist, and you.

Postherpetic neuralgia, trigeminal neuralgia, and RSD are all serious and difficult chronic pain states. Although they are difficult to diagnose and to treat both medically and psychologically, recent research and advances are contributing to a much better understanding of treatment. Your understanding, education, and involvement concerning your pain and your treatment are a key to achieving better physical and mental health.

Further Reading

Melzack, Ronald, and Patrick Wall. *The Challenge of Pain*. New York: Basic Books, Inc., 1983.

"Therapeutic Approaches to Reflex Sympathetic Dystrophy of the Upper Extremity," *Clinical Issues in Regional Anesthesia*, I (January 1985).

I would like to acknowledge David Cohen for his editorial assistance in preparing this chapter.

15

Vocational Rehabilitation and Chronic Pain

with Glenn H. Catalano, M.S.

Every year more than 560,000 workers in this country sustain injuries or illnesses that disable them for at least five months. Approximately half of these people never return to work. Half of those live for more than a decade, being supported by disability benefits even though most are considered capable of further, gainful employment.

—From the *National Institute of Handicapped Research*, May, 1986.

Anyone who has tried to work while suffering from chronic pain will tell you how difficult it is to meet the daily requirements of a regular job. Obviously, a physical laborer who regularly lifts and hauls will be critically hampered by chronic pain. But even a sedentary office worker's productivity will be affected. Research shows that people who have suffered a disabling injury on or off the job show evidence of greater absenteeism, decreased productivity, and pressure from management and co-workers to adequately perform their jobs.

In the event of an acute injury, medical therapy is straightforward—rest, appropriate medications, and perhaps traction and physical therapy. But when the pain drags on for many months and you feel that you are unable to return to your job, other issues come into play. You may begin to wonder if you can ever do the type of work that you did again. Your family relationships may suffer from added financial and emotional burdens. And you may feel lethargic and depressed from lack of activity. Should you return to your old job? Should you attempt to do the same amount of work for the same number of hours? What if you are a warehouseman and your doctor recommends that you not lift over twenty pounds? Or what if you have been doing high-pressure work that you know has been causing or aggravating your headache pain? At this point you find yourself confronted by a complex of decisions that

---

Glenn H. Catalano has had fourteen years' experience as a Rehabilitation Counselor and Supervisor for the Virginia Department of Rehabilitative Services.

must be made about your capabilities, limitations, and desire to return to your former place of employment.

This chapter is about decision making concerning your job, career directions, and career attitudes. Through using the vocational rehabilitation structure already set up in your state, plus a step-by-step decision-making process, you will be able to clarify the issues confronting you and make a decision that you can live with.

Kathleen had a very successful experience working out her back problem with the job. She is a personnel supervisor for a large and busy company, a job that requires hours of driving from job site to job site across the state. She developed her back problem after thirteen years of service, and it looked as though her ability to do the job—including some lifting along with all the driving—would be seriously threatened.

It took Kathleen a while to figure out how she could do her job and cope with back spasms so painful that there were times when she could not stand up. But persistence on her part and a good attitude on the part of her employers paid off in the long run. Her company allowed her to take time off for regular visits to a pain clinic for counseling and biofeedback sessions. She learned stretching and strengthening exercises for her back, which she practiced daily. She learned to relax during the day by mentally rehearsing several relaxation strategies. She patiently negotiated with her company to rearrange some of the workload, and she took care to demonstrate to them her commitment and energy for her work.

Now Kathleen is back on the job, and although she has modified her work schedule, she feels that she is producing as much as she did before her injury. And she is extremely pleased that neither she nor her company lost faith in her ability to cope and work it out.

Evidence tells us that Kathleen is representative of the typical worker in this country. Most disabled workers want to return to work . Moreover, if they are encouraged and counseled early in their recovery process, their chances of returning to their jobs or at least to a job are significantly higher. What can you do to promote your return to work?

You already know what to do for your acute pain. You must follow your doctor's orders carefully, take the needed time off work, get sufficient rest, and take the appropriate medications. You have to allow yourself time to heal.

When you do go back to work, do not try to perform at the same rate of speed that you maintained before your injury. If your employers expect you to resume your usual amount of heavy lifting, talk to your boss and work out a system that will allow you to do as much work as possible, but without pushing yourself to the point of potential reinjury. Carefully follow the rules of good body mechanics (explained in chapter three). Copy the rules below and post them near your work site or desk. Share them with your boss and co-workers.

- Push, don't pull.
- Get help.

- Keep objects close to your body when lifting; lift with the large muscles in your legs, not with the small muscles in your back.
- Assume a broad base of support when lifting and a proper pelvic tilt—feet flat on floor and slightly apart; pelvis tucked up with your back rounded.
- Pay attention to your stress levels. Do deep breathing and other relaxation exercises that you enjoy regularly throughout the day. Don't let the muscular tension build up!

Compensation and Chronic Pain

If you are ready to return to work after your injury but have an on-the-job injury that is currently being litigated, you should check with your attorney first to see if your case will be undermined by your return. The word "litigation" means any legal suit brought for workmen's compensation, social security disability, negligence, and so on. In other words, you need to ask your lawyer if the desired outcome of your suit will be affected by your ability to work.

It is common for people to sue their employer for compensation when an injury happens at work and they are unable to return to their previous job or to any other job that requires the same kind of work. Sam was a laborer in a rural western Virginia rock quarry whose injury left him physically unable to continue the rigorous manual labor involved in his job. He was also unable to find other work at a comparable salary in his isolated area. The compensation he received from his former company was enough to provide for his family while Sam decided what new career to pursue and thought through the possibilities of relocating to an area with more employment opportunities. This is how the system is supposed to work.

But the compensation system can also serve as a disincentive to return to work. Sam's compensation checks are almost as great as the salary he received for the hard work of his old full-time job. If he continues to blame his inability to find new work on his old job injury, it's more than likely that he will continue to receive workmen's compensation benefits for years. Then social security disability takes over, leaving Sam in a position where he may never have to work again. At first glance this prospect may sound ideal, but Sam has actually been having a hard time adjusting to his new role as homemaker, rather than sole breadwinner. He feels awkward and depressed, and his emotions add to his stress—making it even harder for him to begin the slow climb to recovery and better functioning. His bind is that he's dissatisfied with his current life, but he's also literally being paid to be dysfunctional.

Sam is one of hundreds of thousands of people caught up in this bind. It is easy to blame the system for providing ready cash without accountability. And it is easy to blame the workers themselves for taking advantage of the situation and possibly prolonging their disability. But the compensation system is a highly complex one, and the problems it addresses are equally complicated. Blaming the system will only make it more difficult to solve the very real problems of pain and work.

This is the time to take an honest look at your desire to return to work. No amount of counseling, cajoling from your spouse, doctoring, or nursing will get you back to work if you basically don't want to be there.

Task 1. Clarifying Your Commitment to Your Job

This first step will enable you to assess the value you place on your current job and to see it in perspective with other values you hold in life. Write down your answers to the following questions. Try not to debate or qualify your responses. Simply record them as they occur to you.

1. What do I value about my current job?

2. What aspects (apart from the problems concerning my disability) would I change about this job?

3. What job or jobs have I truly enjoyed in the past? (Include any childhood or high school experiences.) What characteristics about those jobs did I enjoy?

4. What activities do you enjoy? List at random, as they occur to you, all of the things that you like to do in your life. You don't have to fill all the blanks; just write until you can't think of anything else. Don't forget to include your hobbies.

_____   _____

_____   _____

_____   _____

_____   _____

_____   _____

_____   _____

_____   _____

_____   _____

_____   _____

_____   _____

Now rank your list by assigning a number to each item in terms of which you value most, second most, and so on.

5. Where did you place your current job on your hiearchy? Did it even make the list? What about your past jobs?

6. What does this list tell you about the value you place on the activities in your life? Where there any surprises for you?

7. What does this list tell you about the amount of time you spend doing the things that are most satisfying to you?

8. Are you willing to make changes in your life so that you can do more things that are satisfying to you? If your current job is highly valued on your list, are you happy to continue to give it top priority?

You may find it helpful to talk out your reactions to this exercise with a counselor or a friend. Sharing your thoughts with your spouse will help you begin problem solving about the next steps to take. Remember, you always have options. You do not have to return to the exact same job, or face compensation and unemployment for the rest of your life. There are other options that you can learn to exercise, if you take time to examine them and have the patience and persistence to work towards them.

If you have decided that you value your present job and want to stick with it, regardless of your disability, then you are ready for step 2. (If you wish to change jobs, skip to step 3.)

Step 2. Problem-Solving Sequence

1. First, make sure that you are committed to your job by answering the questions in step 1 and evaluating your responses.

2. If you're comfortable talking to your boss, go to him or her and explain your desire to return, making it clear that you can continue doing your old job with a few modifications. If you can't work with your boss, then find yourself an advocate. Either contact a counselor at your state's vocational rehabilitation agency, or get a letter from your doctor stating that he or she feels that you can resume employment with some minor modifications to the job. Explain to your doctor that you are clear about your decision to stay on your job and that you want to go back.

3. Get help in assessing what you can and can't do on the job. Find a physical therapist, occupational therapist, or rehabilitation/biomedical engineer through your state vocational rehabilitation agency. Invite that person to come to your work site to help you find ways to modify your job to make the work easier and help prevent reinjury. Here are some examples of common work site modifications:

- Reassignment to a less strenuous job
- Getting help with difficult tasks
- Working longer hours with more frequent breaks
- Getting a special chair with good lumbar support
- Changing the height of a work table

- Getting a device for reaching for distant objects
- Clustering items that you regularly use around your workspace so that you do not have to get up and down repeatedly
- Finding a suitable cart to help you push or pull items
- Finding a stool to prop up your foot when standing for long periods

You may need to have your doctor write a prescription for these rehabilitation professionals so that your insurance will cover the cost of their services.

4. Write up a list of changes you would like to make.

5. Discuss the list with your boss. Introduce your requests by saying, "I still want to work for you. And I feel that I can be a productive worker with a few minor modifications in my work environment."

If you feel that any pending litigation will be an obstacle in solving your work problems, then wait until your suit is settled. Talk the question over with your attorney.

Bob and Tom

Bob, aged 49, sustained severe crush injury to both of his legs while working at a construction job. He underwent very extensive surgical reconstruction of both legs that left him with obvious difficulty in mobility and a severe amount of constant, chronic pain.

After several years of recuperation provided by workmen's compensation, he made an important decision. Even though he had learned how to manage his pain, he knew that it was not going to go away. He could sit at home with it, or he could try to resume full-time employment and be in the same constant pain at work. One factor that swayed him was the thought that he would have more distractions from the pain at work than he would at home. He also missed using his expertise and the companionship of his co-workers.

Bob made a decision to go back, and took the initiative to get himself rehired. He has been working successfully at his former occupation now for over a year, even though his physician had rated him as over 50 percent disabled in his ability to perform his former job. Bob will tell you flatly that he hurts tremendously, all the time, every day. But working does distract him, and for long periods he simply doesn't think about his pain.

Tom is in his 30s and has a back injury from lifting heavy produce in his supermarket job. Tom has been through back surgery and pain control techniques, seen a psychologist, taken medication, and made several other futile attempts to control his pain and get back to work. He has gotten good advice on how to cope and adapt, but Tom always finds reasons why the suggestions won't work. He finally agreed to attend a daily support and educational group at a hospital. Tom had to drive an hour and a half to attend the group. When he got there he would become very anxious and spend his time in the group gesticulating and complaining loudly about his pain. Then he would drive for an hour and a half to get home. Tom put in almost a full day's work participating in this group, but he couldn't see that the energy he was putting out in this context could be transferred to a real job.

Part of Tom's problem was that he was afraid of being reinjured. But a larger part of the problem was that he was holding out for a cure, hoping that someone would find an answer to his pain. This is where Bob and Tom part company. Bob's doctor said, "You're always going to be in pain." So Bob began to view the pain as a new component of his life, one that had to be adjusted to. Tom refused to accept his pain, and so put his life on hold until the day when he would be cured.

Step 3. The Department of Vocational Rehabilitation

If there is no compensation or litigation involved in your chronic pain situation and you want to get back to work, then here is another option.

Apply to the department of vocational rehabilitation in your state. This service is available to all and is not a welfare program. You have already paid for this program out of your taxes! It is designed to help the injured worker resume gainful employment and provides counselors and administrators for you to talk with about your employment options. Sometimes this service can also provide money for you to get retraining in another field.

Note that the people who work for the state rehabilitation agency in your area are working for you—and not for the insurance company that covers workmen's compensation claims, or for the insurance company that your business uses. If you do happen to meet a rehabilitation counselor who works for your employer's insurance agency, keep in mind that this person's primary goal is to get you back to *any* full-time work. Any suggestions that this person makes may not be the best options for you. The state rehabilitation counselor works for a neutral agency, one that is interested in your individual goals. He or she will work with you and your doctor to make a realistic assessment of the extent of your disability, your career goals, and your training needs. The goal is to help you decide what choices will work best. Also note that since this is a state and federally funded program, you can get the same service in every state.

What Services Do You Get?

1. **Physical capacities evaluation.** This is a test of major motor strength—that is, your ability to lift, bend, stoop, and twist over a period of time. The counselor goes over this test with you, and then works with you and your doctor to determine whether you can find a new line of work that will fit your physical and educational capacities.

2. **Developing a rehabilitation program.** You and the counselor will work out an

individualized written rehabilitation program for you to follow and mark your progress.

3. **Contacting potential employers.** If there is work available within your community, the counselor will assist you in contacting potential employers and help you come up with a strategy for job placement. As the client, you will be responsible for going to the prearranged job interviews and getting your new job. The counselor can accompany you, if needed, to help explain to the potential employer your physical capacities and the employer's potential liability if you should have a reinjury. Your counselor will also explain to the employer that disabled workers who return to the workforce are as a rule very motivated people. Evidence shows a lower absenteeism rate among previously injured people once they get back to work.

4. **Job retraining.** If the counselor determines that you are eligible, the state agency will provide funds for job retraining in your area. The state purchases vocational training services from private business, industry, colleges, and universities.

5. **Counseling.** Your counselor is available to talk over any difficulties you may be encountering in trying to make a job shift. He or she understands the difficulties of trying to cope with chronic pain and working and can reinforce positive coping mechanisms for you to remember and follow.

Other Rehabilitation Resources

The National Institute of Handicapped Research reports a rapid growth of rehabilitation programs encouraging return to work. In addition to the federally funded public rehabilitation program, larger companies have begun to employ industrial medical teams to treat and counsel disabled workers. Labor unions are adopting a more comprehensive stance for worker protection. Some are lobbying for additional rehabilitation assurances and sponsoring Projects With Industry (PWI) programs that encourage disabled workers to return to jobs. Some employers offer company rehabilitation offices, where they counsel injured employees, educate supervisors and other staff (in an effort to eliminate attitudinal barriers), and initiate work site modifications.

Private rehabilitation programs are now springing up to provide return-to-work services for business and industry. One such model is The Menninger Foundation's Project Retain in Topeka, Kansas. The project employs a trained rehabilitation counselor to act as liaison between the disabled person and the community and to involve the worker with a multidisciplinary team of professionals from the community.

The Employment and Rehabilitation Institute of California in Anaheim operates another model rehabilitation program called "Work Hardening." This program operates on the principle of early intervention. The disabled worker is sent to the program soon after appropriate medical treatment. The staff works with the client on a daily basis to increase muscle strength and flexibility, improve body mechanics and proper work habits, increase confidence and self-esteem, and adapt to assistive devices or modified work sites. For more information about both of these innovative programs write to them directly:

Gabriel Faimon
Director
Rehabilitation Research and Training Center
The Menninger Foundation
Jayhawk Tower, 9th Floor
700 Jackson
Topeka, Kansas 66603

Leonard Matheson, Ph.D.
Director
Employment and Rehabilitation Institute of California
Anaheim, California 92801

State vocational rehabilitation agencies are not the only public resource available to injured workers. Many colleges and universities offer low-cost or no-cost career exploration programs for individuals wishing to change careers. These programs can provide invaluable guidance in choosing an appropriate alternative career path, and you don't necessarily have to be associated with the university in order to use this type of service. Another point about these services: they are also used by thousands of American workers who decide after twenty to thirty years on the same job that they want to switch careers and embark on an entirely different direction. Instead of considering yourself an injured worker who is unable to resume your former occupation, try seeing yourself as one of the adventurous ones who is setting out to find a more suitable and exciting career. What have you got to lose? What, if not your boredom, sense of isolation, and reduced standard of living?

If you're on workmen's compensation or social security and would like to go back to some form of work activity, then consider volunteer work. This can also be a useful strategy if you've been out of the work force long enough to be unsure of your physical capabilities. There are an infinite number of ways to volunteer, and most nonprofit groups have a desperate need for help. You can look into local hospitals, church groups, youth groups, senior citizen groups, the Red Cross, and on and on. Remember that most jobs in this country are located through contact with other people, and not through the classified ads. Volunteer work is rewarding in itself, but it can also lead to a real job.

A Warning

In the experience of many rehabilitation professionals, the use of drugs and alcohol are a major contributor to the lack of motivation and inability of many injured workers to resume full-time work. Your condition has already placed you in a situation where the potential for drug abuse is extremely high. It has also probably left you alone for many hours during the day while others are at work or school. Many people in this type of situation let their boredom lead them to turn on the TV and drink. Drugs and alcohol kill motivation. *If you begin to suspect that you may be drinking too much or taking too many drugs, you probably are, and should seek professional guidance and counseling.*

Preparing To Return to Work

1. Before returning to work, cut back on medications that make you drowsy, sleepy, or impair your ability to react rapidly. Be sure to consult your doctor about any changes in medication that you think appropriate.

2. Be prepared for new employers to ask questions about your injury and their potential liability if you are injured again.

3. In filling out applications, make sure that you state your injury. While withholding information about previous injury may initially help you obtain employment, if you are injured on your new job and your employer learns of your original injury, be prepared to be fired. Being honest about your injury will mean that you have to prepare a statement about any limitations or special needs you now have.

16

Pain Clinics and Support Groups

It is easy to be confused about what to do and where to go for help when you suffer from chronic pain. Your friends will tell you one thing, you'll read about another thing, and all of it sounds at least plausible. But chronic pain is such a complex subject and so much research still needs to be done to explain the mechanisms behind it and validate the treatments for it that you are bound to be confused by the variety of information you hear. One thing is certain—if you sustain an injury, your first step should be to go to a medical doctor for a complete checkup. Your doctor is the one who can assure you that your acute or chronic injury does not involve any related problems and that tumors can be ruled out as a cause for your headaches. It's preferable to play it safe through a conventional medical check initially, rather than relying on hearsay or one particular treatment. For example, hypnosis for pain relief is best used *after* your doctor and psychologist have thoroughly ruled out any other complicating disorder. The same holds for chiropractic treatments. Both of these approaches to pain can be extremely effective, if they are preceded by a thorough medical work-up.

After you have been medically examined and feel satisfied that you and your doctor understand as much as possible about your pain, then you are free to try any number of other treatments. You may choose to try several simultaneously, or you may settle on just one. In any case, you will have made an educated decision about what is right for you.

At this time there are over 1,000 pain clinics established in this country. If you live in or near a big city, you probably have several to choose from. The increasing number of places that will treat your pain makes it important for you to know what to look for in a comprehensive pain center. In this chapter we look at the characteristics of a multidisciplinary pain center and discuss the pros and cons of outpatient versus inpatient settings. We also examine another useful resource that many pain patients have used—the support group.

Comprehensive Pain Clinics

Pain treatment has become a hot topic these days. So many people have chronic pain that specialty groups, private centers, and pain clinics supported by academic insitutions have sprung up everywhere. There are a lot of people professing skill at "curing" pain—which means you need to exercise caution in choosing a center that is right for you and your situation.

Medicine traditionally excels at treating symptoms, not necessarily the whole person. Medical personnel are trained and accustomed to "fix" the pain, or at least attempt to find a cure for it. As new research and attitudes about pain evolve, psychologists and psychiatrists have increasingly sought to enlarge this traditional medical approach by examining the emotional aspects of treating pain. Neither approach is adequate solely in and of itself. Most experts agree that the best approach is a combination of the two, a blending of physical and psychological therapies that encompasses the whole person.

A group of chronic pain specialists, among them Drs. Harold Carron, Gerald Aronoff, Benjamin Crue, and Steven Brena, have suggested that any adequate pain center will meet these criteria:

1. A pain center should recognize the complexity of chronic pain and its disruptive effect on your emotional, social, and vocational life; the depression and behavioral changes it causes; and the infrequent usefulness of surgical procedures.

2. The complexity of the problem requires a comprehensive therapeutic program, combining surgical with psychosocial methods to deal with potential underlying physiological states. The program should educate you to shake off the dependency and passivity that often accompanies chronic pain in order to regain control of the pain and your life.

3. The full-time director of the center should support this comprehensive approach and be certified in one of the specialties involved in diagnosis and treatment of chronic pain.

4. A staff of therapists trained in the various branches of treatment included in a comprehensive program should be available full time.

5. The center should be professionally qualified to review your medical records and tests, perform additional tests when appropriate for diagnostic purposes, do physical examinations, and set appropriate goals for treatment.

6. The program should be capable of providing these treatment services:

- Drug reduction as well as elimination of narcotics and tranquilizers
- Physical therapy and exercise
- Psychosocial therapy
- Exercises with or without biofeedback to teach relaxation and reduce stress
- Behavior therapy or cognitive therapy for patient and family, to nudge you out of your pain behavior and cycles of negative thinking
- Vocational counseling and rehabilitation
- A research program directed toward improving treatment and measuring its effectiveness
- An admission policy that requires referral from a physician who should be kept informed of your condition, consulted, and advised about recommended post-treatment care

Dr. Brena elaborates on these criteria by advising that people should avoid any overly optimistic doctor who advocates that one form of treament or instrument will end a pain problem. He also advises against using a doctor or center that is noncommunicative, prescribes habituating drugs or routinely distributes them to you without question, or immediately advocates surgery or "cutting out" nerves. Dr. Nelson Hendler, another prominent researcher in the field, cautions that a prospective patient should be wary of anyone who makes exaggerated claims of success or prescribes a single type of treatment for all types of pain. He suggests that people seek out centers with academic affiliations, as these centers tend to have greater access to current research.

For the past three years, the Commission on Accreditation of Rehabilitation Facilities (CARF) has been surveying and accrediting chronic pain programs throughout the country. The Commission currently has 53 programs on their list, which groups clinics into those with inpatient services only, those with outpatient services only, and those with a combination of both. For a free list of approved programs, write to the CARF Report, 2500 North Pantano Road, Tuscon, Arizona 85715. For $25.00, you can also purchase their manual on guidelines for program accreditation. The CARF guidelines are still not fully used throughout the country, so it is difficult to judge a program solely by whether it has been approved by CARF. However, you can get a good idea of the industry standards that CARF has established for pain clinics to follow. And if you are an employer looking for a good program for your employees, you may find it easier to obtain insurance coverage for an accredited program, although there is no guarantee that this will be the case.

Inpatient and Outpatient Centers

Both inpatient and outpatient pain treatment centers work on the principle of reducing or eliminating negative pain behaviors and replacing them with positive, healthy behaviors. The basic idea is that learned pain behaviors such as excessive groaning, complaining, or lethargy can be unlearned. This does not mean that the underlying basis for your pain is questioned, either from an organic or psychological point of view. The principle simply means that there are other reinforcers in your environment that discourage or encourage you to respond to your pain in different ways.

Families can be unwitting reinforcers of pain behavior. Consider the case of John and his wife, Cathy. Cathy learned early to attend to John's every pain complaint with an abundance of sympathy, food, and suggestions that he go to bed. But a time came when John needed to get out of bed and begin a gradual exercise program. At this point, the reinforcer of bed only served to weaken his muscles further and contribute to his immobility and depression. At the pain center, Cathy learned to encourage John to do his exercises and literally to ignore whatever protests he made.

In some cases, a sufferer may unconsciously be "using" pain to get a secondary gain from other family members. If he or she has been feeling neglected, the pain may seem to be the only viable tool to get attention. This was the situation with John and Cathy. Cathy learned at the pain center to pay attention to John's positive activities, such as his carpentry, and shift the focus away from his pain and complaining. John learned that he could get love and support from doing rather than hurting.

Both inpatient and outpatient programs can teach you to understand your pain behaviors, and to set up contingencies in your environment that reinforce healthy behavior. Here are some typical simple reinforcers.

1. Praise and attention for accomplishments
2. Rewards for completing exercises (such as treating yourself to a whirlpool bath at the end of the session)
3. Attention and support from family members encouraged to participate in your activities
4. The replacement of negative attention by family members (such as nagging, threatening, or coercing, all of which can actually reinforce pain and disability) with positive forms of attention such as praise

Inpatient programs have a tighter control over all these contingencies because you are required to stay in or near the clinic for anywhere from ten days to three weeks, depending on the design of the program. The inpatient treatment team works with you daily and rigorously to identify and confront negative behavior and help you relearn positive behaviors as solidly as possible. But the size of the staff and the amount of time involved make these programs very expensive.

In a typical outpatient program the same services are provided, but you do not stay at the clinic itself. After your initial visit, you are scheduled for follow-up visits over a period of from several weeks to a year or more, depending on your needs. Outpatient programs are less expensive and demanding and can ease you into a lifestyle change without disrupting your home or work. The bottom line with whatever type of program you choose, however, is that any program will be useless if you do not transfer the skills you learn to your everyday life. Studies show that the successful cases from both types of programs are people who regularly use their skills. After completing a program, you will be wise to ask your doctor for a referral to a health care professional in your area who can provide you with continuing support and reinforcement.

Support Groups

The word support means just that—you get support from a group of people who have experiences similar to your own and can empathize with you. The use of a support group to help people manage a problem is not a new idea. One of the most well-known and immensely successful support groups is Alcoholics Anonymous, which helped to set the pace for the viability of this type of coping tool in modern society. Support groups that help people deal with chronic pain are a fairly new development, but one that is catching on quickly.

There are many types of support groups. Some may be largely educational, while others may be purely social and unstructured. But strictly defined, a support group is primarily a gathering of sympathetic people who share coping strategies with each other. One of the main forms of support a group can provide is the feeling that you are wholly accepted, with whatever problems or limitations you may have. And as you feel accepted by others, you feel more accepting of yourself.

Several reasons make support groups an extremely useful tool for coping with chronic pain.

First, you are with others who also suffer from chronic pain and can intuitively understand what you're going through. A common statement, often made in anger and frustration, is "You don't understand my pain because you haven't had chronic pain." That argument is usually dissolved very quickly in a group where all the members share the same experience.

Second, veteran members of the group who have coped with the experience of pain can identify the stages of denial and anger in dealing with a chronic condition and ease newer members through them.

Third, a support group gives you a neutral place to express frustration, disappointment, and any other feelings you have about your experience. Sometimes it helps just to be away from your job, home, or hospital to discuss difficulties and gain perspective on your problems.

Last, a support group can be *psychoeducational*; that is, you can learn how others cope. The group can be a place where you experiment with new behavior, such as role-playing assertive situations, handling conflicts, or practicing good listening skills.

Support groups give you a chance to get out and meet new people at little or no cost. They can bridge the gap between terminating therapy or medical counseling and being on your own—there is nothing so lonely as being in a great deal of pain and totally alone. This way you don't have to!

A pain group in my area was spontaneously formed when a graduate student at a university saw a need for such a group in the community. This group of approximately eight members has been meeting twice a month for three years now and is completely voluntary and free of charge. David, who has been a participant since the group started, feels that it has helped him immeasurably since he joined. "After I finished working with my therapist and doctor at a pain clinc, I felt an extreme sense of loss, as if I was left out in the cold with no one to support me. I learned about the group and have been going regularly. It's very reassuring to be with people who understand me and encourage me when things get tough."

Doctors Dan Owens and Doyle Gentry run pain coping groups in their counseling center at Lynchburg, Virginia. They know that people in pain can feel socially isolated and alienated, and so have set up groups to provide a sense of social support that competes with this sense of alienation. Their groups include all ages, races, and educational and social backgrounds, and are not time limited. Members are encouraged to participate in the group for as long as they feel they are benefiting and can reenter the group at any time. The group leader, a therapist, helps to educate group members about chronic pain and facilitates group cohesion and confrontation. By confronting each other's myths about finding a "perfect cure" for their pain and other unhelpful beliefs, group members learn to accept the chronicity of their pain and begin to integrate it into a new lifestyle and sense of self. These successful groups have proven that members eventually learn to stop talking about how much the pain hurts and start talking about coping better.

For free information and help in setting up or locating a chronic pain support group in your area, write to:

National Chronic Pain Outreach Association, Inc.
Dr. Laura Hitchcock, President
4922 Hampden Lane
Bethesda, MD 20814
(301) 652-4948

Further Reading

Holzman, Arnold, and Dennis Turk, eds. *Pain Management*. New York: Pergamon Press, 1986.

17

Relapse and Recovery

It is not unusual for episodes of chronic pain to flare up from time to time, tempting you to feel like you are right back where you started. John had entered a pain clinic program with the set expectation that after a certain period of time his pain condition would completely disappear. And he did enjoy a tremendous decrease in pain while participating in the program, until after about eight weeks when a muscle spasm incapacitated him for several days. He felt despondent at the thought that all the skills he had learned were of no use. He was sure that his pain was returning in full force, never to be controlled again.

By now you are familiar with the ideas presented in this book, and you have probably already identified the errors in John's thinking that led him in unproductive directions. First, he had an unrealistic expectation at the start of the program that his pain would *never* return. Second, at the first sign of pain, he "catastrophized" his setback into a disaster and honestly convinced himself that all he had learned before was useless. Third, by letting his anxiety levels escalate, he experienced increased physical tension. This made his painful spasm worse and made it harder for him to practice his skills.

But for all his doubts, John stuck with it. He learned to control his catastrophic thinking so that the next time he had a pain episode, he was prepared. Every time the negative thoughts surfaced, he argued back that he "controlled the pain rather than the pain controlling him." He learned to religiously follow his doctor's orders about proper medication use and exercise. Staying consistent in the face of intermittent flare-ups and discouragement required real tenacity. But he gained confidence in his ability to use the relaxation skills and programmed himself to use them immediately upon the first sign of pain.

But probably the most important factor in John's comeback was his introduction to a way of thinking about pain relapses that was developed by Dr. Ian Wickram, a behavioral medicine psychologist. Dr. Wickram explains that whenever you make major behavioral changes, there are inevitably some setbacks. But if you sincerely want to cope better, you cannot let those setbacks dictate the rest of your life. Put them into perspective. Accept the fact that there will be times when you cannot cope as well as you'd like and you may need to pull back and regroup. Dr. Wickram has devised the graph on the next page to illustrate his point.

As you make your way along your coping road, you know that you will have "up times" and "down times." The double O's on the graph are those up times, when you feel bursts of energy, well-being, and mastery. But sometimes the pain causes you to slip down to where the double X's are on the graph. These are the times when

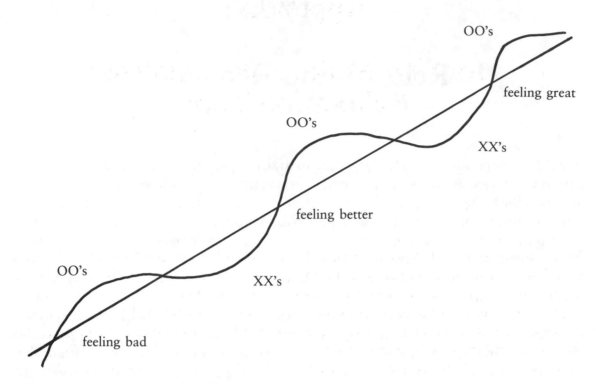

things are not going so well, when you may have a pain relapse and feel depressed and frustrated.

The trick here is to have a plan to get you through those low periods. You might pull out the plan-of-action contract you started at the beginning of this book and review it. Have you strayed from any of your goals and activities? Are there any outdated goals that you could now replace with goals that are more functional? Or perhaps you simply need a boost of support from your friends or counselors. Make an appointment to see your doctor or health care professional who you know will be supportive. If you've tried biofeedback, hypnosis, or another type of pain control program, now might be a good time to make an appointment for a refresher session.

Remember that everything you learn and do adds another coping skill to your reportoire and takes you a step further along the road to recovery. Remind yourself that you do have the stamina to get through any difficult period and that you will eventually improve again. When you tell yourself that, BELIEVE IT! Getting better means holding on to your commitment to healing yourself. The doctors and health care practitioners are only resources. You are the real healer, the one who marshals the helping resources, who learns the essential skills, who keeps on working through the dark days of pain until you gain control of your body and your life again.

Appendix:

How To Make a Personalized Relaxation Tape

by Richard Gevirtz, Ph.D.

Many fine commercial tapes are available to help with relaxation training. Most are based on principles developed by Edmund Jacobson in 1938. Several years ago I was about to give one of the commercial tapes to a client when I realized that I had exhausted my supply. Out of desperation, I recorded a version of the procedure onto a blank cassette and sent the client off to practice. At the next session, I offered her the commercial tape, which she tried but gave back, claiming that she liked her "personalized" tape better. I had been worried about the tape I had made because my voice didn't sound very "professional" and because there was no real script. As it turned out, these "drawbacks" offered certain advantages.

Since this accidental discovery, I have made personalized tapes for clients while observing psychophysiological indications of arousal (skin temperature, electrodermal response, muscle tension, heart rate, and pulse volume). I have discovered that almost all clients can produce a "cultivated low arousal" with the help of a personalized short tape (12 to 18 minutes). People also seem to practice more with personalized tapes and become more inventive in the ways that they use them. These tapes can be adapted to special circumstances and seem to promote generalization better than commercial tapes. Each tape can reflect the physiology and imagination of the specific client. With small cassette recorders so readily available, many applications are possible. I have used tapes for:

- General relaxation training
- Presurgical calming, coping, and relaxation
- Coping with panic attacks while driving
- Coping with agoraphobic fears
- Desensitization of dental phobias
- Prevention of nighttime bruxing
- Test anxiety
- The production of optimal performance in sports or other performance settings
- Hand warming for Raynauds Syndrome (cold hands)
- Muscle relaxation for chronic muscle bracing
- Facial postures for muscle contraction headaches
- Relaxation focus for various other disorders
- General stress management

As you can see, this technique can be a versatile tool to be used with biofeedback and clinical stress management, or by itself.

A Few Cautions

Very few people experience problems with tape-assisted relaxation training, but occasionally a few difficulties can occur.

1. **Parasympathetic rebound.** On rare occasions clients using a relaxation procedure may report nausea, dizziness, and general malaise upon completing a session of relaxation. This response has been documented in the literature as *parasympathetic rebound*, the overreaction of the part of the autonomic nervous system that usually controls digestion and body conservation. This reaction is more likely to occur if the training does not include any active muscle tensing. A simple solution is to include muscle tensing and relaxing in the exercise.

2. **Disturbing thoughts.** Some people experience an uncontrollable flood of thoughts as soon as they begin a relaxation session. It is important not to make these individuals feel "put down" for this. Instead, instruct them to "step back" and observe the thoughts happening to them. I often use the phrase "What you resist will persist" to convey the essence of "passive volition," or learning to purposely "let go."

But note that a person with a serious thought disorder may experience something disturbing and need special care. Caution should be taken with anyone diagnosed as schizophrenic or as having manic-depressive disorders. (I have found, however, that even quite disturbed individuals usually seem to benefit from this sort of training.)

3. **Fear of failure.** Some clients will see their training as an arena of success or failure—and the training will not work if seen as a competitive activity. Great care must be taken to help these clients accept the essentially passive nature of the relaxation response. Biofeedback is more useful with very competitive, goal-oriented people, since they can only make the numbers decrease by learning to "let go."

4. **Giggling or self-consciousness.** Some people can't seem to stop giggling while listening to relaxation instructions. Once the tape is made, however, they usually settle down well on their own. If clients are self-conscious because you are watching them, have them practice when they are alone with the tape.

5. **Diabetic problems.** There are rare reports of diabetics having problems with their usual insulin intake because they have lowered their need for the insulin by using relaxation techniques. Be sure to have your diabetic clients monitor their insulin levels carefully after beginning a course of training.

6. **Extreme drowsiness.** Some people become *profoundly* relaxed and need a transition period to get back into normal functioning. You can build such a period into the tape.

7. **Sleeping.** Some people fall asleep while listening to the tape. If they enter deep sleep, they may not experience the full benefits of the training. One solution is to build in periods of lighter, alerting instructions, along with deepening, relaxing ones. With experimentation you can usually keep the person from going into a deep sleep.

Making a Tape

Have the person for whom you are making the tape relax in a recliner-type chair. While narrating the tape, observe his or her breathing patterns and general demeanor. Be sensitive to any environmental distractions or uncomfortable positions. Observe facial muscle patterns. If possible, monitor physiological parameters. This can be accomplished by using a measure as simple as a little thermometer taped to a finger or as complex as a biofeedback display. Watch breathing. Respiration rates vary but should show some slowing (below twelve breaths per minute).

If you are a pain sufferer making this tape for yourself, you will probably find it difficult to monitor your physical reactions while you speak. But you can check your temperature, notice your breathing and check for overall relaxation while listening to your first tape. Later you can modify the tape to emphasize what seemed to relax you most—lengthening or shortening sections, repeating or deleting phrases, depending on your reaction.

The following script can be used by professionals, but can also be adapted for use by those making tapes for their own use. Speak slowly. Let your voice drop into a low, relaxing cadence.

Sample Script

1. Breathing. Start the relaxation by focusing on your breathing patterns. You're striving for diaphragmatic or "belly" breathing, rather than thoracic or "chest" breathing. Take each breath in deep down into your abdomen, so that your belly expands when you breath in and contracts when you breath out. (*Demonstrate this.*) Take each breath deep down while keeping your chest fairly stable. Imagine that you are breathing in beautiful, clean, pure mountain air and breathing out all the particles of tension in your body. With each breath you purify and relax your whole mind and body. (*Breath deeply while instructing client.*) Now let your breathing slow down and become automatic, but still work to release all the tension in your body. (*Observe breathing patterns and wait for a stable pattern.*)

2. Autogenic phrase. As you settle down to a safe and relaxed state, repeat this phrase over and over again to yourself. You don't have to really believe it or work at it, just let the words repeat silently in your mind: "My arms and legs are heavy and warm, my whole body is calm, quiet, and relaxed." (*Repeat four or five times. Other phrases can be incorporated for individual uses, such as "My jaw muscles are loose and relaxed" and so on.*)

3. Progressive muscle relaxation. Now I want you to concentrate on your muscle tension. To start, tense your left calf and foot tightly for five seconds (*one thousand, two thousand, and so on. Be sure to count this with the client.*). Now relax. Let the tension go. Carefully notice the contrast between a tight muscle and a loose one. Notice a pleasant sort of burning that occurs as the muscle relaxes. Now make that muscle even more relaxed. Notice you can *let go* even more. Let the chair hold up your leg completely. Now try the other leg. Tighten the calf and foot for five seconds (*one* *thousand, two thousand, and so on*). Now you can move to the quadricep, or thigh muscle. First, the left leg; tighten (*one thousand, two thousand, and so on*); relax. Notice the dramatic flow of tension from this large muscle. There's a warm, comforting feeling as the muscle loosens and relaxes. Arms and legs are heavy and warm, the whole body is calm, quiet, and relaxed. (*Repeat for the other thigh muscle.*)

Now concentrate on your lower back. Imagine opening up the lower back and pelvic muscle, sinking deeper in the chair. Focus on letting go of all the muscles in the lower back, pelvis, and abdomen. Feel yourself sinking, slipping, sinking into the chair, as you let the lower portion of your body relax completely. Monitor all the tension in your legs and back, and let go even more.

Begin feeling the relaxed feeling in your legs and back spreading, slowly, to your upper back and chest. First, focus on your shoulder blades. Imagine the distance between them. Now *slowly* feel that distance increase and expand. Slowly feel your shoulders move apart, spreading down and back, down and back. Take a deep breath and let go of the tension in your shoulders as you exhale. With each breath feel calmness in your shoulder, neck, and chest muscles. Let go of any remaining tension and let your shoulders go back and down, back and down. Arms and legs are heavy and warm, whole body calm, quiet, and relaxed.

Let your jaw become relaxed. Imagine that you are on the verge of a smile. Make your face smooth and relaxed. Imagine every muscle in your face smoothing and relaxing with your jaw loosely relaxed. Now let all the muscles in your shoulder, neck, and back let go a bit more. Breathing in beautiful, pure, relaxing air, and letting go of all the tension in your body. As you breathe slowly and deeply, let go of any tension left over in any muscles in your body. Let yourself slip into a calm, quiet, relaxed state.

Recording a Visualization Scene

Before you start the exercise, you should interview the client to determine the optimum scene for that individual. Many people find the following beach scene relaxing, but great individual differences exist. For example, a fair-skinned person may imagine being sunburned on a beach. Be sensitive to your client's unique characteristics. Whatever scene you use, try to involve all the senses, including the *proprioceptive* sense of muscle and joint position. Try to include the person in the scene in one of two ways: (1) from the client's point of view ("Look around you and see the white sand . . .") or (2) from a third person's perspective ("See yourself laying on the sand with no one around you . . ."). Use the pretraining interview to determine ahead of time which of these approaches to use.

If you are making the tape for your own use in relaxation and pain relief, simply choose a scene, either real or imagined, where you feel deeply relaxed. Describe the scene on tape using an approach similar to the beach scene below.

Visualization scene. Imagine yourself on a deserted Carribean beach. It is a crescent-shaped beach with a reef so that the water is calm and clear. There's no one around, the beach is yours. The sand is white and very clean and pure. The water is very warm and a beautiful aqua-blue color. The wind is warm and gentle, cooling you from the warmth of the sun. There's nowhere to go, nothing to do. You can see yourself settle back and enjoy the peace and calm, the sound of the wind in the trees, the gentle lapping of waves on the shore, the sweet salty sea air, the warmth and quiet. See yourself as totally relaxed, quiet, peaceful, with nowhere to go, nothing to do, your whole body calm, quiet, and relaxed. As you lay back and enjoy the serenity, see a person totally at peace, totally safe, totally relaxed.

(Continue the scene to the desired length.)

Now let your mind drift back to the present. As you emerge from your deeply relaxed state, feel yourself become alert and refreshed. Your body remains completely relaxed, but with each breath, your mind becomes more alert. I will count five breaths. With the fifth breath, your eyes will open and you will feel very refreshed and relaxed, alert, but calm. One, two, three, four, five.

Debriefing

Make sure that the client is alert enough to drive. Inquire about hand warmth and muscle relaxation. Find out if anything on the tape was disturbing or distracting. If any problems exist, correct them or do another tape. Remember that it's only 12–14 minutes. If all is well, begin to work out the logistics of when, where, and how the tape will be used. Adherence to a practice regimen is the biggest problem that many clients face. Work as a colleague, not a parent, and find a workable schedule.

Other New Harbinger Self-Help Titles

The Depression Workbook: A Guide for Living With Depression and Manic Depression, $13.95

Risk-Taking for Personal Growth: A Step-by-Step Workbook, $11.95

The Marriage Bed: Renewing Love, Friendship, Trust, and Romance, $11.95

Focal Group Psychotherapy: For Mental Health Professionals, $44.95

Hot Water Therapy: How to Save Your Back, Neck & Shoulders in Ten Minutes a Day of Exercise, $11.95

Older & Wiser: A Workbook for Coping With Aging, $12.95

Prisoners of Belief: Exposing & Changing Beliefs that Control Your Life, $10.95

Be Sick Well: A Healthy Approach to Chronic Illness, $11.95

Men & Grief: A Guide for Men Surviving the Death of a Loved One., $11.95

When the Bough Breaks: A Helping Guide for Parents of Sexually Abused Childern, $11.95

Love Addiction: A Guide to Emotional Independence, $11.95

When Once Is Not Enough: Help for Obsessive Compulsives, $11.95

The New Three Minute Meditator, $9.95

Getting to Sleep, $10.95

The Relaxation & Stress Reduction Workbook, 3rd Edition, $13.95

Leader's Guide to the Relaxation & Stress Reduction Workbook, $19.95

Beyond Grief: A Guide for Recovering from the Death of a Loved One, $10.95

Thoughts & Feelings: The Art of Cognitive Stress Intervention, $13.95

Messages: The Communication Skills Book, $12.95

The Divorce Book, $11.95

Hypnosis for Change: A Manual of Proven Techniques, 2nd Edition, $12.95

The Deadly Diet: Recovering from Anorexia & Bulimia, $11.95

Self-Esteem, $12.95

Chronic Pain Control Workbook, $13.95

Rekindling Desire: Bringing Your Sexual Relationship Back to Life, $12.95

Life Without Fear: Anxiety and Its Cure, $10.95

Visualization for Change, $12.95

Guideposts to Meaning: Discovering What Really Matters, $11.95

Videotape: Clinical Hypnosis for Stress & Anxiety Reduction, $24.95

Starting Out Right: Essential Parenting Skills for Your Child's First Seven Years, $12.95

Big Kids: A Parent's Guide to Weight Control for Children, $11.95

My Parent's Keeper: Adult Children of the Emotionally Disturbed, $11.95

When Anger Hurts, $12.95

Free of the Shadows: Recovering from Sexual Violence, $12.95

Resolving Conflict With Others and Within Yourself, $12.95

Lifetime Weight Control, $11.95

The Anxiety & Phobia Workbook, $13.95

Love and Renewal: A Couple's Guide to Commitment, $12.95

The Habit Control Workbook, $12.95

Call **toll free, 1-800-748-6273**, to order books. Have your Visa or Mastercard number ready.

Or send a check for the titles you want to New Harbinger Publications, 5674 Shattuck Avenue, Oakland, CA 94609. Include $2.00 for the first book and 50¢ for each additional book, to cover shipping and handling. (California residents please include appropriate sales tax.) Allow four to six weeks for delivery.

Or write for a free catalog of all our quality self-help publications. For orders over $20 call 1-800-748-6273. Have your Visa or Mastercard number ready.

Prices subject to change without notice.